Letts
Framework FOCUS

English
KS3 Classbook

George Kulbacki

Framework key: W = Word level, S = Sentence level, R = Reading, Wr = Writing, SL = Speaking and Listening Objectives listed in bold type are Key Objectives.

Framework key: W = Word level, S = Sentence level, R = Reading, Wr = Writing, SL = Speaking and Listening
Objectives listed in bold type are Key Objectives.

YEAR 9 Contents

Framework key: W = Word level, S = Sentence level, R = Reading, Wr = Writing, SL = Speaking and Listening

How to use this book

LETTS KS3 ENGLISH CLASSBOOK

The Letts KS3 English Classbook is designed to give complete coverage of all Key Objectives for Years 7, 8 and 9 as set out in the Framework for Teaching English.

Each unit begins with an outline of the key points to be covered, followed by a brief starter activity, more detailed developmental activities, and finally a review section. All units feature an extract from a fiction or non-fiction text. These extracts have at times been trimmed, in order to focus on the key features of the genre being demonstrated.

ICONS

- Throughout the book you will see a number of icons being used.

- After each question or activity, an icon suggests how many people should be involved in finding a solution:

    🎲 This means you should work on your own.

    🎲🎲 This indicates that you should work with a partner.

    🎲🎲🎲 When you see this icon, you will be working in groups of three or four people.

    🎲🎲🎲🎲 Activities marked with this icon will involve the whole class.

- Important words are defined in a Key Words box, where you see this symbol: 🔑. All key words are listed and defined again in the glossary at the back of the book.

- Certain questions are marked with a star: ✴. This symbol indicates that the question is deliberately more challenging.

- Questions which would be suitable for completion as homework are marked: 🏠.

UNIT 1 What are you?

- To listen to and recall a number of points.
- To talk confidently and fluently in a group and whole class discussion.
- To infer and deduce meanings in a text.

STARTER

1

A **metaphor** is a comparison in which one thing is said to be another. The words 'as' or 'like' are not used, for example, 'the child is an angel', or 'my bedroom is a tip'. Metaphors make descriptions of people, places and objects interesting and memorable.

Complete the following metaphors. The first one has been done for you.

a The surface of the lake is _a mirror._
b The footballer is _____
c The dancer is _____
d The schoolboy is _____
e My brother/sister is _____
f The garden is _____
g The inside of my bag is _____

INTRODUCTION

The following verses are taken from a poem by the Liverpool poet Roger McGough. In it he is comparing a person to a number of unusual objects. Notice how he develops his comparisons in an interesting and often startling manner.

2

How does the poet feel about the person he is describing? Explain your answer by referring to the words in the poem.

What You Are

you are the cat's paw
among the silence of midnight goldfish

you are the teddybear (as good as new)
found beside a roadside accident

you are the green
whose depths I cannot fathom

you are the sweetfresh grass that goes sour
and rots beneath children's feet

you are the apple for teacher
left in a damp cloakroom

you are the ivy
which muffles my walls

you are a derelict canal
where the tincans whistle no tunes

you are the distance
between you and me
measured in tears

Roger McGough

DEVELOPMENT

3 Speaking and listening

Think about the type of person you are. What are your interests? What type of personality do you have? What do you look like? Write down what you would be if you were each of the following:

- colour
- animal
- place
- flower or plant.

Now ask the person next to you what they wrote about themselves. Remember their answers. Go round the rest of the class and ask people for their answers. Your teacher will ask you if you can remember what people have said.

4 Writing

Think of other comparisons you could make to describe yourself (for instance, a character from a book or film, food, a song and so on). Complete your own personal fact file using all the metaphors from today's lesson.

5 Writing

Look back at the poem 'What You Are' and the results of your work in Activities 3 and 4. You are going to develop your ideas further by writing a poem with the title 'What Am I?'. You could begin by completing the following unfinished sentences:

I am the colour _____
Because I am ...

If I was an animal I would be _____
Because I ...

If I was a place I would be _____
Because I am ...

6 Writing

See how many verses you can write about yourself using and extending the techniques and ideas we have discussed in this unit.

REVIEW

Some of you will be asked to read your poems to the rest of the class.

- Have you learnt anything about your classmates?
- Would you have chosen the same metaphors (colour, animal, place, etc.) for them as they have chosen for themselves?

UNIT 2 An early memory

AIMS

- To make the retelling of an anecdote exciting and entertaining.
- To examine the interesting choice of language in an anecdote.

STARTER

1

Do you know any dialect words that are used in the area in which you live? Write them down with their meanings.

- A **dialect** is a form of language that is different from standard English in its vocabulary, grammar and pronunciation.
- **Slang** is language that is not used in standard English or in formal contexts (e.g. 'mega' or 'wicked').
- A **simile** is a comparison that uses the words 'like' or 'as' (e.g. 'he was running like a madman').
- An **anecdote** is a short, amusing description, generally spoken, of an interesting event or incident, often from the narrator's past.

INTRODUCTION

In the extract on page 9, the comedian Billy Connolly describes the excitement of one of his childhood games. Look closely at how he chooses language which makes this anecdote entertaining for the reader.

2

Work out the meaning of these dialect words: 'wee', 'parish boots', 'tackety' and 'back green'.

DEVELOPMENT

3 Language

Look up the following words in a dictionary and use each one in a sentence:

- legendary
- initiation
- void
- midden.

4 Language

Produce a **slang** dictionary.

5 Language

Pick out at least one simile from the passage and explain its meaning.

6 Reading

Describe the Big Sui and what made it special.

7 Reading

Which words and phrases does Billy Connolly use to make his story amusing and exciting?

8 Language

What do you think are the key features of an anecdote? Give examples from the extract.

9 Speaking and listening

Describe an amusing or memorable event that you have experienced. Don't forget to get the order of events clear and include some humour.

10 Writing

Imagine you are Geordie Sinclair. Write your version of events – don't forget to make your account amusing and exciting.

Jumping Big Sui

There used to be these air raid shelters all over the place and we would leap around on top of them. There was the 'Shelter-to-Shelter' jump, which was legendary. They were like mountaineering passes and routes: the White Patch, the Wee Sui and the Big Sui, which was short for suicide.

The Day I jumped the Big Sui ... oh, the feeling. It was like suddenly maturing, like the Indian brave's initiation rites, passing into manhood. And being able to jump the Big Sui was no mean feat. Maybe it was because I was a wee boy, but it seemed like one hell of a distance to jump. It was from the top of the air raid shelter, across a void with railings in the middle of it that divided one back court from another, and then you had to land on top of this midden with a sloped roof. You had to stop dead there or you were right off over the other side.

Geordie Sinclair's attempt at it I remember well. Geordie was wearing these boots that a lot of the boys wore at the time. Parish boots they were called; all studded and tackety and funny. And he was running like a madman, like a dervish, across the shelter, then leapt into the air and Did the Big Sui. But when he hit the midden, he went into an incredibly fast slide and ended up in mid-air in a sitting position, with a trail of sparks coming from his studs. Landed right on his arse in the back green.

Billy Connolly

11 Writing 🏠

Write a passage about a day when you achieved something special. Try to use as many features of an anecdote as possible.

REVIEW

Your teacher might ask you to retell your anecdote to the rest of the class.

UNIT 3 A day I'll never forget

AIMS

- To understand how a writer creates a vivid picture through an interesting combination of details.
- To examine how a writer uses the senses to create effects and mood.
- To scan a text for particular information.

STARTER

1

List the five senses on the board. Now brainstorm a list of things you could perceive with each sense in a garden (e.g. for 'sight' you could write 'flowers', 'colour', 'grass', 'trees'). Make your observations more interesting by adding adjectives (e.g. 'red roses').

INTRODUCTION

In the following extract from *The Secret Garden*, Colin, an invalid, is taken outside for the first time he can remember by his friends Mary and Dickon. Look closely at the author's thoughtful attention to detail, colour and use of the senses, particularly sight.

2

Scan the passage and pick out the writer's use of at least three senses to describe the garden. Write down the relevant phrases you have chosen.

The Secret Garden

Dickon began to push the wheeled-chair slowly and steadily. Mistress Mary walked beside it and Colin leaned back and lifted his face to the sky. The arch of it looked very high and 5 the small snowy clouds seemed like white birds floating on outspread wings below its crystal blueness. The wind swept in soft big breaths down from the moor and was strange with a 10 wild clear-scented sweetness. Colin kept lifting his thin chest to draw it in, and his big eyes looked as if it were they which were listening – listening, instead of his ears. 15

'There are so many sounds of singing and humming and calling out,' he said. 'What is that scent the puffs of wind bring?'

'It's gorse on th' moor that's openin' 20 out,' answered Dickon. 'Eh! th' bees are at it wonderful today.'

Not a human creature was to be caught sight of in the paths they took. In fact every gardener or gardener's lad 25 had been witched away. But they wound in and out among the shrubbery and out and round the fountain beds, following their carefully planned route for the mere mysterious 30

pleasure of it. But when at last they
turned into the Long Walk by the ivied
walls, the excited sense of an
approaching thrill made them, for
some curious reason they could not   35
have explained, begin to speak in
whispers.

'This is it,' breathed Mary. 'This is
where I used to walk up and down and
wonder and wonder.'   40

'Is it?' cried Colin, and his eyes began
to search the ivy with eager
curiousness. 'But I can see nothing,' he
whispered. 'There is no door.'

'That's what I thought,' said Mary.   45

Then there was a lovely, breathless
silence and the chair wheeled on.

'That is the garden where Ben
Weatherstaff works,' said Mary.

'Is it?' said Colin.   50

A few yards more and Mary
whispered again.

'This is where the robin flew over the
wall,' she said.

'Is it?' cried Colin. 'Oh! I wish he'd   55
come again!'

'And that,' said Mary with solemn
delight, pointing under a big lilac
bush, 'is where he perched on the little
heap of earth and showed me the key.'   60

Then Colin sat up.

'Where? Where? There?' he cried, and
his eyes were as big as the wolf's in Red
Riding Hood, when Red Riding Hood
felt called upon to remark on them.   65
Dickon stood still and the wheeled-
chair stopped.

'And this,' said Mary, stepping on to
the bed close to the ivy, 'is where I
went to talk to him when he chirped at   70
me from the top of the wall. And this is
the ivy the wind blew back,' and she
took hold of the hanging green
curtain.

'Oh! is it –' gasped Colin.   75

'And here is the handle, and here is
the door. Dickon, push him in – push
him in quickly!'

And Dickon did it with one strong,
steady, splendid push.   80

But Colin had actually dropped back
against his cushions, even though he
gasped with delight, and he had
covered his eyes with his hands and

held them there, shutting out 85
everything until they were inside and
the chair stopped as if by magic and
the door was closed. Not till then did
he take them away and look round and
round and round as Dickon and Mary 90
had done. And over walls and earth
and trees and swinging sprays and
tendrils the fair green veil of tender
little leaves had crept, and in the grass
under the trees and the grey urns in 95
the alcoves and here and there
everywhere, were touches or splashes
of gold and purple and white and the
trees were showing pink and snow
above his head, and there were 100
fluttering of wings and faint sweet
pipes and humming and scents and
scents. And the sun fell warm upon his
face like a hand with a lovely touch.
And in wonder Mary and Dickon stood 105
and stared at him. He looked so
strange and different because a pink
glow of colour had actually crept all
over him – ivory face and neck and
hands and all. 110

'I shall get well! I shall get well!' he
cried out. 'Mary! Dickon! I shall get
well! And I shall live for ever and ever
and ever!'

Frances Hodgson Burnett

DEVELOPMENT

3 Language

In lines 68–74 the following verbs are used to describe Mary's encounter with a robin:

**stepping   went   talk   chirped
blew   took**

See if you can rewrite the passage replacing the original verbs with others of similar meaning.

4 Reading

Pick out at least two phrases that show Colin is excited at the prospect of seeing the garden for the first time.

5 Reading

Writers use interesting detail to build up a vivid picture in the reader's mind. From the passage, make a list of all the things you can find in Mary's garden.

6 Reading

What is Colin's reaction when he sees the secret garden? Look closely at the way the visit affects his physical appearance and how he feels.

7 Writing

Write an account called 'A Day I'll Never Forget' about a day you really enjoyed.

- Try to develop a real sense of excitement and pleasure.
- Try to use verbs, adjectives and the senses imaginatively in your account.

REVIEW

Recap the five senses. Quickly brainstorm things you can sense with each one in your classroom.

UNIT 4 — A day I'd rather forget

AIMS

- To plan, structure and develop your own story.
- To examine ways of improving your own writing.
- To investigate homophones.

STARTER

1

Where are you likely to come across the following types of non-fiction texts?

**report   review   instruction   profile
chronicle   obituary**

INTRODUCTION

Look closely at the following extract about visiting the doctor, taken from Roald Dahl's *Boy*. Think about the techniques and language used to make this incident horrific and shocking.

2

How is Roald Dahl's experience different from the way operations are performed nowadays?

Boy

The doctor was bending over me. In his hand he held that long shiny steel instrument. [...] It was about the thickness and length of a pencil, and like most pencils it had a lot of sides to it. Toward the end, the metal became much thinner, and at the very end of the thin bit of metal there was a tiny blade set at an angle. The blade wasn't more than a centimetre long, very small, very sharp and very shiny.

'Open your mouth,' the doctor said, speaking Norwegian. [...] 'It won't take two seconds.' [...] He spoke gently, and I was seduced by his voice. Like an ass, I opened my mouth.

The tiny blade flashed in the bright light and disappeared into my mouth. It went high up into the roof of my mouth, and the hand that held the blade gave four or five very quick little twists and the next moment, out of my mouth into the basin came tumbling a whole mass of flesh and blood. [...]

'Those were your adenoids,' I heard the doctor saying.

I sat there gasping. The roof of my mouth seemed to be on fire. I grabbed my mother's hand and held on to it tight. I

couldn't believe that anyone would do this to me.

'Stay where you are,' the doctor said. 'You'll be all right in a minute.'

Blood was still coming out of my mouth and dripping into the basin the nurse was holding. 'Spit it all out,' she said, 'there's a good boy.' [...]

The nurse wiped my lips and washed my face with a wet flannel. Then they lifted me out of the chair and stood me on my feet. I felt a bit groggy.

'We'll get you home,' my mother said, taking my hand. [...] We walked the full half-hour journey back to my grandparents' house, and when we arrived at last, I can remember as clearly as anything my grandmother saying, 'Let him sit down in that chair and rest for a while. After all, he's had an operation.'

Roald Dahl

DEVELOPMENT

3 Language

Homophones are words which are spelt differently but which sound the same (e.g. 'their' and 'there', 'flower' and 'flour', 'so' and 'sow').

Find a homophone for each of the following words.

- steel
- whole
- heard
- would

4 Language

Use each of the following homophones in a sentence.

- birth/berth
- cell/sell
- stair/stare

5 Reading

What did the doctor use to remove the adenoids? Describe it carefully.

6 Reading

Pick out at least two phrases which show that the writer was stunned by what had happened to him.

7 Reading

Work out where the following sections of the passage begin and end:

- introduction
- middle
- ending.

8 Writing

Write an account with the title 'A Day I'd Rather Forget'. Consider:

- the build-up of tension
- attention to detail
- the characters' feelings
- a surprising ending.

Use a thesaurus to find some new words to use in your writing.

9 Writing

Read through your account. Try to write a second draft, then proofread it.

REVIEW

What do you think are the main ingredients of an interesting anecdote or a good story?

AIMS

- To recognise the origins and types of prefixes.
- To use prefixes correctly and accurately.

STARTER

1

> **Prefixes** are placed at the start of a root word to change its meaning. For example: 'mis' is added to 'fortune' to make 'misfortune', 'dis' is added to 'obey' to make 'disobey'.

Work out which of the following are prefixes and should go at the start of a word.

able	ful	est	un	dis
ing	extra	anti	ex	

DEVELOPMENT

Prefixes for opposites

In the following examples, prefixes are added to produce an **antonym** (opposite):

'il' (='not') is added to 'legal' to make 'illegal'.

'un'(= 'not') is added to 'helpful' to make 'unhelpful'.

2

See how many words you can find with the following prefixes.

e.g. anti (= 'not') ➡ anticlockwise, antifreeze, antiseptic

a in (= 'not') ➡ _____

_____

b mis (= 'wrong') ➡ _____

_____

c un (= 'not') ➡ _____

_____

Greek and Latin prefixes

Many prefixes come from the classical languages Greek and Latin.
For example, the Greek prefix 'bio' (= 'life') is added to 'ology' to make the word 'biology'. The prefix 'mono' (= 'one') is added to 'tone' to make 'monotone'.

3

See if you can find any words with the following Greek prefixes.
e.g. auto (= 'self') ➡ autobiography, autograph, autopilot

a micro (= 'small') ➡ _____

_____

b para (= 'along with') ➡ _____

_____

c tele (= 'distant') ➡ _____

_____

4

See if you can work out what the following Latin prefixes mean.

a circ/circum – circle, circus, circumference

b aqua/aque – aquatic, aquarium, aqueduct

c audi – audible, auditorium, audience

d bi – bicycle, bilingual, binary

e trans – transatlantic, transcontinental, transcribe

Old English prefixes

There are numerous Old English prefixes. Some of the best-known ones are:

- be (= around)
- fore (= before)
- mid (= middle)
- out (= surpassing)
- over (= too much)

5

The prefix 'be' can be used to form words like 'befriend', 'bedeck', 'beside'. See if you can add any of the other Old English prefixes to the root words below.

a active

b arm

c crowded

d do

e drive

f father

g pace

h paid

i term

6

Correct the prefix in the following words.

**unagree   misallow   inaware
disfortune   subcoat   infaithful
misapprove   misappear
inprofessional   disunderstood**

REVIEW

How can knowing the meaning of a prefix help you when reading a difficult text? Brainstorm some more words with prefixes.

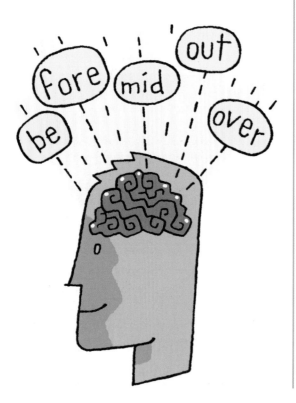

UNIT 6

The happiest days of your life

AIMS

- To consider how poetry is organised before planning and writing your own poem.
- To write a poem thinking about structure, rhyme and rhythm.

STARTER

1

Look closely at the two poems. Think about what makes a piece of writing a poem. Write down as many things to think about when writing poetry as you can – consider rhyme, rhythm, organisation/structure, sound effects, imagery, language, themes, etc.

INTRODUCTION

The subject of school often inspires poets and other writers. In these two poems each writer makes lunch and break times sound interesting and lively. Which original rhyme is the first poem based on?

School Dinner Rhyme

Sing a song of sixty pence –
A lump of stodgy nosh,
A plate of meatless meat pie
Soaked in greasy slosh;
Queue up for your junk food,
Fried hamburger brick,
Frozen chips and Choc-o-chew
Or spotty dotted sick.

Ian Serraillier

2

The poet clearly does not have happy memories of school dinners. Pick out two adjectives which make school dinners appear unappetising.

Morning Break

Andrew Flag plays football
Jane swings from the bars
Chucker Peach climbs drainpipes
Spike is seeing stars

Little Paul's a Martian
Anne walks on her toes
Ian Dump fights Kenny
Russell picks his nose

Dopey Di does hopscotch
Curly drives a train
Maddox-Brown and Thompson
Stuff shoes down the drain.

Lisa Thin throws netballs
Ranji stands and stares
Nuttall from the first year
Shouts and spits and swears

Dick Fish fires his ray gun
Gaz has stamps to swop
Dave and Dan are robbers
Teacher is the cop

Betty Blob pulls faces
Basher falls … and dies
Tracey shows her knickers
Loony swallows flies

(continued)

Faye sits in a puddle
Trev is eating mud
Skinhead has a nose bleed
– pints and pints of blood

Robbo Lump pings marbles
Ahmed hands out cake
What a lot of nonsense
During
     Morning
        Break

Wes Magee

3

Find at least two games which are being played in the poem 'Morning Break'.

4

Make a list of the different things that are being eaten in the poem.

DEVELOPMENT

5 Language

> 📖 **Compound words** are made of two words that are put together (e.g. 'arm' + 'chair' = 'armchair', 'step' + 'ladder' = 'stepladder').

Pick out at least four compound words from the poem 'Morning Break'.

6 Language

Think of as many other compound words as you can.

7 Writing

Write a poem about your school or an imaginary school. It could be about a lesson, break, friends, teachers, examinations, assembly, school uniform, a trip, daydreaming in lessons, etc. Before you start, brainstorm your chosen topic and write all your ideas down. Comment on and include:

- unusual details and observations
- appearances, movement and behaviour
- colours, sounds and smells
- feelings
- imaginative use of adjectives, verbs and adverbs
- comparisons – similes and metaphors to bring your subject to life.

When you start writing your poem, think about rhyme, rhythm and stanzas.

8 Writing

Word process your poem. With the help of your teacher, put all the class's poems together in an anthology or in a class display.

9 Writing

Find a poem you have really enjoyed reading. Write a few sentences explaining why you have enjoyed reading this poem so much.

REVIEW

Think about what poetry is. What are the most important things to remember when writing a poem? Some of you will be asked to read out your school poems. Why are poems easier to read out loud than some other types of writing?

UNIT 7 First day at school

AIMS

- To think of strategies for learning new spellings.
- To improve reading skills and understand how a writer creates ideas and moods in a text.

STARTER

 A **mnemonic** is a rhyme or saying that helps you learn a spelling or fact (e.g. 'i' before 'e' except after 'c').

1

Think of a suitable mnemonic for at least two of the following words.

accommodation business character conscience environment favourite February library separate Wednesday

2

Think of ways of learning spellings other than using mnemonics. For instance, a word like 'environment' could be broken up into two parts: 'environ' and 'ment'.

INTRODUCTION

In this extract from Laurie Lee's *Cider With Rosie* we can clearly visualise the hustle and bustle of a village school. How does the writer show how he feels about his first day at school?

Cider With Rosie

The morning came, without any warning, when my sisters surrounded me, wrapped me in scarves, tied up my bootlaces, thrust a cap on my head, and stuffed a baked potato in my pocket.

'What's this?' I said.

'You're starting school today.'

'I ain't. I'm stopping 'ome.'

'Now, come on, Loll. You're a big boy now.'

'I ain't.'

'You are.'

'Boo-hoo.'

They picked me up bodily, kicking and bawling, and carried me up to the road.

'Boys who don't go to school get put into boxes, and turn into rabbits, and get chopped up Sundays.'

I felt this was overdoing it rather, but I said no more after that. I arrived at the school just three feet tall and fatly wrapped in my scarves. The playground roared like a rodeo, and the potato burned through my thigh. Old boots, ragged stockings, torn trousers and skirts, went skating and skidding around me. The rabble closed in; I was encircled; grit flew in my face like shrapnel. Tall girls with frizzled hair, and huge boys with sharp elbows, began to prod me with hideous interest. They plucked at my scarves, spun me round like a top, screwed my nose, and stole my potato.

I was rescued at last by a gracious lady – the sixteen-year-old junior-teacher – who boxed a few ears and dried my face and led me off to The Infants. I spent that first day picking holes in paper, then went home in a smouldering temper [...].

But after a week I felt like a veteran and grew as ruthless as anyone else. Somebody had stolen my baked potato, so I swiped somebody else's apple...

Laurie Lee

3

Match up these words from the text with their correct definition.
Word
rabble
veteran
bodily
smouldering
Definition
burning slowly
with the whole bulk of your body
crowd of noisy and aggressive people
person with a lot of experience

DEVELOPMENT

4 Reading
How did the writer's sisters get him to school on his first day?

5 Reading
How did the writer feel when he arrived at school?

6 Reading
By the end of his first week at school the writer's attitude had changed. Pick out at least two phrases from the text that suggest this change.

7 Reading
Pick out any words or phrases that suggest that the other children behaved in an unfriendly or threatening manner.

8 Speaking and listening
Think back to your infant and primary school days. Discuss things you liked and disliked – make a list.

9 Writing
Complete a descriptive piece of writing called 'My First Day at School'. Think about:
- paragraph topics
- how you felt
- the appearance of your new school
- what happened to you
- who you met
- interesting vocabulary and expression – adjectives and similes.

10 Writing
Read through the account you wrote in class. Which of Lee's techniques could you use to make your work more interesting?

REVIEW

Share your account about starting school with the rest of the class. Have you managed to get your feelings across in a lively and imaginative way?

UNIT 8 My primary school

AIMS

- To use evidence in a text to support a personal reading response.
- To understand how characters are portrayed in writing.
- To use suffixes correctly.

STARTER

1

Why do writers use similes? Think of some of your own similes which could be used to describe people you know.

INTRODUCTION

In the following passage, Matilda Wormwood starts school. Look closely at how Roald Dahl describes Miss Honey and Miss Trunchbull.

2

Find as many similes in the passage as you can. How does the author's use of similes make you feel about Miss Honey and Miss Trunchbull?

Matilda

The village school for younger children was a bleak brick building called Crunchem Hall Primary School. It had about two hundred and fifty pupils aged from five to just under twelve years old. The head teacher, the boss, the supreme commander of this establishment was a formidable middle-aged lady whose name was Miss Trunchbull.

Naturally Matilda was put in the bottom class, where there were eighteen other small boys and girls about the same age as her. Their teacher was called Miss Honey, and she could not have been more than twenty-three or twenty-four. She had a lovely pale oval madonna face with blue eyes and her hair was light-brown. Her body was so slim and fragile one got the feeling that if she fell over she would smash into a thousand pieces, like a porcelain figure. [...] Some curious warmth that was almost tangible shone out of Miss Honey's face when she spoke to a confused and homesick newcomer to the class.

Miss Trunchbull, the Headmistress, was something else altogether. She was a gigantic holy terror, a fierce tyrannical monster who frightened the life out of the pupils and teachers alike. There was an aura of menace about her even at a distance, and when she came up close you

could almost feel the dangerous heat radiating from her as from a red-hot rod of metal. When she marched – Miss Trunchbull never walked, she always marched like a storm-trooper with long strides and arms aswinging – when she marched along a corridor you could actually hear her snorting as she went, and if a group of children happened to be in her path, she ploughed right on through them like a tank, with small people bouncing off her to left and right. Thank goodness we don't meet many people like her in this world, although they do exist and all of us are likely to come across at least one of them in a lifetime. If you ever do, you should behave as you would if you met an enraged rhinoceros out in the bush – climb up the nearest tree and stay there until it has gone away.

Roald Dahl

DEVELOPMENT

3 Language

'Gigantic' has the suffix 'ic' and 'tyrannical' has the suffix 'al'. Try to think of or find as many words as possible with the 'ic' and 'al' suffixes. Set out your answers in two columns: e.g.

ic	al
acidic	additional

4 Language

See if you can think of or find any words with the 'ary' and 'ist' suffixes (e.g. 'anniversary' and 'artist').

5 Reading

How many pupils went to Crunchem Hall Primary School?

6 Reading

Describe the appearance of Miss Honey.

7 Reading

Miss Honey is clearly very likeable. Pick out at least two words or phrases which show this.

8 Reading

What are the main differences between Miss Trunchbull and Miss Honey? Explain your answer in an extended paragraph, giving evidence from the passage.

9 Writing

Think about your own primary school. Write a detailed description of your favourite teacher. Consider:

- their appearance
- their personality
- why they were good at their job
- why you liked them.

10 Writing

Design a poster or short flyer advertising your primary school. Use the following headings:

- Location
- Facilities
- Teachers
- Clubs and Activities/Trips
- Special Events.

REVIEW

As a class, brainstorm the most important things to remember when describing people.

UNIT 9

My secondary school

AIMS

- To think about the style and structure necessary for an advice leaflet.
- To organise the layout of an advice leaflet.

STARTER

1

Write a definition for these words, which you might come across in your Year 7 English course.

**consonant   expression   plural
vocabulary   vowel**

INTRODUCTION

What were your first impressions of your secondary school? Jimmy Stewart, the boy in this extract, has been educated at home before going to his new school.

2

Many of the verbs in lines 17–22 convey a strong sense of movement and noise. Using a thesaurus rewrite those lines, changing the original verbs to other verbs of similar meaning.

The Dragon In The Garden

Cronton Comprehensive's a boys' school. There's one at Farley for girls. The kids go to them when they're eleven and leave when they're fourteen to go to Barnton Senior Comprehensive. [...]   5

In a corner of the playground I met loneliness for the first time in my life. Loneliness isn't being alone but wondering why you have to be alone. I had rarely known other kids, I had   10 always been alone, yet in those first moments at school I felt loneliness flood through me as I watched the hundreds of boys. My brain ached as their uproar beat against it. They and I were all   15 wearing the same uniform, but they were different from me. They were rough savages, screaming their war-cries and rushing into brutal battle, and they were happy in a way I had never known. They   20 were happy shouting at each other, wrestling each other, hating each other.

Then one of them spotted me and, like a dog catching a strange scent, he swerved and stopped in front of me. He   25 was smaller than I was and younger and his thick glasses gave him the look of an owl.

'You a new kid?' he asked.

I nodded.   30

'What's your name?'

'Stewart,' I said. He was shooting his questions at me like bullets and I didn't like them.

'Stewart what?' he asked.   35

'Jimmy Stewart.'

'Jimmy Stewart,' he said as if tasting the name. Then he went into a convulsive dance and started screaming, 'Jimmy Stewpot! Jimmy Stewpot!'   40

> *'He's a new kid!' he yelled. 'His name's Jimmy Stewpot!' [...]*
>
> *I could see dozens of pairs of eyes and I knew how zoo animals must feel on Sunday afternoons when people press* 45 *close to the cages. There was a dull kind of interest in all the eyes; interest and animosity, but no friendliness. I felt lonelier than ever.*
>
> Reginald Maddock

DEVELOPMENT

3 Reading

How does Jimmy feel when he is in the corner of the playground?

4 Reading

Describe the appearance of the boy who first notices Jimmy.

5 Reading

How does Jimmy feel about the behaviour of the other boys towards him?

6 Speaking and listening

Discuss similarities and differences between your primary and secondary schools and make notes.

7 Language

Imagine an advice leaflet written for Year 6 pupils about to start secondary school. How might the writing in such a leaflet be different to that in a story? Write down five rules for producing an advice leaflet.

8 Language

Design a layout for your advice leaflet. Be sure to think about the different section headings you might need.

9 Writing

Now write your advice leaflet for Year 6 pupils about to start your secondary school. You may wish to focus on:

- how Year 6 pupils may be treated by older pupils and their new teachers
- the main differences between primary and secondary school
- secondary school subjects
- uniform
- facilities
- eating arrangements
- clubs, activities and trips
- your overall impressions of the school
- advice for new pupils.

10 Writing

Create a questionnaire which could be given to other Year 7 pupils, asking them what it was like coming to a new school and what problems, if any, they encountered.

REVIEW

Share your outline or draft for your leaflet with the class. What are the key ingredients of a successful advice leaflet? How can you improve the layout, language and content of your own leaflet?

UNIT 10 Nouns

AIMS

- To learn about different types of nouns.
- To build up vocabulary by identifying the groups described by various collective nouns.

STARTER

1

Write down each of the following in a list.

- the name of your school
- one of the items in your school bag
- an emotion or feeling (e.g. happiness or misery)
- the word for a group of eleven football players

You should have four nouns. Next to each word write down the type of noun it is (e.g. concrete, abstract, proper, collective).

DEVELOPMENT

Proper nouns are the names of people, places, books and films (e.g. John, London, Lord of the Rings, Matilda). Proper nouns also include the names of organisations, days of the week, months and people's titles (e.g. The Football League, Friday, April, The Prince of Wales, etc.). Proper nouns always begin with a capital letter.

Concrete nouns are objects you can touch (e.g. cat, book, chair, shoe). Concrete nouns, which are sometimes referred to as common nouns, always have a physical existence and appearance.

Abstract nouns are feelings and qualities which don't have physical properties (e.g. excitement, sadness, confusion, etc.). Abstract nouns name emotions, properties and ideas that we cannot see.

A **collective noun** is the special name given to a collection of objects, animals or people (e.g. a **bouquet** of flowers, a **herd** of cows, a **class** of schoolchildren).

2

Pick out the proper nouns from the following list.

**The Daily Mirror   book   dog
Preston North End   May   trousers
Prime Minister   goat   Somerset
road   Tim Henman   France**

3

Make up your own list of ten proper nouns.

4

Put the following nouns in two columns, one headed 'Concrete Nouns', the other, 'Abstract Nouns'.

**flower   anger   love   magazine
television   arrogance   water
success   disappointment
intelligence   pain   computer
embarrassment**

5

Now think of five concrete nouns and five abstract nouns of your own.

6

Using a dictionary and your knowledge of English, match the following collective nouns with their correct group.

Collective noun

1 crowd

2 staff

3 congregation

4 pride

5 shoal

6 anthology

7 library

8 choir

9 squadron

10 pack

11 convoy

12 troupe

13 archipelago

14 constellation

15 copse

Group

a trees

b spectators

c stars

d singers

e books

f poems

g cards

h planes

i trucks

j worshippers

k fish

l lions

m acrobats

n teachers

o islands

7

See if you can find out which groups of animals and birds the following collective nouns belong to.

flock flight swarm gaggle nye cete covey

UNIT 11 Treasure island adventure

AIMS

● To look at and understand the use of simple and complex sentences.
● To write a story with an interesting opening and exciting conclusion.

STARTER

1

> *A **simple sentence** is made up of a single clause (e.g. The boy walked down the street). A **complex sentence** contains a main clause and one or more subordinate clauses (e.g. The boy walked down the street passing several shops before entering the newsagent's where he bought a mountain of his favourite sweets).*

What are the advantages and disadvantages of using simple and complex sentences for both readers and writers?

INTRODUCTION

In the following extract from *Treasure Island*, by Robert Louis Stevenson, Jim Hawkins sees the island where Captain Flint's treasure is supposedly buried. Jim thinks the island looks sinister and dangerous. His initial misgivings are soon proved correct …

2

The writer's use of complex sentences allows him to build up interesting and detailed images. But what effects or changes in atmosphere can be achieved by using short sentences?

Treasure Island

The appearance of the island when I came on deck next morning was altogether changed. Although the breeze had now utterly failed, we had made a great deal of way during the night, and were now lying becalmed about half a mile to the south-east of the low eastern coast. Grey-coloured woods covered a large part of the surface. This even tint was indeed broken up by streaks of yellow sandbreak in the lower lands, and by many tall trees of the pine family, out-topping the others – some singly, some in clumps; but the general colouring was uniform and sad.

The hills ran up clear above the vegetation in spires of naked rock. All were strangely shaped, and the Spy-glass, which was by three or four hundred feet the tallest on the island, was likewise the strangest in configuration, running up sheer from almost every side, and then suddenly cut off at the top like a pedestal to put a statue on. [...]

Perhaps it was the look of the island with its grey, melancholy woods, and wild stone spires, and the surf that we could both see and hear foaming and thundering on the steep beach – at least, although the sun shone bright and hot,

and the shore birds were fishing and crying all around us, and you would have thought anyone would have been glad to get to land after being so long at sea, my heart sank, as the saying is, into my boots; and from that first look onward, I hated the very thought of Treasure Island.

Robert Louis Stevenson

Word bank

configuration – shape
pedestal – the base of a column
melancholy – depressing or miserable

DEVELOPMENT

3 Language

Write down a complex sentence from the text. Now rewrite it, developing the same ideas in simple sentences.

4 Reading

Draw a map of Treasure Island. Include as many features from the passage as you can.

5 Speaking and listening

Imagine you have been marooned on a desert island with some of your classmates. Discuss what problems you might encounter and write a list of them.

6 Speaking and listening

Make a list of at least ten dos and don'ts which you think might make life on your desert island easier and help you survive.

7 Writing

Write a story called 'Treasure Island Adventure' which describes your struggle for survival on the island and your eventual rescue.

Before you begin, brainstorm your ideas under these headings.

- Arrival on the island
- Friends and enemies
- Geography and wildlife
- What goes wrong?
- Overcoming a crisis
- Rescue

Begin your story with a strong and dramatic opening. Try to use longer complex sentences when building up detailed descriptive passages. Shorter simple sentences are often useful when building up a mood of tension and excitement.

8 Writing

Proof-read and edit your first draft, then rewrite your story neatly, paying special attention to handwriting, spelling, punctuation and paragraphs.

REVIEW

Your teacher will ask some of you to read out your 'Treasure Island Adventure' stories. Did the stories you have heard have strong beginnings, interesting twists and convincing endings? Was there a build-up of tension and excitement towards the end?

UNIT 12 Balloon debate

AIMS

- To use group discussion for solving problems.
- To improvise a short dramatic role play.
- To recognise the cues to start a new paragraph.

> A **noun phrase** is a group of words including a noun. The other words generally add interest to the noun and may include adjectives (e.g. 'the bike' might become 'the gleaming new mountain bike').

STARTER

1

Expand two of the following into detailed noun phrases.

- a footballer
- the dog
- the schoolboy
- my friend

INTRODUCTION

In the following extract from *The Wizard of Oz* Dorothy is desperate to return to her home in Kansas. Unfortunately, things do not go according to plan.

The Wizard of Oz

For three days Dorothy heard nothing from Oz. These were sad days for the little girl, although her friends were all quite happy and contented. [...]

On the fourth day, to her great joy, Oz sent for her, and when she entered the Throne Room he greeted her pleasantly:

'Sit down, my dear; I think I have found the way to get you out of this country [...] You see, when I came to this country it was in a balloon. You also came through the air, being carried by a cyclone. So I believe the best way to get across the desert will be through the air. Now, it is quite beyond my powers to make a cyclone; but I've been thinking the matter over, and I believe I can make a balloon.'

'How?' asked Dorothy.

'A balloon,' said Oz, 'is made of silk, which is coated with glue to keep the gas in it. I have plenty of silk in the Palace, so it will be no trouble to make the balloon. But in all this country there is no gas to fill the balloon with, to make it float.'

'If it won't float,' remarked Dorothy, 'it will be of no use to us.'

'True,' answered Oz. 'But there is another way to make it float, which is to fill it with hot air. Hot air isn't as good as gas, for if the

it would be caught in the silken bag. Gradually the balloon swelled out and rose into the air, until finally the basket just touched the ground.

Then Oz got into the basket and said to all the people in a loud voice:

'I am now going away to make a visit. While I am gone the Scarecrow will rule over you. I command you to obey him as you would me.'

The balloon was by this time tugging hard at the rope that held it to the ground, for the air within it was hot, and this made it so much lighter in weight than the air without that it pulled hard to rise into the sky.

'Come, Dorothy!' cried the Wizard. 'Hurry up, or the balloon will fly away.'

'I can't find Toto anywhere,' replied Dorothy, who did not wish to leave her little dog behind. Toto had run into the crowd to bark at a kitten, and Dorothy at last found him. She picked him up and ran towards the balloon.

She was within a few steps of it, and Oz was holding out his hands to help her into the basket, when, crack! went the ropes, and the balloon rose into the air without her.

air should get cold the balloon would come down in the desert, and we should be lost.'

'We!' exclaimed the girl. 'Are you going with me?'

'Yes, of course,' replied Oz. [...]

'I shall be glad to have your company,' said Dorothy.

'Thank you,' he answered. 'Now, if you will help me sew the silk together, we will begin to work on our balloon.' [...]

When it was all ready, Oz sent word to his people that he was going to make a visit to a great brother Wizard who lived in the clouds. [...]

The Tin Woodman had chopped a big pile of wood, and now he made a fire of it, and Oz held the bottom of the balloon over the fire so that the hot air that arose from

L. Frank Baum

2

Much of the extract is in the form of dialogue between Dorothy and Oz. Write a list of words which have been used instead of 'said'. Can you add more words to this list?

DEVELOPMENT

3 Reading

How had Oz arrived in the country?

4 Reading

How did Oz propose to make his balloon float?

5 Reading

Explain how the balloon left without Dorothy.

6 Language

Look at the paragraph beginnings and discuss why a new paragraph is needed each time.

7 Speaking and listening

Imagine that you are going on a celebrity balloon flight. List five famous people who are going to go with you. Include a pop star, a film actor, a soap star, a member of the royal family and a sports personality.

8 Speaking and listening

While you are up in the air you run into problems. The pilot tells you that you must jettison two celebrity passengers. Who should you jettison and why? Discuss your reasons.

9 Speaking and listening

You now only have enough helium for one celebrity passenger to stay on board. Who is going to stay alive? Improvise one of the following as a role play:

a discuss who is going to sacrifice their life and why

b tell one of the celebrities that they must leave the balloon and explain why.

10 Writing

Write a diary entry describing the day when you had to tell your celebrity guests that their company was no longer desirable on the balloon ride.

REVIEW

Act out some of the role plays in which you break the bad news to your celebrity passengers. How did you decide who should stay and who should go? Did you base your decisions on a person's usefulness or on other aspects?

AIMS

- To recognise the differences between formal and informal use of language.
- To comment on how a writer manipulates language to create interesting settings, characters and moods.
- To write a newspaper report, using the correct conventions.

STARTER

1

Arrange the following words into two columns: one for words with two syllables and the other for words with three.

although   alcohol   argument atmosphere   believe   conclusion conscience   creation   definite diamond   embarrass   enquire jealous   lovely   nervous performance   people   safety strategy   Wednesday

> A **syllable** is part of a word which consists of one beat. For instance 'like' has one syllable, 'liking' has two, and 'likeable' has three.

INTRODUCTION

The following poem was written for performance by the popular 1950s comedian Stanley Holloway. It is about a family holiday that goes tragically wrong. As you are reading the poem can you spot any unusual spellings that may help a performer pronounce words in a particular way?

The Lion and Albert

There's a famous seaside place called Blackpool,
That's noted for fresh air and fun,
And Mr. and Mrs. Ramsbottom
Went there with young Albert, their son.

A grand little lad was young Albert,
All dressed in his best; quite a swell
With a stick with an 'orse's 'ead 'andle,
The finest that Woolworth's could sell.

They didn't think much to the Ocean:
The waves, they was fiddlin' and small,
There was no wrecks and nobody drownded,
Fact, nothing to laugh at at all.

So, seeking for further amusement,
They paid and went into the Zoo,
Where they'd Lions and Tigers and Camels,
And old ale and sandwiches too.

There were one great big Lion called Wallace;
His nose were all covered with scars –
He lay in a somnolent posture
With the side of his face on the bars.

Now Albert had heard about Lions,
How they were ferocious and wild –
To see Wallace lying so peaceful,
Well, it didn't seem right to the child.

So straightway the brave little feller,
Not showing a morsel of fear,
Took his stick with its 'orse's 'ead 'andle
And pushed it in Wallace's ear.

You could see that the Lion didn't like it,
For giving a kind of a roll,
He pulled Albert inside the cage with 'im,
And swallowed the little lad 'ole.

Then Pa, who had seen the occurrence,
And didn't know what to do next,
Said 'Mother! Yon Lion's 'et Albert,'
And Mother said 'Well, I am vexed!'

Then Mr. and Mrs. Ramsbottom –
Quite rightly, when all's said and done –
Complained to the Animal Keeper
That the Lion had eaten their son.

The keeper was quite nice about it;
He said 'What a nasty mishap.
Are you sure it's *your* boy he's eaten?'
Pa said 'Am I sure? There's his cap!'

The manager had to be sent for.
He came and he said 'What's to do?'
Pa said 'Yon Lion's 'et Albert,
And 'im in his Sunday clothes, too.'

The Mother said, 'Right's right, young feller;
I think it's a shame and a sin
For a lion to go and eat Albert,
And after we've paid to come in.'

The manager wanted no trouble,
He took out his purse right away,
Saying 'How much to settle the matter?'
And Pa said 'What do you usually pay?'

But Mother had turned a bit awkward
When she thought where her Albert had gone.
She said 'No! someone's got to be
    summonsed' –
So that was decided upon.

Then off they went to the P'lice Station,
In front of the Magistrate chap;
They told 'im what happened to Albert,
And proved it by showing his cap.

The Magistrate gave his opinion
That no one was really to blame
And he said that he hoped the Ramsbottoms
Would have further sons to their name.

At that Mother got proper blazing,
'And thank you sir, kindly,' said she.
'What, waste all our lives raising children
To feed ruddy Lions? Not me!'

Marriott Edgar

2

There are several amusing lines in the poem. Pick out two separate lines and try to explain why they are funny.

DEVELOPMENT

3 Language

Rewrite the following phrases in standard English.

a 'a stick with an 'orse's 'ead 'andle'
b 'The waves, they was fiddlin''
c 'the brave little feller'
d 'swallowed the little lad 'ole'
e 'Yon lion's 'et Albert'
f 'Well, I am vexed'
g 'proper blazing'

4 Reading

Describe young Albert.

5 Reading

Why were the Ramsbottoms disappointed when they first arrived in Blackpool?

6 Reading

Why did Albert poke his stick in Wallace's ear?

7 Reading

Do you think Mrs Ramsbottom's reaction after Wallace had eaten her son is normal? Write a short paragraph explaining your response.

8 Speaking and listening

Act out an interview with Mr or Mrs Ramsbottom for a TV news report. It is important to distinguish between the standard speech of your news reporter and the less formal speech of Mr and Mrs Ramsbottom.

9 Writing

Write a newspaper report about the incident in the poem. Include:

- facts about the incident
- details about the incident
- opinions
- eyewitness accounts.

You should answer these questions:

- **What** happened?
- **When** did it happen?
- **Where** did it happen?
- **Who** was involved?
- **How** and **why** did it happen?

Don't forget to write in short, clear sentences, organising your writing into paragraphs.

10 Writing

Write about something memorable or amusing that happened to you on holiday. Make your account exciting and interesting by using varied expression and vocabulary.

REVIEW

There is a sequel to 'The Lion and Albert' called 'Albert Comes Back'. Can you imagine what might happen in this poem?

Homophones

AIMS

- To improve spelling and usage of many high frequency words which are easily confused.
- To learn new vocabulary and to use it accurately.

STARTER

1

> A **homophone** is a word that sounds the same as another word but is spelt differently (e.g. allowed/aloud; are/our; beach/beech; been/bean).

Write a sentence using each of the following homophones correctly.

a there/their/they're
b where/were/wear
c two/too/to

DEVELOPMENT

2

Match up the following homophones with the correct definition.

Homophone

1	blue	**11**	dear
2	blew	**12**	deer
3	bored	**13**	flour
4	board	**14**	flower
5	break	**15**	hair
6	brake	**16**	hare
7	cell	**17**	hole
8	sell	**18**	whole
9	cereal	**19**	peace
10	serial	**20**	piece

Definition

- **a** a wide piece of wood
- **b** a part of something
- **c** brightly coloured part of plant
- **d** a gap or hollow place
- **e** tranquillity or calm
- **f** the total thing
- **g** used for baking
- **h** the colour of the sky or sea
- **i** a mechanism for stopping a vehicle
- **j** Rudolph is a type of this animal
- **k** to exchange for money
- **l** fine threadlike stuff on your head
- **m** a room in a prison
- **n** completely uninterested
- **o** grain eaten at breakfast perhaps
- **p** past tense of blow
- **q** to smash into pieces
- **r** a series of connected TV programmes
- **s** an affectionate start to a letter
- **t** a rabbit-like mammal with long ears

3

Write sentences using the following homophones.

a	grate/great	**h**	herd/heard
b	key/quay	**i**	leak/leek
c	slay/sleigh	**j**	steal/steel
d	sum/some	**k**	tail/tale
e	through/threw	**l**	waist/waste
f	week/weak	**m**	wholly/holy
g	wring/ring		

4

*A **homograph** is a word that can be pronounced differently and has different meanings although its spelling stays the same (e.g. I bought my dog a new **lead**. My bag is as heavy as **lead**.)*

Use the following homographs in sentences which show their different meanings.

a read
b tear
c bow
d sow

5

The following words and homophones are easily confused. Go through them and make sure you know the difference between them. Use a dictionary to work out their meaning or ask your teacher if necessary.

a a lot/allot
b advise/advice
c affect/effect
d allowed/aloud
e bought/brought
f breath/breathe
g braking/breaking
h check/cheque
i choose/chose
j cloth/clothe
k conscience/conscious
l course/coarse
m our/are
n practice/practise
o quiet/quite
p site/sight
q source/sauce
r threw/through

6

Here are some more easily confused words. Use a dictionary to help you put them in sentences of your own.

a continual/continuous
b ensure/insure
c fate/fete
d formally/formerly
e goal/gaol
f knead/need
g license/licence
h main/mane
i muscle/mussel
j past/passed
k stationary/stationery
l storey/story
m vain/vein

REVIEW

What rules and strategies can you think of to help you remember how to spell some of the more difficult words you have come across in this unit?

UNIT 15 Gollum

AIMS

- To extract information from a text and work out meanings.
- To understand how a writer builds up a mood of tension and excitement.

STARTER

1

🔬 **Onomatopoeia** *occurs when words are used which sound like the noise they are describing (e.g. bang, baa, crash, squelch, rustle).*

Write down as many onomatopoeic words as you can.

INTRODUCTION

In the following passage from *The Hobbit* Bilbo Baggins has his first encounter with the vile creature Gollum. Consider how the writer builds up an unpleasant and dangerous image of Gollum.

2

Using a thesaurus find an alternative verb for each of the following.

**paddled   dangling   grabbed
throttled   prowling   lurking
tunnelling   flummoxed   thrusting**

The Hobbit

Deep down here by the dark water lived old Gollum, a small slimy creature. I don't know where he came from, nor who or what he was. He was a Gollum – as dark as darkness, except for two big round pale eyes in his thin face. He had a little boat, and he rowed about quite quietly on the lake; for lake it was, wide and deep and deadly cold. He paddled it with large feet dangling over the side, but never a ripple did he make. Not he. He was looking out of his pale lamp-like eyes for blind fish, which he grabbed with his long fingers as quick as thinking. He liked meat too. Goblin he thought good, when he could get it; but he took care they never found him out. He just throttled them from behind, if they

ever came down alone anywhere near the edge of the water, while he was prowling about. They very seldom did, for they had a feeling that something unpleasant was lurking down there, down at the very roots of the mountain. They had come on the lake, when they were tunnelling down long ago, and they found they could go no further; so there their road ended in that direction, and there was no reason to go that way – unless the Great Goblin sent them. Sometimes he took a fancy for fish from the lake, and sometimes neither goblin nor fish came back.

Actually Gollum lived on a slimy island of rock in the middle of the lake. He was watching Bilbo now from the distance with his pale eyes like telescopes. Bilbo could not see him, but he was wondering a lot about Bilbo, for he could see that he was no goblin at all.

Gollum got into his boat and shot off from the island, while Bilbo was sitting on the brink altogether flummoxed and at the end of his way and his wits. Suddenly up came Gollum and whispered and hissed:

'Bless us and splash us, my preciousss! I guess it's a choice feast; at least a tasty morsel it'd make us, gollum!' And when he said *gollum* he made a horrible swallowing noise in his throat. That is how he got his name, though he always called himself 'my precious'.

The hobbit jumped nearly out of his skin when the hiss came in his ears, and he suddenly saw the pale eyes sticking out at him.

'Who are you?' he said, thrusting his dagger in front of him.

J.R.R. Tolkien

DEVELOPMENT

3 Reading

How did Gollum get his name?

4 Reading

Describe Gollum in as much detail as you can.

5 Reading

How does Gollum move his boat around?

6 Reading

How does the writer reveal that this creature hisses?

7 Reading

What is meant by the simile 'pale eyes like telescopes'?

8 Speaking and listening

Discuss how the writer builds up feelings of tension and excitement.

9 Writing

Continue the story. How do you think Bilbo escapes from Gollum? Try to create a dark and sinister atmosphere, and maintain an element of tension.

10 Writing

Write a story called 'A Dangerous Situation', about coming face to face with a menacing person or creature. Remember to develop:

- a tense and exciting atmosphere
- lively and varied vocabulary
- interesting and imaginative descriptive passages.

REVIEW

Think about why Tolkein's description of Gollum is so successful and exciting. What techniques have you learnt from reading this passage and by writing your continuation of the story?

UNIT 16 Monster madness

AIMS

- To look at how alliteration is used to create interesting effects.
- To plan and write a monster poem which uses some of the techniques learnt in this unit.

STARTER

1

> **Alliteration** is a sound effect found in writing, usually in poetry, when words close to each other begin with the same letter (e.g. 'He **g**obbles **g**reen **g**ottles').

Look at the following examples of alliteration.

Angelic Anna ate an apple and an aubergine.

Creative Colin can colour carefully with crayons.

Write a sentence or phrase including your first name in which most of the words begin with the same letter as your name. Go round the class and find out what other people have written about themselves. Put some of the lines together to form a short poem.

INTRODUCTION

Read the following poems carefully. Think about which lines you like the most. Which is your favourite example of alliteration from the poems?

The Muddy, Mucky, Murky Mouch

On a small asteroid
in the terrible void
dwells a filthy old slouch,
the vile m-m-m-Mouch.
He sleeps in spaghetti,
looks just like a yeti,
and his grotty green wig
would embarrass a pig.
He enjoys a good splosh
in tomato juice squash,
while from swimming in sludge
he's the colour of fudge.
He gobbles green gottles,
swigs pond ooze from bottles
and the stench of his breath
scares all known germs to death.
He's a jumbo sized pest,
falls asleep fully dressed,
and far, far out in Space
he's the last of his race.
The vile m-m-m-Mouch
doesn't run, jump or crouch,
but squats, gnarled as a gnome,
on his asteroid home.

Wes Magee

The Blob

And ... and what is it like?

Oh, it's scary and fatbumped
and spike-eared and groany.
It's hairy and face-splumped
and bolshie and bony.

And ... and where does it live?

Oh, in comets and spaceships
and pulsars and blackholes.
In craters and sheepdips
and caverns and northpoles.

And ... what does it eat?

Oh, roast rocks and fishlegs
and x-rays and mooncrust.
Then steelmeat and sun-eggs
and lava and spacedust.

And ... who are its enemies?

Oh, Zonkers and Moonquakes
and Sunquarks and Zigbags.
Dumb Duncers and Milkshakes
and Smogsters and Wigwags.

And ... what does it wear?

Not a thing! It's bare!

Wes Magee

2

Examine closely how Wes Magee combines alliteration, a whole range of imaginative ideas and many unusual word choices.

DEVELOPMENT

3 Reading

Describe the appearance of the Muddy, Mucky, Murky Mouch.

4 Reading

Where does the Muddy, Mucky, Murky Mouch live?

5 Reading

Pick out two examples of alliteration from the poem.

6 Reading

Draw a picture of the Muddy, Mucky, Murky Mouch and label it in a way suitable for a reference book for space travellers.

7 Reading

Create a menu for The Blob's favourite restaurant. Use some of his favourite food from the poem and make up some of your own dishes.

8 Reading

Which monster do you think is the most dangerous and frightening? Give reasons for your answer.

9 Language

There are lots of compound words in 'The Blob'. Some are made up, such as 'steelmeat' ('steel' + 'meat'). Some are real words, like 'spaceships' ('space' + 'ships'). Make a list of real and made up compound words from the poem.

10 Writing

Think of a name for a monster. Now write a monster poem, using the same structure as 'The Blob'. Can you think of any unusual words, phrases or ideas which are suitably horrible for a successful monster poem?

11 Writing

Imagine your monster comes to visit you. Write a short account of what happens.

REVIEW

Your teacher will ask you to read out some of your poems. Have you managed to use alliteration and unusual compound words? Are your monsters as horrible as The Blob and the Muddy, Mucky, Murky Mouch?

AIMS

- To examine non-fiction writing in order to understand its form and function.
- To produce a piece of writing using available information and applying any techniques you have learnt.

ghost   monster   witch
ghoul   castle   forest

STARTER

1

> An **adjective** is used to describe a noun and enhance its meaning (e.g. small pointed ears, a big red bus).

Put two suitable adjectives in front of the following nouns.

INTRODUCTION

A werewolf is a mythical creature, created when a human being transforms into a wolf at the time of the full moon. If you were to come face to face with a werewolf, which piece of advice from the fact file below do you think would be the most useful in protecting you?

2

Pick out any words and phrases from the passage which you would typically find in a piece of non-fiction writing.

Monster Werewolf – FACT FILE

1 A werewolf is said to be rather like a vampire when they are both in human form. They have small, pointed ears, hair on the palms of their clawed hands and eyebrows that meet in the middle. The werewolf, however, has the ring finger of each hand a little longer than the middle finger – in humans and vampires the middle finger is longer.

2 Superstitious people believe that if you sleep outdoors when a full moon falls on a Friday, then you may turn into a werewolf. Eating the plant wolfbane can have this effect too.

3 Human shape-changers can take many forms depending on where in the world they are: in Africa people believed in were-leopards, in India weretigers, in Scandinavia, werebears.

4 Wereanimal stories are often linked with stories of witchcraft. The theory was that witches could turn themselves into animals whenever they wanted.

5 If attacked by a werewolf then, Canadians say, a good defence is to speak the name of Christ. The French recommend taking three drops of the wolf's blood. The most famous method, favoured by film-makers, is to take the silver from a church crucifix, mould it into the shape of a bullet and shoot the werewolf.

6 Werewolves are believed to grow hair *inside* their bodies. Sadly one suspect died in Italy in 1541 when his accusers tried to prove this by cutting him open. He was innocent of course – but that was no comfort to the dead man's family.

7 If a werewolf is wounded in its wolf form then its human form will suffer a similar wound. For example, cut off the wolf's paw and it becomes a man with a missing hand. This is known as *wound-doubling*.

Terry Deary

DEVELOPMENT

3 Language

Match each monster to its correct definition.

**zombie Big Foot centaur Cyclops
Minotaur griffin Medusa troll**

a large, hairy North American creature resembling a yeti

b a creature resembling a man from the waist up and a horse from the waist down

c a giant or dwarf from Scandinavian mythology

d a soulless corpse brought to life by witchcraft

e a mythical creature with an eagle's head and wings and a lion's body

f one-eyed monster from Greek mythology

g a woman from Greek mythology who turns an onlooker to stone – has hair consisting of snakes

h a half-bull, half-man monster from Greek mythology

4 Reading

How is a werewolf different from a vampire or a human?

5 Reading

How might you turn into a werewolf?

6 Reading

Describe two methods of defending yourself against werewolves.

7 Writing

Write a short werewolf survival guide using some of the information from the extract. Before you start writing, think about the sections you will need.

8 Writing

Write a fact file for a monster of your choice. Either go to your nearest library or search the Internet for information. Think about:

- the layout – use appropriate section headings
- the language – keep it simple and direct.

9 Speaking and listening

You discover that one of your friends is either a werewolf or a vampire. Act out a conversation in which you accuse them of behaving in a peculiar way.

10 Writing

Write a short story about coming face to face with a werewolf. Do you have to use any of the techniques described in this unit to protect yourself?

REVIEW

Read out some extracts from your survival guides to the class. Have you used language suitable for a piece of non-fiction writing? What improvements could you make to your own writing?

UNIT 18 Blackmangle arrives: Help!

AIMS

- To continue to develop strategies for learning spellings.
- To plan and develop an interesting children's story suitable for young readers.

STARTER

1

Invent ways to make learning the following words easier (e.g. mnemonics or splitting the words up into roots, affixes or syllables).

beautiful   beginning   conscious disappear   embarrass   furthermore

> An **affix** is part of a word such as a prefix or a suffix. It is added to change word class or meaning. For example, the suffix 'ing' is added to the noun 'interest' to form an adjective – 'interesting'; the prefix 'un' is added to 'interesting' to give it the opposite meaning – 'uninteresting'.

INTRODUCTION

The comedian Spike Milligan was famous for his unusual comedy and outrageous ideas. Pick out two features which indicate that this story about a wicked giant is aimed at children.

2

Do you think children would find the story scary?

Blackmangle arrives: Help!

One day a great shadow fell over King Big-Twytt's castle, and everyone thought it was night time. Then they realised that it was the shadow of Blackmangle.   5

'You didn't tell me he was a giant,' said Sir Nobonk.

Blackmangle let out a great roar: 'Come out and fight!'

Sir Nobonk went out and looked up.   10 'You'll have to wait, we haven't had breakfast yet.'

'Well, hurry up,' said Blackmangle, 'I'm waiting to kill you.'

'If you kill me,' said Sir Nobonk, 'I'll   15 never speak to you again.'

Blackmangle sat on the grass and waited. It was a hot day. Little Willy rushed in and said to King Big-Twytt, 'Blackmangle has fallen asleep, we   20 must wake him up.'

'Why?' said King Big-Twytt.

'Because,' said Little Willy, 'Big Bill is underneath him.'

'No,' said the Wizard, 'while he is   25

asleep he is not dangerous – we must try and keep him asleep.'

'How?' said Sir Nobonk.

'Follow me, I will show you,' said the Wizard.   30

The Wizard put a ladder up against Blackmangle and they all climbed up on to his belly. [...] Wizard said: 'Head for his nose.' [...]

'Where are you going?' asked Sir   35
Nobonk.

'I've got to get to his brain,' said the Wizard. 'Once I reach it I can find the piece that makes him bad and switch it off.'

So they all followed the Wizard up the 40
giant's nose, and soon they were in the giant's brain! Different parts were marked 'Good bit', 'Bad bit', 'Naughty bit', 'Nice bit', 'Don't-want-to-go-to-bed bit', 'Eating-too-much-jelly bit', and   45
'Smelly-poo' bit.

'Ah,' said the Wizard and pointed to a bit marked 'Killing dragon bit'. He saw a switch on it marked ON-OFF. He reached up and put it to OFF, then he   50
switched all the bad bits off. All the giant's body shook like an earthquake!

They all ran down his nose, and on to his belly which was shaking like a jelly! [...] Then the giant woke up.   55

'Hello, everybody,' he said. 'What a lovely day, let's go and pick blackberries.' He was ever so kind and polite.

'You've done it,' said Sir Nobonk to the Wizard and gave him a chocolate medal. 60

Spike Milligan

DEVELOPMENT

3 Language

Rewrite lines 31–34, changing the atmosphere from light-hearted to tense by putting in these adjectives.

**evil   murderous   huge   threatening
vile   wicked   gruesome   hideous
loathsome   monstrous   terrible
repulsive   spiteful**

4 Reading

How does Sir Nobonk stop Blackmangle attacking him?

5 Reading

Explain the Wizard's plan for stopping Blackmangle being bad.

6 Reading

How does Blackmangle change by the end of the story?

7 Writing

Write a story suitable for younger children involving an encounter with a horrible creature or monster. Think about:

- whether your story is going to be funny or frightening
- what is going to happen – a paragraph plan is useful
- suitable ideas and language for children.

8 Speaking and listening

If you have a younger brother or sister try out your story on them. What was their reaction?

REVIEW

What makes a story frightening or funny? Swap stories with a partner and pick out any passages you think are funny or frightening.

UNIT 19 A note about witches

AIMS

- To think about how an information sheet or advice leaflet is organised.
- To organise and write an information sheet or advice leaflet suitable for young children, taking into consideration suitable layout and language.

STARTER

1

Change the following present tense verb forms into the past tense (e.g 'wear' becomes 'wore').

ride forget spend think say choose understand catches go

Can you think of any more verbs with irregular past tense forms?

> A **verb** is a word which describes an action (e.g. I **walk** to school, I **enjoy** reading). Verbs change form according to the tense involved, for example we **walked** (past tense), we **will walk** (future tense), we **are walking** (present continuous).

INTRODUCTION

Most children are fascinated by witches and magic from a very early age. How many stories can you think of which involve witches, either good or bad? In his popular story 'The Witches' Roald Dahl makes it absolutely clear that the danger posed by witches is no laughing matter.

A NOTE ABOUT WITCHES

In fairy-tales, witches always wear silly black hats and black cloaks, and they ride on broomsticks.

But this is not a fairy-tale. This is about REAL WITCHES.

The most important thing you should know about REAL WITCHES is this. Listen very carefully. Never forget what is coming next.

REAL WITCHES dress in ordinary clothes and look very much like ordinary women. They live in ordinary houses and they work in ORDINARY JOBS.

That is why they are so hard to catch.

A REAL WITCH hates children with a red-hot sizzling hatred that is more sizzling and red-hot than any hatred you could possibly imagine.

A REAL WITCH spends all her time plotting to get rid of the children in her particular territory. Her passion is to do away with them, one by one. It is all she thinks about the whole day long. Even if she is working as a cashier in a supermarket or typing letters for a businessman or driving round in a fancy car (and she could be doing any of these things), her mind will always be plotting and scheming and churning and burning and whizzing and phizzing with murderous bloodthirsty thoughts.

'Which child,' she says to herself all day

long, 'exactly which child shall I choose for my next squelching?'

A REAL WITCH gets the same pleasure from squelching a child as *you* get from eating a plateful of strawberries and thick cream.

She reckons on doing away with one child a week. Anything less than that and she becomes grumpy.

One child a week is fifty-two a year.

Squish them and squiggle them and make them disappear.

That is the motto of all witches.

Very carefully a victim is chosen. Then the witch stalks the wretched child like a hunter stalking a little bird in the forest. She treads softly. She moves quietly. She gets closer and closer. Then at last, when everything is ready ... *phwisst*! ... and she swoops! Sparks fly. Flames leap. Oil boils. Rats howl. Skin shrivels. And the child disappears.

A witch, you must understand, does not knock children on the head or stick knives into them or shoot at them with a pistol. People who do those things get caught by the police.

A witch never gets caught. Don't forget that she has magic in her fingers and devilry dancing in her blood. She can make stones jump about like frogs and she can make tongues of flame go flickering across the surface of the water. These magic powers are very frightening.

Luckily, there are not a great number of REAL WITCHES in the world today. But there are still quite enough to make you nervous. In England, there are probably about one hundred of them altogether. Some countries have more, others have not quite so many. No country in the world is completely free from WITCHES.

Roald Dahl

2

If a young child read this passage would they feel happy, sad, worried, excited, reassured, frightened or vulnerable?

DEVELOPMENT

3 Language

Pick out one example of repetition and explain why the writer has used it.

4 Language

Pick out five words that are onomatopoeic and describe the overall impression of witches Roald Dahl is trying to convey.

5 Reading

Why are Real Witches difficult to catch?

6 Reading

How does a Real Witch spend her time?

7 Reading

How many children does a Real Witch try to get rid of in a year?

8 Reading

Why does a Real Witch never get caught?

9 Reading

How many Real Witches are there in England?

10 Speaking and listening

Brainstorm ideas about what a successful information or advice sheet should have. Consider:

- language
- layout and organisation
- presentational appeal.

11 Writing

Produce an information sheet about the dangers of witches. You might wish to offer some advice about how to deal with them.

Before you start, plan the layout. Don't forget to:

- think about the sections you need
- keep your language simple and direct
- think about bullet points, bold type and fonts
- think about illustrations or graphics
- use interesting and appropriate headings and subheadings

Look at the extract if you run out of ideas.

12 Writing

You find out an adult you know is really a witch. Write a letter to a friend describing their suspicious behaviour and refer to any evidence you have uncovered.

REVIEW

Look at each other's work and see if anybody has come up with any unusual, interesting or imaginative advice. What rules do you need to remember when writing an information sheet or advice leaflet?

UNIT 20 Spells and potions

AIMS

- To look at how language has changed and to examine the meaning of familiar and unfamiliar words in a Shakespeare text.
- To identify how sentence structure and punctuation are different in older texts.

STARTER

1

Plan a school dinner menu for your worst enemy, featuring the most disgusting things you can think of.

INTRODUCTION

The following extract is probably the most famous witches' scene in the whole of English literature. Think about the overall atmosphere and impression Shakespeare creates by combining a list of gruesome and disgusting ingredients.

Macbeth – Act 4 Scene 1

An isolated place. Thunder. Enter the three witches with a cauldron.

1ST WITCH: Thrice the brindled cat hath mew'd.
2ND WITCH: Thrice and once the hedge-pig whin'd.
3RD WITCH: Harpier cries, 'Tis time, 'tis time.'
1ST WITCH: Round about the cauldron go:
In the poison'd entrails throw.
Toad, that under cold stone
Days and nights has thirty-one
Swelter'd venom sleeping got,
Boil thou first i'th' charmèd pot.
ALL: Double, double toil and trouble;
Fire burn, and cauldron bubble.
2ND WITCH: Fillet of a fenny snake,
In the cauldron boil and bake:
Eye of newt, and toe of frog,
Wool of bat, and tongue of dog,
Adder's fork, and blind-worm's sting,
Lizard's leg, and howlet's wing,

For a charm of powerful trouble,
Like a hell-broth, boil and bubble.
ALL: Double, double toil and trouble,
Fire burn and cauldron bubble.
3ᴿᴰ WITCH: Scale of dragon, tooth of wolf,
Witches' mummy, maw and gulf
Of the ravin'd salt-sea shark,
Root of hemlock digg'd i'th' dark;
Liver of blaspheming Jew,
Gall of goat, and slips of yew,
Sliver'd in the moon's eclipse;
Nose of Turk, and Tartar's lips,
Finger of birth-strangled babe,
Ditch-deliver'd by a drab,
Make the gruel thick and slab.
Add thereto a tiger's chaudron
For th'ingredient of our cauldron.
ALL: Double, double toil and trouble;
Fire burn and cauldron bubble.
2ᴺᴰ WITCH: Cool it with a baboon's blood,
Then the charm is firm and good.

William Shakespeare

2

Much of this spell is written in rhyming couplets (pairs of lines that rhyme). Why do think Shakespeare did this? What effect was he trying to achieve in this scene?

DEVELOPMENT

3 Language

Match up these words from the passage with their modern-day meaning.

a	brindled cat	1	hedgehog
b	hedge-pig	2	striped cat
c	howlet	3	mummified corpse
d	mummy	4	young owl
e	maw	5	throat
f	gulf	6	stomach
g	drab	7	entrails
h	chaudron	8	prostitute

4 Language

Syntax is concerned with the order of words in a sentence. In modern English a sentence is generally made up of a subject, then a verb and finally an object, for example 'The girl read the book' (subject = the girl, verb = read, object = the book).

In older texts, such as *Macbeth*, the verb often came at the end of a sentence or line. Rewrite the following in modern English.
a 'Thrice and once the hedge-pig whin'd'
b 'In the cauldron boil and bake'
c 'In the poison'd entrails throw'

5 Language

Many words in the extract are shortened by using an apostrophe. Write the full form of the following words.

**poison'd   'tis   ravin'd   sliver'd
i'th'   th'ingredient   deliver'd**

6 Speaking and listening

In groups of three, read the passage in a lively manner, thinking about rhythm and expression.

7 Writing

Rewrite this spell for a modern recipe book. How would it be set out? What headings do you need?

8 Writing

Write your own spell. Think up some gruesome ingredients to go into the potion. What will your spell do? What will you chant when you are stirring your potion?

REVIEW

Why do you think the witches were so popular in Shakespeare's play? What is it about their language that makes them so appealing to an audience, despite their evil characteristics?

UNIT 21 | A lesson in magic

AIMS

- To read a short extract and examine the feelings of different characters.
- To plan and write a story with an effective opening, clear structure and satisfying ending.

STARTER

1

Work out which three school subjects these words are from.

alkaline desert addition combustion landscape element decimal particles estimate rural subtraction urban laboratory vertical weather

Put the words in three columns and make sure you can spell them using the 'Look, Say, Cover, Write, Check' technique.

> **Technical language** includes the words needed to help you understand a particular subject. For instance, in ICT you need words like 'hardware', 'icon', 'password', etc.

INTRODUCTION

This extract from *Harry Potter and the Philosopher's Stone* describes a Potions lesson with a new teacher who is very hard to please. Read it through and consider what the characters think of each other.

2

What are Harry and Ron's initial impressions of Potions lessons and Professor Snape? What is Professor Snape's attitude towards his new pupils, particularly Harry?

The Potions Master

Snape finished calling the names and looked up at the class. His eyes were black like Hagrid's, but they had none of Hagrid's warmth. They were cold and empty and made you think of dark tunnels.

'You are here to learn the subtle science and exact art of potionmaking,' he began. He spoke in barely more than a whisper, but they caught every word – like Professor McGonagall, Snape had the gift of keeping a class silent without effort. 'As there is little foolish wand-waving here, many of you will hardly believe this is magic. I don't expect you will really understand the beauty of the softly simmering cauldron with its shimmering fumes, the delicate power of liquids that creep through human veins, bewitching the mind, ensnaring the senses ... I can teach you how to bottle fame, brew glory, even stopper death – if you aren't as big a bunch of dunderheads as I usually have to teach.'

More silence followed this little speech. Harry and Ron exchanged looks with raised eyebrows. Hermione Granger was on the edge of her seat and looked desperate to start proving that she wasn't a dunderhead.

'Potter!' said Snape suddenly. 'What would I get if I added powdered root of asphodel to an infusion of wormwood?'

Powdered root of what to an infusion of what? Harry glanced at Ron, who looked as stumped as he was; Hermione's hand had shot into the air.

'I don't know, sir,' said Harry.

Snape's lips curled into a sneer.

'Tut, tut – fame clearly isn't everything.'

He ignored Hermione's hand.

'Let's try again. Potter, where would you look if I told you to find me a bezoar?'

Hermione stretched her hand as high into the air as it would go without her leaving her seat, but Harry didn't have the faintest idea what a bezoar was. He tried not to look at Malfoy, Crabbe and Goyle, who were shaking with laughter.

'I don't know, sir.'

'Thought you wouldn't open a book before coming, eh, Potter?'

Harry forced himself to keep looking straight into those cold eyes. He *had* looked through his books at the Dursleys', but did Snape expect him to remember everything in *One Thousand Magical Herbs and Fungi*?

Snape was still ignoring Hermione's quivering hand.

'What is the difference, Potter, between monkshood and wolfsbane?'

At this, Hermione stood up, her hand stretching towards the dungeon ceiling.

'I don't know,' said Harry quietly. 'I think Hermione does, though, why don't you try her?'

A few people laughed; Harry caught Seamus's eye and Seamus winked. Snape, however, was not pleased.

'Sit down,' he snapped at Hermione. 'For your information, Potter, asphodel and wormwood make a sleeping potion so powerful it is known as the Draught of Living Death. A bezoar is a stone taken from the stomach of a goat and it will save you from most poisons. As for monkshood and wolfsbane, they are the same plant, which also goes by the name of aconite. Well? Why aren't you all copying that down?'

There was a sudden rummaging for quills and parchment. Over the noise, Snape said, 'And a point will be taken from Gryffindor house for your cheek, Potter.'

J.K. Rowling

DEVELOPMENT

3 Reading

Comment on Harry's performance in this Potions lesson.

4 Reading

What are monkshood and wolfsbane?

5 Reading

According to Professor Snape, what can you do with asphodel and wormwood?

6 Reading

What are your impressions of Professor Snape?

7 Speaking and listening

Act out the conversation Ron and Harry have after the lesson. Discuss your first impressions of your new teacher.

8 Writing

Write a story called 'The Spell that Goes Wrong'. Before you start, think about:

- what your spell is supposed to do
- who you are going to use it on and why
- what goes wrong
- how you put things right
- an interesting opening paragraph
- characters and setting
- building up atmosphere and tension
- a satisfying ending.

Let a friend read your first draft. Can they suggest any improvements?

9 Writing

Make a list of technical vocabulary you might need for a Potions lesson (there are lots of examples in the extract).

REVIEW

Have you ever been in a situation like Harry? How did you feel? You may be asked to read your story out loud – did you manage to get across how the character was feeling?

UNIT 22 Connectives

AIMS

- To use connectives correctly and accurately.
- To understand how connectives can be used to change simple sentences into complex sentences.

STARTER

1

Unscramble the following connectives.

**dan tub hent efrat eebsuac
os gouhht hilew lagouhht rof
lintu ety sa ro hwen**

Write sentences using three of the connectives you have managed to unscramble.

> A **connective** is a word, such as 'and', which joins together words and phrases to create a longer and more complex sentence. For example: I like fish **and** chips with just a splash of vinegar, **but** not too much, **and also** a pinch of salt.

DEVELOPMENT

2

Join these simple sentences together and make one complex or compound sentence using **and** or **but**.

a I like chocolate. I enjoy eating sweets.
b I love cricket. I hate football.
c The teacher entered the classroom. She greeted the children.
d I looked at the magazines in the newsagents. I didn't buy anything.

e At the moment I am the reserve goalkeeper for the girls' football team. One day I hope to be in the starting eleven.

3

Now join these sentences. This time, use **then** or **when**.

a Yesterday I went to school. On the way home I visited my grandmother.
b It is time to go home. The bell goes at 3.30.
c When I get home I am going to do my homework. I am going to watch Blue Peter.
d My mum lets me go out to play. I've finished my homework.

4

Try joining the following sentences using either **because** or **although**.

a I support Arsenal. My dad comes from North London.
b I love ice cream. I don't mind cheesecake.
c I am not going to school today. I am not feeling very well.
d My mum would like us to go to Spain for our holiday this year. My dad would rather go to Portugal.

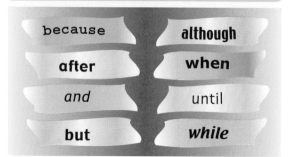

because   although
after   when
and   until
but   while

5

Complete the following paragraph about Meg Shelton, the Lancashire witch. Use the connectives in the box – you can use each one more than once.

> **and   but   as   which
> when   after   because**

Meg Shelton was a crafty old witch _____ her real name was Margery Hilton. She lived in a cottage at Cuckoo Hall near Wesham, Lancashire _____ was alive in the seventeenth century. Meg could turn herself into many different animals, _____ helped her steal food from neighbouring farms. On one occasion she turned herself into a hare _____ was bitten by a black dog _____ she was being chased, _____ is how she got her limp. Meg was buried on 2nd May, 1705 by torchlight, _____ even so she would not rest quietly _____ she managed to scratch her way to the surface.

_____ Meg was buried again her head was pointed downwards.

_____ they buried her they placed a huge boulder on her grave, _____ is still at St Anne's Churchyard, Woodplumpton, Preston to this day.

6

Write a paragraph about the day you visited Meg Shelton's grave using as many different connectives as you can.

7

Make up a story about a place near your home being haunted or having a legend like the one involving Meg Shelton. Try to use connectives in your writing.

REVIEW

Why is the use of connectives important? How will using connectives improve your speech and writing?

Meg Shelton's grave at Woodplumpton.

UNIT 23 Inventors

AIMS

- To look at how information is presented in non-fiction writing.
- To present factual information and structure it appropriately.
- To prepare and deliver a speech.

STARTER

1

Non-fiction writing is generally clear and to the point. Which of these words might describe a non-fiction text?

**clear descriptive direct slang
standard English formal informal
emotional chronological
third person recount fictitious
factual biased past tense
active verbs accurate fantasy**

> An **active verb** has a subject that performs the action (e.g. John Logie Baird (subject) **invented** (active verb) the television). Writing that uses active verbs is generally more direct than writing that uses passive verbs.

INTRODUCTION

Look at the following biography of the inventor John Logie Baird and consider what a young inventor could learn from his early struggles and his eventual remarkable success.

2

Pick out any words which you might consider to be technical or scientific.

John Logie Baird
Pioneer of TV – watch this channel!
1888–1946

Baird was a Scottish electrical engineer. In 1918 he had to give up his job with the Clyde Valley Electrical Company due to poor health which dogged him all his life. He marketed a patent sock, then jam, then honey, then soap. Each new business promised to be a success and each one failed due to his lousy health. He then had a nervous breakdown.

In 1922 he moved to Hastings. By this time people must have thought that he'd gone completely mad. He was determined to develop the first ever television. His first attempt was a crazy contraption: the lamp was mounted in a biscuit tin, the motor in a tea-chest, the scanning disc was cut from cardboard and the whole thing was stuck together with knitting needles, sealing wax and string. With this equipment, in 1924, he transmitted the world's first ever television image across several feet of his meagre, rented room. It was a picture of a Maltese cross. He moved to London, still struggling against sickness and poverty, and in 1926 – success at last! He showed his mad contraption to fifty scientists – the first public showing of a television. By 1928 he'd transmitted pictures between London and New York.

(from Who's Who in Science and Technology)

DEVELOPMENT

3 Language

Rewrite the second paragraph in four or five complex sentences. Use a variety of connectives.

4 Language

Based on the description of John Logie Baird's first attempt to build a TV, write a set of instructions for how to build your own television.

5 Reading

What are the main events in John Logie Baird's life? Write them down in chronological order starting each new line with a key date.

6 Speaking and listening

Imagine that you are John Logie Baird. Prepare a speech to convince fellow scientists about the merits of your new invention, the television. Perform your speech to the class.

7 Writing

Write a magazine article with the title 'TV: Good or Bad?'. Consider the following:

- the advantages and disadvantages of TV
- the effects of watching too much TV
- .how TV can benefit people your age.

Remember to plan your article.

- Write a list of possible paragraph topics.
- Devise potential sections.
- Start with a lively introduction.
- Finish off with a conclusion answering the original question.

8 Reading and writing

Find out as much information as you can about a famous inventor. Write a short biography in a format of your choice (e.g. a chronological account, a fact file, a report for a science textbook or a magazine article).

REVIEW

What are the main ingredients of non-fiction writing? How is non-fiction writing different from most types of fictional writing?

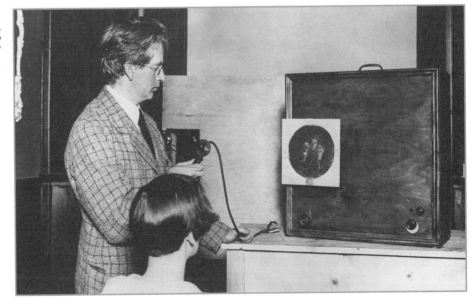

John Logie Baird demonstrating an early television set.

UNIT 24 The inventing room

AIMS

- To plan an advertising campaign.
- To write, plan and perform a TV commercial.

STARTER

1

> A **slogan** is a catchphrase or saying normally associated with a product or advertising campaign (e.g. 'Just do it' for Nike sportswear or 'Because I'm worth it' for L'Oréal hair products).

How many advertising slogans can you think of from TV, radio or magazines?

INTRODUCTION

This extract from *Charlie and the Chocolate Factory* is about Charlie Bucket's experiences in Wonka's Inventing Room, where he witnesses some sensational creations. How does Roald Dahl bring his description of the room to life?

2

Why do you think Roald Dahl invented such ridiculous names as 'Oompa-Loompas' and 'Willy Wonka' as part of his stories?

DEVELOPMENT

3 Language

Pick out three examples of onomatopoeia from the text.

4 Language

Pick out two adjectives which describe each of the following.

- colour
- size
- feel

The Inventing Room – Everlasting Gobstoppers and Hair Toffee

Charlie Bucket stared around the gigantic room in which he now found himself. The place was like a witch's kitchen! All about him black metal pots were boiling and bubbling on huge stoves, and kettles were hissing and pans were sizzling, and strange iron machines were clanking and spluttering, and there were pipes running all over the ceiling and walls, and the whole place was filled with smoke and steam and delicious rich smells.

Mr Wonka himself had suddenly become even more excited than usual, and anyone could see that this was the room he loved best of all. He was hopping about among the saucepans and the machines like a child among his Christmas presents, not knowing which thing to look at first. He lifted the lid from a huge pot and took a sniff; then he rushed over and dipped a finger into a barrel of sticky yellow stuff and had a taste; then he skipped across to one of the machines and turned half a dozen knobs this way and that; then he peered anxiously through the glass door of a gigantic oven, rubbing his hands and cackling with delight at what he saw inside. Then he ran over to another machine, a small shiny affair that kept going *phut-phut-phut-phut-phut*, and every time it went *phut*, a large green marble dropped out of it into a basket on the floor. At least it looked like a marble.

'Everlasting Gobstoppers!' cried Mr Wonka

proudly. 'They're completely new! I am inventing them for children who are given very little pocket money. You can put an Everlasting Gobstopper in your mouth and you can suck it and suck it and suck it and suck it and it will *never* get any smaller!'

'It's like gum!' cried Violet Beauregarde.

'It is *not* like gum,' Mr Wonka said. 'Gum is for chewing, and if you tried chewing one of these Gobstoppers here you'd break your teeth off! And they *never* get any smaller! They *never* disappear! *NEVER*! At least I don't think they do. There's one of them being tested this very moment in the Testing Room next door. An Oompa-Loompa is sucking it. He's been sucking it for very nearly a year now without stopping, and it's still just as good as ever!'

'Now, over here,' Mr Wonka went on, skipping excitedly across the room to the opposite wall, 'over here I am inventing a completely new line in toffees!' He stopped beside a large saucepan. The saucepan was full of a thick gooey purplish treacle, boiling and bubbling. By standing on his toes, little Charlie could just see inside it.

'That's Hair Toffee!' cried Mr Wonka. 'You eat just one tiny bit of that, and in exactly half an hour a brand-new luscious thick silky beautiful crop of hair will start growing out all over the top of your head! And a moustache! And a beard!'

'A beard!' cried Veruca Salt. 'Who wants a beard, for heaven's sake?'

'It would suit you very well,' said Mr Wonka.

Roald Dahl

5 Reading

How does Roald Dahl show Mr Wonka's excitement when he enters the Inventing Room? Pick out individual words and phrases.

6 Reading

Describe an Everlasting Gobstopper.

7 Reading

What is Hair Toffee like? Pick out the adjectives used to describe it.

8 Writing

Design a magazine or poster advertisement for a new sweet, toffee or chocolate bar.

- Explain why it is so good.
- Describe any special ingredients.
- Draw and design a wrapper.
- Think of a suitable advertising slogan.

9 Speaking and listening

Plan, write and act out a TV commercial for one of your new products. Include in your script:

- directions for actors and cameramen
- description of the setting, atmosphere and music
- your slogan.

10 Writing

Write a description of your favourite food. Try to use adjectives to make it sound as enticing as possible.

REVIEW

Look at each other's advertisements and commercials. Would you buy any products invented by your class? If so, which ones and why? What techniques do advertisers use to make their TV commercials and magazine advertisements appeal to young people?

UNIT 25 The Time Machine

AIMS

- To write an evocative, descriptive piece.
- To work out the meaning of new words or discover their meaning using a dictionary or thesaurus.

STARTER

1

> **Synonyms** are words with the same or similar meaning (e.g. worried/anxious; big/large; small/tiny; gorgeous/beautiful).

Using a thesaurus find synonyms for the following words.

**cold   hot   weird   dark
quick   horrid   lovely**

INTRODUCTION

The Time Machine by H.G. Wells is the story of a time traveller who reaches the future after inventing an incredible time machine. In the following extract, he describes the sensation of time travelling.

The Time Machine

'I am afraid I cannot convey the peculiar sensations of time travelling. They are excessively unpleasant. There is a feeling exactly like that one has upon a switchback – of a helpless headlong motion! I felt the same horrible anticipation, too, of an imminent smash. As I put on pace, night followed day like the flapping of a black wing. The dim suggestion of the laboratory seemed presently to fall away from me, and I saw the sun hopping swiftly across the sky, leaping it every minute, and every minute marking a day. I suppose the laboratory had been destroyed and I had come into the open air. I had a dim impression of scaffolding, but I was already going too fast to be conscious of any moving things. The slowest snail that ever crawled dashed by too fast for me. The twinkling succession of darkness and light was excessively painful to the eye. Then, in the intermittent darknesses, I saw the moon spinning swiftly through her quarters from new to full, and had a faint glimpse of the circling stars. Presently, as I went on, still gaining velocity, the palpitation of night and day merged into one continuous greyness; the sky took on a wonderful deepness of blue, a splendid luminous colour like that of early twilight; the jerking sun became a streak of fire, a brilliant arch, in space; the moon a fainter fluctuating band; and I could see nothing of the stars, save now and then a brighter circle flickering in the blue.'

H.G. Wells

2

How does the time traveller create a sensation of speed and the passage of time?

DEVELOPMENT

3 Language

This passage follows on from the extract. Put the words below in the right place.

> vague   speed   hillside   stands
> vapour   dreams   faster   hands
> passed   surface   eyes

'The landscape was misty and

_____(a). I was still on the

_____(b) upon which this house

now _____(c), and the shoulder

rose above me grey and dim. I saw trees

growing and changing like puffs of

_____(d), now brown, now green;

they grew, spread, shivered, and

_____ (e) away. I saw huge

buildings rise up faint and fair, and

pass like _____ (f). The whole

_____ (g) of the earth seemed

changed – melting and flowing under

my _____(h). The little _____(i)

upon the dials that registered my

_____(j) raced round faster and

_____(k).'

4 Language

Using a dictionary or thesaurus, match up these words from the extract with their correct synonym.

Word	Synonym
convey	extremely
excessively	express
anticipation	aware
imminent	interrupted
conscious	forthcoming
intermittent	expectation

5 Reading

Find phrases from the text which show:

- that time travelling is an unpleasant activity
- how the landscape changes during time travel
- that time passes very quickly when time travelling.

6 Writing

Imagine that you are a time traveller. Describe the sensations of time travel in a paragraph suitable for a teenage magazine.

7 Writing

Write a diary entry describing your first journey through time. Think about:

- whereabouts you end up in time
- what happens
- who you meet.

REVIEW

The Time Machine first appeared in serial form during 1894–95. How has written English changed over the past hundred years? Do you find the language of The Time Machine difficult? If so, why?

UNIT 26 Professor Branestawm's dictionary

AIMS

- To investigate the meanings of new words using a variety of techniques.
- To use some of these techniques to consider meaning when thinking up new words of your own.

STARTER

1

> The **denotation** of a word is its main or primary meaning. It is the first definition of a word in a dictionary (e.g. the denotation of 'call' is generally 'to speak at volume in order to attract someone's attention'). However, **connotations** (or secondary meanings) of 'call' include 'bird song', 'a wake-up message' and 'to telephone someone'.

Using a dictionary find the denotation of each of the following words.

**court   game   root
press   quarter   pack**

Find a connotation for each word.

INTRODUCTION

Professor Branestawm is the master of ingenious inventions and unusual contraptions. He has even managed to invent new meanings for many everyday words. As you read through the following examples think of the sounds within each word.

2

Using a dictionary if necessary write down the correct definition of five of the words in the extract.

Professor Branestawm's Dictionary

A

Aaron. What a wig has.

abandon. What a hat has.

abate. Something for catching fish.

abominable. A piece of explosive swallowed by a male cow.

abundance. A waltz for cakes.

accident. Mark made by a chopper.

account. A countess's husband.

accountant. Insect who is good at figures.

acquire. Group of singers.

addition. What a dinner table has.

allocate. A greeting for Catherine.

allotment. A good deal is intended.

also. Everybody stitch.

analyse. Ann doesn't tell the truth.

Norman Hunter

DEVELOPMENT

3 Language

New English words and phrases are constantly being created to fulfil the demands of the increasingly complex and technological world. Here are some which have appeared over recent years.

clone   information superhighway virtual reality   alcopop   yuppie walkman   website modem   Eurozone

Use five of these words in sentences of your own. See if you can find out when each word was used for the first time.

4 Reading

Explain how three of Professor Branestawm's definitions work. For example, the definition 'everybody stitch' for 'also' comes from the sound 'all' (everybody) in the first syllable and the sound 'sew' (stitch) in the second syllable. It sounds like a command telling everybody to sew or 'stitch'.

5 Speaking and listening

Using the techniques employed by Professor Branestawm in making his dictionary, make up new definitions for the following words (e.g. the definition of 'carpet' could be 'a pet you keep in a car').

capsize   cargo   catchword   catkin forty   handsome   hatred   igloo inward   manage   mango   mankind minimum   syllable   tango   thinking wayward   winsome

6 Writing

Think of new words for the following inventions.

a   a robotic teacher
b   a bicycle that flies
c   a skateboard without wheels
d   a solar-powered toothbrush
e   a pocketsize DVD player
f   a pen that never runs out
g   trainers that make you run very fast
h   a T-shirt that warms up in the cold
i   perfume that makes you disappear
j   glasses that help you see in the dark

7 Writing

Write a promotional leaflet for an invention that you think might appeal to people your own age. Give your invention a catchy name, explain what it does and how it works. How will your invention improve people's lives?

REVIEW

By now you should have some knowledge of how words come into the language. As a class, compare some of the words you invented in Question 6. Describe how you came to invent them.

AIMS

- To recognise different types of suffixes and understand how they might change words.
- To use suffixes correctly and accurately, thereby improving spelling.

STARTER

1

Suffixes are a type of affix or part of a word. Suffixes are placed at the end of a word to change its meaning or word class. For example, 'ate' is added to 'affection' (a noun) to make 'affectionate' (an adjective).
You may have to knock the 'e' or 'y' off some words when you add the suffix.

Add the suffixes 'al' or 'ary' to the following words and write a definition for each new word.

**accident   addition   mission
occasion   person   exception
nation   revolution   station
season   sensation**

DEVELOPMENT

Vowel suffixes
A vowel suffix begins with a vowel.

2

Add the suffix 'ic' to the following words to change their meanings and word class (i.e. from a noun to an adjective). You may have to add or take away some letters to create the correct form from the original word.

**acid   allergy   drama   energy
photograph   science**

3

Add the suffix 'ible' or 'able' to the following words.

**adore   agree   enjoy   force   like
excite   laugh   manage   respect
reverse   value**

4

Work out which suffix should be added to the following words to give the word for a person who does a particular job. Should it be 'er' or 'or'?

**act   paint   edit   profess   write
teach   drive   build   clean   bank**

5

Which suffix can be added to the following words – 'ion' or 'ian'?

**complete   music   magic
devote   electric   explode
statistic   tactic   promote
reduce   distribute   confuse**

Consonant suffixes
A consonant suffix begins with a consonant.

6

Think of as many words as you can which end in the consonant suffixes 'ly', 'ful' and 'less'. Create three columns in your exercise book. Only use a dictionary if you get stuck.

ly	ful	less

Changing words

7

One word can adopt many different suffixes. Some words can be changed into several forms by adding different suffixes (e.g. 'heavy' can be changed into 'heavier', 'heaviest', 'heavily', 'heaviness').
See how many different forms you can make from the following words by changing their suffixes.

happy   lazy   pretty

8

Think of a rule for what you need to do to words ending in 'y' when adding a suffix.

9

Look at the following words and add an appropriate suffix to change them.

**achieve   beauty   care   fanatic
free   hope   lone   love   home
realise   tear   trendy   vary   watch**

See if you can change each word more than once.

10

Rewrite the following sentences by correcting the suffix.

- **a** My brother is a musical.
- **b** The firework went off with a loud explosition.
- **c** The car was stationery.
- **d** I got a promotive at work.
- **e** My mother always puts pasta in a storeful jar.
- **f** I went to the opticion to get my eyes tested.
- **g** The soldiers stood to attension.
- **h** My compass helped me find the right directian.
- **i** She is very beautisome.
- **j** I am allergist to peanuts.

REVIEW

What rules can you think of when adding suffixes? For instance, what might you have to do if adding a vowel suffix to a word ending in 'e' or 'y'? There are lots of suffixes we haven't looked at in this unit. Can you think of any?

UNIT 28 The diary of Anne Frank

AIMS

- To make a speech about your hopes and dreams.
- To write a diary extract describing what you and your family would miss if you had your freedom taken away.

STARTER

1

Write down a list of five 'likes' and five 'dislikes'. Give your lists to your teacher, who will read them out. Can you guess who wrote each one?

> ♪ A **diary** involves writing a personal account of the events of each day, describing experiences and the writer's thoughts and feelings.

INTRODUCTION

In *The Diary of a Young Girl* Anne writes about her experience of being in hiding with her family during the Nazi occupation of Holland. Read the extract, looking at how Anne describes the intensity of people's hopes and dreams.

The diary of a Young Girl

Friday, 23rd July, 1943

Dear Kitty,

Let me tell you, just for fun, what we each want to do first when we're able to go outside again.

Margot and Mr van Daan wish, above all else, to have a hot bath, filled to the brim, which they can lie in for more than half an hour. Mrs van Daan would like a cake, Dusssel can think of nothing but seeing his Charlotte, and Mother is dying for a cup of real coffee. Father would like to visit Mr Voskuijl, Peter would go into town, and as for me, I'd be so overjoyed I wouldn't know where to begin.

Most of all I long to have a home of our own, to be able to move around freely and have someone help me with my homework again, at last. In other words, to go back to school!

Bep has offered to get us some fruit, at so-called bargain prices: grapes 2.50 guilders a pound, gooseberries 70 cents a pound, one peach 50 cents, melons 75 cents a pound. No wonder the papers write every evening in big, fat letters: 'Play Fair and Keep Prices Down'!

Yours,
Anne

Anne Frank

2

What evidence is there in the text to suggest that life was very different in 1943?

DEVELOPMENT

3 Language

Writing in diaries tends to be informal, with use of contractions instead of full forms (e.g. 'I'm' instead of 'I am'). Contract the following words.

should not
will not
shall not
you will
would not
I will
you are
do not

4 Speaking and listening

Plan a short speech beginning 'I wish...' in which you describe something you would really like to happen. For example, it could be going on a dream holiday, winning the lottery or finding a cure for a disease.

Practise making your speech to a partner before you deliver it to the whole class. Describe your wish clearly and explain why you want it so badly. Think about:

● speaking clearly
● trying not to sound like you are reading
● putting feeling into your speech.

5 Writing

Write your own diary entry for yesterday, describing what happened to you. Don't forget to include some thoughts and feelings.

6 Speaking and listening

Find out what your family and friends would really miss if they had to go into hiding like Anne and her family.

7 Writing

Imagine that you are in Anne Frank's situation. Write a diary extract describing what you and your family would miss more than anything. What would each of you do first after things get back to normal?

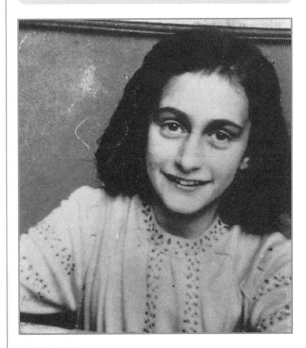

REVIEW

What would people in your class miss most of all if they had their freedom taken away from them or their lives changed in a time of war or conflict? Share some of your writing with the rest of the class.

UNIT 29 Carrie's War

AIMS

- To look at how a writer develops the mood and feelings of a character.
- To explore in the form of a story how you would react in a difficult situation.
- To use role play to express your feelings in a difficult situation.

STARTER

1

> **Attributes** are the qualities or features given to characters by writers. For instance, Harry Potter has the positive attributes of loyalty, bravery and honesty, whilst Draco Malfoy has more negative attributes, such as being devious and bullying.

Put the following attributes into three categories: positive, negative, and neutral.

cheerful plump fierce angry skinny ugly pretty handsome stout slender scrawny slight

Think of some more words to go in each list.

INTRODUCTION

This extract is about Carrie and Nick, who are sent to live in the safety of a Welsh village during the Second World War. Look at how the writer builds up a strong feeling of anxiety as Carrie waits to see which family she will end up with.

2

Describe some of the thoughts and feelings Carrie experiences in the passage.

Carrie's War

Nick clung to Carrie's sleeve as they went through the door into a long, dark room with pointed windows. It was crowded and noisy. Someone said to Carrie, 'Would you like a cup of tea, bach? And a bit of cake, now?' She was a cheerful, plump woman with a sing-song Welsh voice. Carrie shook her head; she felt cake would choke her. 'Stand by there, then,' the woman said. 'There by the wall with the others, and someone will choose you.'

Carrie looked round, bewildered, and saw Albert Sandwich. She whispered, 'What's happening?' and he said, 'A kind of cattle auction, it seems.'

He sounded calmly disgusted. He gave Carrie her suitcase, then marched to the end of the hall, sat down on his own, and took a book out of his pocket.

Carrie wished she could do that. Sit down and read as if nothing else mattered. But she had already begun to feel ill with shame at the fear that no one would choose her, the way she always felt when they picked teams at school. Suppose she was left to the last! She dragged Nick into the line of waiting children and stood, eyes on the ground, hardly daring to breathe. [...]

Nick's hand tightened in hers. She looked at his white face and the traces of sick round his mouth and wanted to shake him. No one would take home a boy who looked like that, so pale and delicate. They would think he was bound to get ill and be a trouble to them. She said in a low, fierce voice, 'Why don't you smile and look nice,' and he blinked with surprise, looking so small and so sweet that she softened. She said, 'Oh it's all right, I'm not cross, I won't leave you.'

Minutes passed, feeling like hours. Children left the line and were taken away. Only unwanted ones left, Carrie thought. She and Nick, and a few tough-looking boys, and an ugly girl with a squint who had two little sisters. And Albert Sandwich who was still sitting quietly on his suitcase, reading his book and taking no notice. *He* didn't care! Carrie tossed her head and hummed under her breath to show she didn't either.

Someone had stopped in front of her. Someone said, 'Surely you can take two, Miss Evans?'

'Two girls, perhaps. Not a boy and a girl, I'm afraid. I've only the one room, see, and my brother's particular.'

Particular about what, Carrie wondered. But Miss Evans looked nice; a little like a red squirrel Carrie had once seen, peering round a tree in a park. Reddish brown hair and bright, button eyes, and a shy, quivering look.

Carrie said, 'Nick sleeps in my room at home because he has bad dreams sometimes. I always look after him and he's no trouble at all.'

Miss Evans looked doubtful. 'Well, I don't know what my brother will say. Perhaps I can chance it.'

Nina Bawden

DEVELOPMENT

3 Language

The word 'nice' is often overused. Rephrase the following, replacing 'nice' with a different word.

a Why don't you smile and look nice?
b Miss Evans looked nice.

4 Language

Pick out words and phrases from the passage which show two of the following emotions.

confusion   worry   shame   relief

5 Reading

What is the atmosphere like in the room at the start of the extract?

6 Reading

Describe the woman who talks to Carrie at the beginning of the passage. How does she treat Carrie?

7 Reading

Why does Carrie think that no one would want to take Nick home?

8 Reading

How does Albert Sandwich behave while he is in the room?

9 Speaking and listening

Imagine you are evacuated into a stranger's home and have to share a bedroom with one of the children of the house. Act out your first conversation.

10 Writing

Write a story in which you are evacuated to a stranger's home in another part of the country. You should write about:

- how you feel
- differences from your own home
- people you meet
- problems you encounter
- how you overcome any difficulties.

11 Reading

Find out as much as you can about one of the following aspects of life in the Second World War:

- rationing and food
- air raids
- evacuees.

REVIEW

Share your writing with each other and think about how each writer manages to show their emotions.

Conflict

AIMS

- To find evidence in a text to show how atmosphere and meaning are developed.
- To comment in writing on how setting, atmosphere and character are carefully developed through word choice.
- To develop critical reflection skills and personal responses to texts.

STARTER

1

> 🎵 **Genre** is the type, style or category of a piece of writing. The three main literary genres are poetry, drama (plays) and prose. Each of these can be subdivided into other genres.

Consider the genre of prose or story writing. How many different types of story are there? Write a list and see if you can think of an example of each type.

INTRODUCTION

The following story gives you an impression of what life was like for some people during the Second World War – look out for the different feelings Rosie experiences through the story.

2

Which genre does the story fit into?

DEVELOPMENT

3 Language

Pick out any words and phrases that suggest that this story takes place during the Second World War.

Rosie

Rosie cut down Lime Street, walking fast. Not easy in the blackout. But there was a moon tonight, flirting with the clouds. A bomber's moon.

Rose was an ARP warden; air-raid patrol, a full-timer and proud of it. She liked being one of the few woman wardens, even if she'd had to lie about her age to get in. She was only eighteen, but big with it.

She liked the comradeship of the Warden's Post. She liked all the new people she met.

Before the War, she'd been a mother's help. A comfy life, but not a lot of thrills. Changing nappies; wheeling prams round Seffie Park. She'd loved the babies and they had loved her, but it hadn't been getting her anywhere.

Now she was meeting new people from morning 'til night. And she usually called in at some dance, after she came off duty. Strange, dancing in her warden's uniform; but there were plenty of girls in uniform now, Wrens and Waafs.

She met such interesting fellers. Tonight's bloke had lived in Australia and caught crocodiles with his bare hands to sell to zoos. Last week she'd met a cheerful undertaker, serving with the Irish Guards. The way he'd eyed her, she hadn't been sure he wasn't measuring her up for a coffin!

She liked a good time; but she wasn't a good-time girl. She always went home before eleven. Alone. That way, fellers didn't get the wrong idea.

Liverpool was safe enough. Nothing worse than some amorous drunk you had to hold up while he was talking to you. Easy enough to get away from *them*; they usually fell over when you let go of them.

The worst thing that could happen was you might fall into one of those great gaping pigswill bins in the dark, stinking of potato peelings and boiled-out fish-heads.

It was lonely, out on the streets. Her sharp

footsteps echoed off the tall buildings, but her gas mask case and tin hat banged against her bottom reassuringly.

And the pubs might be dark, but they were full to bursting behind their blackout curtains; roared-out choruses of *We'll Meet Again* and *Roll out the Barrel* cheered her on her way.

Mind you, the war was terrible for some people; like those poor people down that shelter in Mellor Street. The bomb had burst outside the door and killed them all with the blast. With hardly a mark on them, even the little kids.

But Mellor Street wasn't in Rosie's district and you only worried about your own district now. Rosie's district had had a few bombs, a few people buried under the rubble. But she'd helped to dig them out with her bare hands, working shoulder to shoulder with the fellers; and held their hands till the ambulance came. She'd cheered them up and that made her feel good.

Rosie hurried on. The pubs were further apart now and even the alleys were silent. Just the odd moggie, poor things, scavenging at the pigswill bins.

She was just bending down to stroke one when the siren went. For the third time that day. Rosie got the usual sinking feeling in her gut, but she wasn't all that worried. Air-raid sirens couldn't kill you. She listened intently, through the dying drone of the siren, for the sound of bombers' engines …

And heard nothing.

She'd carry on for a bit, try and get home before anything happened. Her ma would worry if she was caught out in a raid. Ma might even leave the shelter and come looking for her, as far as the chippie in Scobie Street. Then batter Rosie over the ear when she found her, for causing so much worry.

'G'night, moggie. Best of British Luck!'

Her footsteps quickened; the gas mask banged harder against her bottom, as if urging her on.

She'd gone nearly half a mile before she heard the bombers coming. She was in a district she hardly knew. Really poor people, to judge from the state of their doors and windows. But you couldn't be choosy when the bombers came. You just ran for the nearest brick street-shelter with its concrete-slab roof.

Not many shelters round here. Poor people were always the worst looked after. Bet the toffs had shelters, and to spare, up Croxteth way …

She ran and ran. Turned a corner by a chapel with bombed-out windows. Saw the three brass balls of a pawnbroker's … Then a great square shelter loomed up.

She made the doorway, just as the first guns opened up overhead, turning the night white-black, white-black. Making a noise like some daft kid banging a tin tray right in your ear that echoed across the whole sky after.

Then she heard the shrapnel shrieking down like dead rockets on Bonfire Night. And ducked through the blackout curtain into the shelter.

There was room by the door, on the slatted benches. She flung herself into it, to get her breath back. She must cut down on the ciggies; except it was hard to refuse when the men wardens offered them, friendly-like.

Still panting, she looked around.

And sighed. It seemed a totally miserable sort of shelter.

People huddled together in a dim blue light. Silent except for the racking cough and the dismal wail of a baby at the far end.

Some shelters were really jolly. Fellers brought a fiddle or a squeeze-box, and you could have a good sing-song to drown the noise of the bombs. In some of the bigger ones there was dancing – a good knees-up as those Cockneys called it. In some there was even a drop to drink, or people passing round home-made toffee and biscuits.

Some even had buskers, doing their spoon-bashing or playing the *Air on a G String* on a musical saw. Or telling rude jokes that made the mums scream with laughter, and then tell their kids to put their hands over their ears so they couldn't hear.

But this was a bunch of real miserable sods. Looked really sorry for themselves. Nothing but cough, cough, wheeze and snore.

Might as well be dead, Rosie thought. Where there's life there's hope …

She caught the eye of an old feller opposite. She said, just to say something, 'Big raid tonight. I expect they're copping it down the Dingle. Hope they don't hit the off-licence!'

The old man nodded, friendly enough; but he didn't say anything. Then he pursed his lips and shook his head, as if he was afraid she might wake the kid he was nursing on his lap.

God, even the kids were spiritless. In the shelter at home they were always yelling for a condensed-milk buttie, or punching each other and chasing round the whole shelter, and getting their ears battered all the way round. What was the matter with this lot? Had they left their sense of humour at the pawnbroker's up the road?

So she told the only really dirty joke she knew. If that didn't get them laughing, it would take a thousand-pound bomb to shift them …

Again, the old man raised a finger to his lips.

Rotten old killjoy. Like the deacons in chapel when she was a kid. Children should be seen and not heard. No giggling in the House of God.

Cripes, she thought, this isn't a chapel, it's only a shelter. There must be somebody lively, further down …

She turned her head and shouted, 'Are we downhearted?'

In her home shelter, the yell of 'No!' would have raised the concrete roof two feet in the air, and made the Liver Birds rock on their perches.

Here, nothing. Silence.

Cough, cough. Wheeze. Snore. They might as well be dead.

Chin up, she thought. Grin and bear it. Never say die.

But she didn't actually say any of those things. A chill was working into her, even through her thick warden's greatcoat. She shivered. And shivered again.

This shelter's damp, she thought. They've all caught bronchitis. She studied them intently in the dim blue light. They did look sort of ill; wrinkled, poverty-battered faces, mouths hanging open to show ill-fitting false teeth.

Unemployment, she thought, scrimping and saving and spreading marge on bread then scraping it off again. Years and years when hardly anybody's boat ever came in. Poor Liverpool! Let the poor souls rest in peace …

She shivered again. Shut up, Rosie, they haven't all been as lucky as you. The babies you looked after might have been boring, but at least you got four square meals a day, and a hottie in a nice clean bed at night. Count your blessings. Don't despise those who are worse off …

And then it began to bother her.

Where *was* that blue light coming from?

Normally the light in a shelter was yellow. Candles burning. Kids showing off their torches, flicking them round the ceiling. Or the hurricane lamps that the ARP laid on.

But the light was always *yellow*.

You only got blue lights in hospitals and factories, where they had mains electricity.

And there was no electricity in shelters. It was forbidden in law, in case the shelter was hit by a bomb and the broken electric cable-ends fried everyone to death.

So where *was* the blue light coming from?

Rosie stared around her.

It seemed to be coming from the people themselves. From their clothes, hands, faces … all over them.

'Where's the blue light coming from?' she shouted at the old man, a sudden cold fear gripping her heart.

With a ghastly little smile he raised his cap to her. Under his cap, his domed bald head was broken. Cracked open like an egg. Stuff oozing out.

She was up and out running before she knew her legs had moved. Running through streets as bright as day with searchlights, shells and bombs exploding. But still she ran. She would have run into the mouth of Hell itself to get away from that shelter …

It was the singing that stopped her in the end. *'There'll be bluebirds over, the White Cliffs of Dover …'*

Another shelter. An accordion playing. People bellowing their lungs out.

She staggered inside. Every face turned to look at her. Interested grinning faces.

'Ey, whacker,' said the warden by the door. 'Catch your breath. You look like you've seen a ghost.'

When Rosie finally caught her breath, luxuriating in the *yellow* candle-light, the hot breath from the singing, the little kids tripping over her legs, she asked the warden, 'Do you know a street near here, wi' a bombed-out chapel and a pawnbrokers?'

He flinched, as if at some quite unbearably horrible memory.

'You mean Mellor … Street?' he asked.

Robert Westall

---

4 Language

What clues does the writer give to show that something unusual is about to happen?

5 Language

This story has a tense and frightening atmosphere at times. Find four words or phrases that have a strong effect on the reader. How does each make you feel?

6 Reading

Why did Rosie like being an ARP warden?

7 Reading

How did Rosie know that poor people lived in the district in which she found herself after the air raid siren sounded?

8 Reading

How did people entertain themselves in the air raid shelter during a raid?

9 Reading

Describe the atmosphere of the air raid shelter Rosie found herself in.

10 Reading

How was the atmosphere in the second shelter different from the first shelter?

11 Reading

Explain the ending of the story. Where had Rosie been and what had she seen?

12 Reading

What is the overall effect of the text? Discuss what you like and dislike about it with a partner.

13 Speaking and listening

Discuss which possessions you would take into an air raid shelter knowing that your home might be destroyed in the raid.

14 Speaking and listening

Discuss and agree on a set of rules to go inside an air raid shelter.

15 Writing

Write a diary extract in which you describe being in an air raid shelter. You may wish to set it in modern times. How would it feel to be in an air raid shelter while bombs were going off? What would people do nowadays to entertain themselves? What might you see when you stepped outside in the morning?

16 Writing

Think of a list of questions you could ask someone who experienced the Second World War, to build up a picture of what the war was like.

REVIEW

Share your writing with the rest of the class. How effectively have you managed to portray the atmosphere in the shelters?

AIMS

- To recognise different types of adjectives.
- To use adjectives accurately and effectively.

STARTER

1

Put each of the following nouns next to an appropriate group of adjectives.

> **house   sky   girl   man**
> **boat   book   forest**
> **dog   flower   mountain**

a blue cloudy summer
b haunted derelict uninhabited
c brown shaggy mongrel
d high snow-capped rocky
e dense dark threatening
f interesting exciting hardback
g sleek fast sailing
h grumpy bad-tempered bald
i delicate colourful scented
j pretty happy bubbly

> - An **adjective** is a word which describes a noun. For example:
>   He was an **old** man. The man was **old**.
>   It was a **beautiful blue** sky.
> - Adjectives which are placed before a noun are known as **attributive**. These adjectives are said to **modify** the noun (e.g. My **new** teacher. The **yellow** flower.)
> - Adjectives which are placed after a noun are known as **predicative**. These adjectives are said to **qualify** the noun (e.g. The girl is **clever**. The cat is **cute**.)

DEVELOPMENT

2

Pick out the adjectives in the following sentence and decide whether they are attributive or predicative.

a It was a beautiful day.
b The man was old.
c I scored a fantastic goal.
d My school uniform is blue.
e Homework is easy.
f The large lazy cat woke up.
g Football is boring.
h My mum is funny.
i She wore a dark purple sweatshirt.
j The bright sun shone in the blue sky.

Adjectives and the senses

Many adjectives often appeal to the senses of the reader and can be put into the following categories:

 VISUAL (sight) – e.g. big, blue, bright

 AUDITORY (hearing) – e.g. loud, tuneful

 GUSTATORY (taste) – e.g. sweet, sour, savoury

 TACTILE (touch) – e.g. rough, hot, soft

 OLFACTORY (smell) – e.g. aromatic, malodorous

3

Find four suitable adjectives from the list below to go with each of the nouns in the box.

> **diamond   snowflake   curry   toffee**

gleaming   bright   delicious fragrant   sparkling   spicy   sticky delicate   white   sugary   light dazzling   sweet   tasty   frosty hot   chewy   precious mouthwatering

4

Using a thesaurus, find four adjectives to go with these nouns.

skin   eyes   liquid   glass   music

Creating atmosphere

Adjectives describe features and characteristics of nouns and make them more interesting. They make descriptions more vivid, often adding atmosphere. For example, the sentence 'The pupil walked into the classroom' can be made more interesting by adding adjectives: 'The **tall aggressive** pupil marched into the **large noisy** classroom.'

5

Expand the following sentences using imaginative adjectives that add atmosphere and interest.

a A ghost appeared in the hallway.
b The footballer scored a goal.
c The girl walked into the room.
d A soldier attacked the enemy.
e The man walked through the market.
f The teacher came into the playground.

6

Put the following adjectives in the correct spaces.

> **childhood   large   plastic   holiday delicious   blue   fishing   fantastic wonderful   family   bright   golden**

When I think of _____ holidays I always remember _____ sunshine and _____ beaches. The _____ car was always packed with _____ buckets, _____ nets and _____ picnic hampers full of Mum's _____ sandwiches. When we arrived at our _____ destination the sea was always _____ and the weather was _____. It was a _____ time.

7

Try and think of four adjectives for each of the following nouns.

car   film   castle   cat   cloud playground   pizza   bag   hair

8

Write a descriptive paragraph on two of the following, using as many interesting adjectives as you can.

- a lake in the country
- a busy shopping centre
- a deserted beach
- a noisy sports arena

REVIEW

Read through some of the passages written by your class and pick out any interesting or striking adjectives. How does using adjectives help the reader?

UNIT 32 Introducing comics

AIMS

- To examine some characters from popular comics.
- To think about some of the techniques used in comics for telling stories.

STARTER

1

Look at the front cover of *Classics From The Comics*. See if you can match up the name of each character with the picture.

Desperate Dan   Dennis the Menace
Puss and Boots   Walter   Lord Snooty

> A **comic** is a type of magazine which contains stories about cartoon-type characters told in pictures with a small amount of writing.
>
> The **media** is the means by which information is communicated to a large audience. The media includes TV, radio, film, newspapers, magazines, comics, advertising and the Internet.

INTRODUCTION

Comics are an important and popular part of the media and are generally thought of as light entertainment. They are usually eye-catching, often funny and should be very easy to read. Comic storylines are often simple and very easy to follow.

2

If you were to add a speech bubble to one of the characters on the cover of this comic, what might they be saying?

DEVELOPMENT

3 Language

Look at the names of the comics surrounding the picture (*Beano, Dandy, Sparky, Beezer, Cracker, Topper, Buzz, Nutty*). Choose three of these words and find out what they mean. Why are they suitable names for a comic? What feelings and ideas does each word suggest?

4 Language

Pick out two examples of onomatopoeia. How does onomatopoeia help in our understanding of what two comic characters are doing?

5 Language

Think about the name 'Dennis the Menace'. Why is it a good name for a comic character?

6 Reading

Look at the black and white cat Puss and the brown dog Boots. How would you describe their relationship and feelings towards each other? Explain your answer by finding evidence from the cover to support your ideas.

7 Reading

How is the catamaran moving? How do we know?

8 Reading

What is Dennis the Menace doing to Walter? What do you think each boy is like? Give reasons for your answer.

9 Speaking and listening

Write out a conversation between Dennis and Walter in the form of a script. Then read it out using the appropriate voices. Think about:

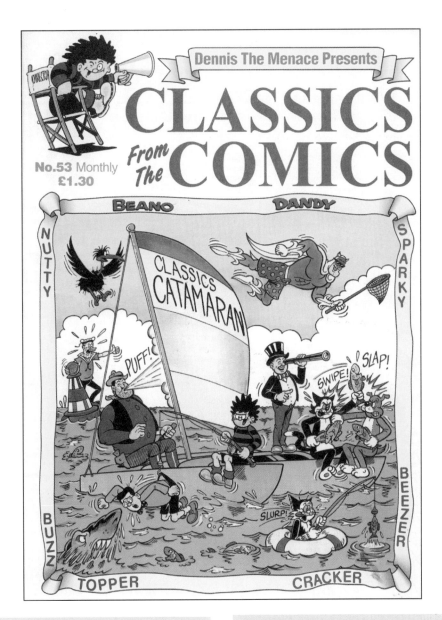

● the type of person each character is
● why Dennis should want to feed Walter to a shark.

10 Writing

Write a short script containing the conversation Puss and Boots have as they slap each other about the head with the fish. Make notes for a storyboard.

11 Writing

Write a comic strip story involving one or more characters from the cover of *Classics From The Comics*. You may wish to produce your work in the form of a storyboard.

REVIEW

What have you learnt about comic characters from this unit? Think about their names, appearance and behaviour. What is the advantage of the comic form over the book form?

UNIT 33 Narrative I spy

AIMS

- To continue looking at techniques used in producing comic strips.
- To employ some of the techniques used in producing a comic strip.

STARTER

1

Which of the following language features would you find in a comic?

complex sentences	narrative
direct language	description
onomatopoeia	close ups
action shots	bold print
thought bubbles	capital letters
speech bubbles	paragraphs
continuous writing	chapters

INTRODUCTION

*A **stereotype** is a fixed set of ideas about what a particular group of people is like. Very often, stereotypes are very unfair (e.g. in the eyes of a pupil a stereotypical teacher might be someone who reads a lot, gives orders and punishes children for being naughty). There are many stereotypes to be found in literature and the media, particularly in comics, cartoons and magazines.*

I Spy was a popular character in the comic *Sparky*. The extract on page 77 features many stereotypical characters and some classic 'comic' techniques.

2

Which of the characters are stereotypical? What stereotypes do they represent?

DEVELOPMENT

3 Language

What are the biggest words on the page? What do the words suggest? Why have they been enlarged?

4 Language

Read the speech bubble:

'YOU HAFF ME BUT YOU HAFF NOT GOT ZE PLANS! HAR-HAR!'

What do these words tell us about the 'horrible villain'? Where might he come from? Where do you think this particular stereotype of a villain might originate from?

5 Language

Can you pick out any technical language used by the pilot? What is the effect of using technical language here?

6 Reading

Describe the character I Spy. Is there anything about his appearance that might suggest that:

- he wants to hide his real identity
- he is a stereotypical spy
- he is a ridiculous figure
- he relies on special gadgets.

7 Reading

Is there anything in the appearance of the villain that suggests he is a villain?

8 Reading

How is it obvious without even reading this comic strip that I Spy is the central character? How does he stand out?

9 Writing

Rewrite the comic strip in the form of a story using sentences and paragraphs. Write a paragraph plan before you start.

10 Writing

Produce a fact file for I Spy. Use the following headings.

- Name
- Job
- Favourite coat
- Best hat
- Gadgets
- Likes
- Dislikes
- Ambitions

Can you think of anything else you might add?

11 Writing

Look again at the frame in which I Spy and his boss discover the plans have gone. Do you think this story could develop in a different way? Rewrite the ending in either comic strip form or in normal story form.

REVIEW

Events in comics are often very extraordinary and obviously would not happen in real life. Is there anything in 'Operation Security' which is far-fetched? Are there any typical comic techniques used in the extract which might be found in other comics you have read?

UNIT 34 A comic character

AIMS

- To take a closer look at how characters are developed by comic strip writers.
- To develop your own comic character and storyline.

STARTER

1

Comic and cartoon characters can have both positive and negative characteristics. They can be ridiculous, funny, evil, villains, super heroes, bullies, wimps, sly, naughty, clever, victims, clumsy, dangerous, pranksters, accident prone, supernatural, monsters, eccentric, powerful, friendly, hostile or stupid. Which of these words fit two of the following comic and cartoon characters?

- Superman
- Bart Simpson
- Angelica from *Rugrats*
- Tom from *Tom and Jerry*
- The Incredible Hulk

INTRODUCTION

Beryl the Peril is a classic character from the comic *Topper*. Occasionally she is a peril or danger to her friends and neighbours, but more often than not she is a danger to herself. Things often go wrong for Beryl and those around her.

2

Why are the following words in bold on the comic page opposite?

- **TRICK FLOWER**   - **SQUAWK**
- **VULTURE**

DEVELOPMENT

3 Language

Think about the title 'Beryl the Peril'. How do the two words 'Beryl' and 'Peril' go together? Why is 'Peril' an appropriate word to describe Beryl?

4 Language

Punctuation plays a significant part in this comic story. Comment on the use of exclamation marks, explaining how they help the reader to imagine how each character speaks.

5 Reading

How has the artist made the main character – Beryl – stand out? Where does she generally stand in each frame?

6 Reading

What type of person is Beryl? What do you think the other characters think of her? Give reasons for your answer.

7 Reading

How is Beryl's father like his daughter?

8 Speaking and listening

Act out the conversation between Beryl and her aunt in which Beryl explains the events of her day.

9 Writing

Invent two characters suitable for a comic story. Make them very different from each other. Consider the following:

- their appearance and any unusual physical features that make them stand out
- their behaviour, manners and habits
- their style of speech

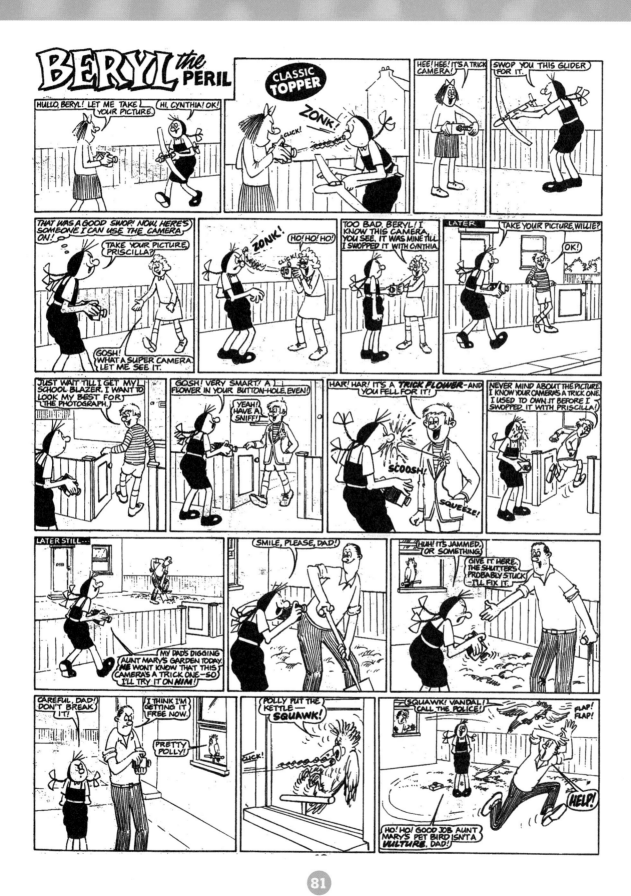

● their peculiarities, special powers, gifts or weaknesses.

Describe your character in a short paragraph. Try to see the characters in your mind's eye as you work on them. You may wish to draw each character and label your drawing. Are their characteristics and appearance suitable for a character of their particular type?

10 Writing 🏠

A **narrative** is a text which tells a story, very often in a simple chronological form. Narratives can be fictional (e.g. comics, fairy stories) or non-fictional (e.g. diaries, biographies and autobiographies).

Plan and write a short narrative involving your two characters which would be suitable for a comic of your choice. Set out your writing in a short paragraph or as a numbered sequence of sentences, each of which could represent one frame of your story. Consider the plot carefully, particularly the beginning and ending. What problems arise and how are they solved?

Remember: don't make your narrative too complicated – keep it simple.

REVIEW

Have a look at each other's comic characters and think about the type of stories they could be involved in. Brainstorm a list of words which could be used to describe a successful character from a comic.

UNIT 35 Creating a class comic

AIMS

- To produce your own comic strip using a storyboard.
- To create a class comic either for a classroom display or for publication.

STARTER

1

> A **storyboard** is an interpretation of an idea in pictorial form. It may be the plan of a story, advertisement, TV or film scene produced in chronological order. The plan is explained in pictures, frame by frame, with each picture representing an event or a camera shot.

Match these classic comic characters with the correct description.

Billy Whizz	**Winker Watson**
Colonel Blink	**Hungry Horace**
Roger the Dodger	**Jimmy Jinx**
Calamity Kate	
Baron von Reichs Pudding	

- a short-sighted eccentric retired army officer
- a boy obsessed with food
- a public schoolboy who is always playing tricks on his teachers
- a ridiculous German First World War fighter pilot
- a boy who is always naughty
- a girl whose plans always go wrong
- a boy who runs very fast

What clues did you find in the name of each character to help you with this activity?

INTRODUCTION

Desperate Dan from the *Dandy* is one of the most popular and best-known British comic characters. His immense, almost superhuman strength often compensated for his limited ability in other areas. How much respect do young Danny and Katey have for their Uncle Dan?

2

What do think Desperate Dan is going to do his niece and nephew?

DEVELOPMENT

3 Language

Why are some of the words in the speech bubbles in larger, bold letters? What does it suggest about how some of these words should be spoken?

4 Language

Find four onomatopoeic words from the extract.

5 Language

Which of the following words best describe the language of the comic?

formal informal descriptive conversational direct simple complex

Choose two words from the list and find a phrase or sentence from the text that could be used to support each choice.

6 Reading

Look closely at the character of Desperate Dan. What impressions are formed by:

- his appearance

- his behaviour when trying to catch the rat
- the attitude of his nephew and niece towards him
- the way he deals with his nephew and niece at the end of the story?

7 Reading

Describe the teacher in the comic. Think about:

- his appearance
- his actions
- whether he looks and acts like any of your teachers.

8 Reading

How is the reader supposed to feel about the teacher hitting the class bully? How has the artist made the class bully look mean?

9 Reading

In what way is this teacher stereotypical? Do you think teachers like this ever existed in real life, or do they just appear in stories?

10 Speaking and listening

Act out one of the following situations.

- Danny and Katey's conversation with their teacher when they arrive back at school.
- What happens when Desperate Dan gets Danny and Katey home.

11 Writing

Imagine that your class has been asked to produce a new comic suitable for pupils in your year group. In it, you are going to have a range of new characters and comic strips.

First of all you must form an editorial team. This is a group of people who will decide:

- the title of the comic and its intended audience (e.g. boys, girls or both)
- which characters and stories will be included
- the type, style or genre of your comic (e.g. action, fantasy, funny, mixed appeal, etc.)
- the jobs people will have to do (e.g. designer, artist, writer, proofreader, editor, etc.).

Once you have decided these issues at your first editorial meeting, you can start producing your comic. Your teacher will give you blank storyboard grids to help you plan and write stories and develop ideas and characters.

You may wish to start off with everyone planning or writing their own story. Remember that stories can be greatly improved by sharing and discussing ideas.

Eventually you might want to publish your comic by putting it together for a wall display or getting your teacher to photocopy it so that you can distribute it to your friends at school.

12 Reading/Writing

Research one of the following superhero comic characters. Write a short description of them in the form of a fact file for your comic.

**X Men   Elektra   Spiderman
The Incredible Hulk   Captain America
Judge Dredd**

REVIEW

What is the most difficult part of producing a comic? How did using the storyboard help? What comic book features did you include in the layout? In what ways are your stories and characters typical of those that might appear in a comic?

AIMS

- To carry out an investigation and present the findings in the style of a TV news report.
- To examine the facts of a case and present an explanation of what happened in the form of a talk and dramatic role play.

STARTER

1

> A **fact** is a piece of information which can be proved to be true (e.g. Paris is the capital of France, the Fire of London took place in 1666).

Think of five facts about yourself. Then think of five facts about your school.

INTRODUCTION

There are many interpretations of the mystery of the *Mary Celeste*: piracy, mutiny by the crew, alien abduction. Read the extract on page 87 and consider the facts.

2

What do you think is the most sensible interpretation of the facts?

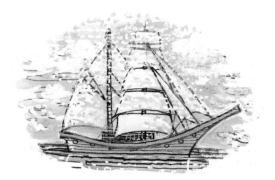

DEVELOPMENT

3 Language

Find out the meaning of the following words.

**brigantine   cargo
navigation   binnacle**

4 Language

Using a thesaurus find as many synonyms as you can for the word 'boat'.

5 Writing

Write a short paragraph describing what happened to the *Mary Celeste* using the following connectives.

**and   but   then
furthermore   eventually**

6 Reading

Find four facts from the first paragraph.

7 Reading

What evidence was there to suggest that the ship was highly seaworthy?

8 Speaking and listening

Look at the evidence and discuss what you think happened to the people on board.

9 Speaking and listening

Present a TV news report about the mystery. Include:

- a description of the facts
- interviews with members of the boarding party
- possible interpretations about what happened.

Mary Celeste

The facts of the most famous sea mystery are that two cargo-carrying brigantines set sail from New York in November 1872. Captain Briggs commanded the *Mary Celeste*, heading for Genoa; his friend Captain Moorhouse sailed for Gibraltar on the *Dei Gratia* a week later. [...]

A month later, on 7 November, Captain Moorhouse sighted the *Mary Celeste* in the Azores some 950 kilometres west of Gibraltar. Her sails were set, but she was sailing with the wind so erratically that he sent a boarding party to investigate.

The ship was completely deserted. The only lifeboat was missing, apparently having been launched rather than washed away in one of the storms that had obviously hit the ship during the voyage (the binnacle was knocked out of place and the glass on the compass was shattered).

The deck cabins were tightly battened down with planks but rainwater had come through to soak bedding and floors. Even so, the ship was highly seaworthy. There was about a metre of water in the hold – not enough to be dangerous – and evidence that the pumps had been recently checked. The cargo of 1,700 barrels of commercial alcohol was intact, there were six months' provisions in the stores, and an adequate supply of fresh water. [...] Oliver Deveau, leader of the boarding party, told the enquiry later: 'There seemed to be everything left behind in the cabins as if left in a great hurry, but everything in its place.'

To this day, the mystery of the *Mary Celeste* is why she was abandoned, presumably by lifeboat, without the crew taking the basic necessities for survival.

Francis Hitching

10 Writing

Imagine you are the man who led the boarding party onto the *Mary Celeste*. Write a diary extract for that day, trying to develop a tense atmosphere.

11 Reading

The *Mary Celeste* was abandoned in an area known as the Bermuda Triangle. Try to find out about any other strange mysteries from the Bermuda Triangle for your news report.

REVIEW

Perform your news report for the rest of the class. Are the reports you have seen realistic? If not, how could they be changed to make them appear more like the real thing?

UNIT 37 Peer pressure

AIMS

- To look at how people persuade others to take a course of action.
- To vary the style and formality of speech and writing to suit different circumstances.
- To express a personal view, adding persuasive emphasis to key points.

STARTER

1

What information do you need to include in a script to help actors with their performance?

> **Drama** is a genre of literature connected with plays and performance, both in the theatre and in film, radio and television. Drama is generally presented as a script before being turned into a performance.

INTRODUCTION

The extract from David Calcutt's play *The Terrible Fate of Humpty Dumpty* on page 89 shows what can happen when somebody is persuaded to perform a highly dangerous stunt. As you read, think about how the dialogue is set out and how the stage directions are made to stand out.

2

What advice about speech, positioning and actions has the writer given the actors?

DEVELOPMENT

3 Language

How does the writer make the speech realistic?

4 Reading

What do Stubbs' lines tell us about his character?

5 Reading

Closely examine what Sammy says. What is his role in this scene?

6 Speaking and listening

Improvise a script in which some children try to persuade a friend to do something they don't want to do. Remember to keep your language informal.

7 Speaking and listening

Imagine you are being bullied. Improvise a conversation with a parent or teacher about your problem. You might need to use slightly more formal language.

8 Writing

Write a formal essay outlining your views on how bullying should be dealt with in school. Be persuasive to get across your main points.

9 Writing

Write a letter to an agony aunt about problems with your friendships. Swap letters with a friend and write replies.

REVIEW

Why is it important to alter the way you speak in different situations? How would your headteacher react if you spoke to him or her as you speak to your friends?

The Terrible Fate of Humpty Dumpty

(On waste ground, STUBBS, with THE MEMBERS OF HIS GANG – JIMMY, PETE, KATHY, KAY, JANET and TRACEY – are surrounding TERRY DUMPTON. SAMMY stands to one side. THE GROUP suddenly comes to life as the introductory music fades.)

PETE *(To TERRY.)* See my frisbee, Humpty? My best frisbee, this is. I've had this frisbee for ages. I love it. I'd hate to lose it. I'd go mad if I lost this frisbee. Want to see how it works?…

(PETE throws the frisbee into the air. Then he says:)

… Oh dear. It's got stuck in the pylon. What am I going to do now?

STUBBS You'll have to get it back, Pete.

PETE I know. Only trouble is, I'm scared of heights. Can't stand them. I get a nosebleed just going to the top of the stairs.

STUBBS You'll have to get somebody to fetch it down for you, then.

PETE That's right. Who, though?

(STUBBS points at TERRY.)

STUBBS Him! …

(There is a pause. Then STUBBS says)

… All right, Humpty? Up you go. Get Pete's frisbee back for him …

(There is tension. Then STUBBS continues)

… Go on. Climb the pylon. Get it back …

(TERRY stares up at the pylon. STUBBS goes on)

… Perhaps you ain't our mate, then. Perhaps you don't like us at all. That means you're the kind of person who'd sneak on us.

(He walks towards TERRY.)

TERRY All right, I'll get it.

SAMMY Don't, Terry.

STUBBS Shurrup, Sammy.

SAMMY It's dangerous.

KATHY You wanna go up there instead?

(There is a pause.)

STUBBS Go on.

(TERRY starts to climb they pylon. Egged on by PETE, THE MEMBERS OF THE GANG start to chant 'Humpty Dumpty!' over and over again, and then shout comments up at TERRY. SAMMY runs forward.)

SAMMY Don't, Terry. Come down.

STUBBS Shurrup, Sammy, unless you wanna go up there after him.

(The noise continues. Lights suddenly flash on and off. TERRY hangs dead from the pylon. THE MEMBERS OF THE GANG stare up in silence.)

David Calcutt

UNIT 38 Caring for animals

AIMS

- To discuss and research an area or issue of your choice.
- To give a talk or presentation connected to your issue, answering any questions.

STARTER

1

Write a profile of the person who might be interested in visiting the website opposite.

> An **audience** is a group of people who listen to and watch a performance of a play, concert or presentation. It can also mean the group of people you are aiming at when presenting information, ideas, speech or writing.

INTRODUCTION

Sadly, the neglect of animals is an all too familiar news story. Read the web report from the BBC on page 91.

2

How does the writer bring home the scale of the problem?

DEVELOPMENT

3 Language

Why are short paragraphs used rather than longer paragraphs containing several sentences?

4 Language

Which of the following sentences describing the language of this website is true?

a The language is informal and contains lots of slang.

b There are lots of adjectives.

c Many passive verbs are used and the language is vague.

d There are very few clauses in each sentence thereby making the meaning clear and to the point.

5 Reading

According to animal protection specialists what causes most cases of animal cruelty?

6 Reading

What does the RSPCA think would reduce the suffering of animals?

7 Reading

What would the RSPCA want animal owners to provide by law?

8 Speaking and listening

Choose an issue or topic you feel very strongly about. You are going to give a presentation to your class about your chosen topic.

- Decide how to research your topic/issue.
- Give each other tasks or roles which reflect your expertise or ability.
- Agree a timescale for when tasks should be completed.
- Decide how you are going to structure your presentation.
- Think about whether you may require any props or visual aids.

Practise and rehearse your presentation.

'Animal-loving' UK's tale of neglect

The Royal Society for the Prevention of Cruelty to Animals (RSPCA), which covers England and Wales, wants new laws to reduce suffering.

It believes most cases of animal cruelty could very easily be avoided.

Of 1,977 convictions secured under the 1911 Protection of Animals Act last year, 1,761 (89%) were classified as basic neglect charges

Updating the law

The society wants the government to introduce a 'duty of care' to help reduce the suffering.

This would place upon all animal owners a legal responsibility to provide:

- adequate food and water
- appropriate shelter
- access to proper veterinary treatment when needed
- proper room for the animals to exhibit normal behaviour
- protection against mental suffering and distress.

During 2001 the society's staff rescued or picked up more than 195,000 animals, and answered more than 1,500,000 telephone calls. But the RSPCA says it is frustrated that so many cases could have been prevented if legislation had allowed it to act

Rate falls

The number of cruelty complaints investigated (123,156) and the number of animals rescued (11,947) were both slightly lower than in 2000.

Prosecutions and convictions both showed a slight drop as well. There were 871 cases involving cruelty to dogs (1,175 in 2000), and 289 involving cats (256).

One case prosecuted by the RSPCA involved a puppy whose throat was slashed up to 15 times, leaving the jugular vein exposed. The man convicted was imprisoned for two months. The puppy recovered.

http://news.bbc.co.uk/1/hi/sci/tech/1958109.stm
Alex Kirby

---

9 Speaking and listening

Listen to presentations given by your classmates. Ask them questions on anything you didn't understand or would like to know more about.

10 Reading/Writing

Do some more research on your chosen topic. Write a short report suitable for publication on a website.

REVIEW

What are the most important points to remember when planning a presentation? What could you have changed to make your presentation better?

AIMS

- To investigate the spelling of several high frequency words and also look at some new vocabulary.
- To develop some spelling strategies for learning new words.
- To use a dictionary effectively.

STARTER

1

The following words have been misspelled. Write them out correctly, checking the spelling in a dictionary if you need to.

accomodation assesment begining neccessary possesion sucess

Use each word in a sentence.

DEVELOPMENT

By the end of Year 7 your teacher will expect you to have learned how to spell the following groups of words. Each week you will be asked to learn all the words in at least one group for homework. You might find it helpful to think of a suitable strategy to help you learn each word.

1 Words beginning 'au'
audible audience August author automatic autumn audition

2 Words beginning 'be'
beautiful become behaviour believe beneath benefits between

3 Words beginning 'con'
concentrated conclusion conscience consequence continue continuous

4 Words beginning 'de'
decide decision definite deliberate design development

5 Words beginning 'en'
energy engine enormous enquire entrance environment

6 Words beginning 'ex'
example excess exercise exhibition explanation extraordinary extreme

7 Words beginning 'ge'
generous gentle geography gesture genre German germinate

8 Words beginning 'he'
health heard heaven hedge height heritage

9 Words beginning 'im'
imaginary imaginative immediate impatient important improvise

10 Words beginning 'in'
incident increase individual industrial influence interesting interrupt

11 Words beginning 'mi'
mighty miscellaneous miserable mischief mission mixture

12 Words beginning 'pa'
parallel participation passage passenger patience pattern

13 Words beginning 'qu'
questionnaire queen queue quit quite quiet

14 Words beginning 're'
reaction receive reference relief remember research resources

15 Words beginning 'se'
secondary secretive sensible separate sequence serious

16 Words beginning 'str'
straight stranger strategy strength stretch structure

17 Words beginning 'su'
success suddenly surely suppose surprise survey

18 Words beginning 'te'
technique technology temporary terrible terrific texture

19 Words beginning 'we'
wealthy weary Wednesday weight
weird welcome

20 Words beginning 'ir'
irrational irregular irresistible
irresponsible irrigate irritate

21 Words beginning 'un'
unfortunate unfounded unhelpful
unlikely unrealistic unreasonable

22 Words ending 'ing'
beginning dining disgusting
dropping hiding winning writing

23 Words ending 'tion'
attention direction fiction fraction
proportion reduction creation

24 Words ending 'sion'
collision conclusion decision
exclusion explosion extension

25 Words ending 'ssion'
discussion admission passion
percussion possession profession

26 Words ending 'ous'
devious envious fabulous
marvellous obvious serious

27 Words with 'ough'
although cough drought enough
though thought

28 Words with 'ie'
buried fierce fried lieutenant
piece sieve varieties

29 Words with 'ei'
beige deceive height receipt
receive their weight

30 Words with 'ight'
lighter mighty nightmare sight
tighten tonight

31 Words with 'ite'
bite definite ignite infinite invite kite

32 Words with 'ea'
appear disappear health measures
peaceful steal tearful

33 Soft 'c' words
celebrate centre ceremony
certificate conceive ferocity

34 Words with 'oun'
bounty counter countries found
hound pound sounds

35 Words ending 'ly'
cautiously correctly hurriedly
lovely unexpectedly vitally

36 Words ending 'ity'
ability agility availability
charity probability sanity

37 Words ending 'ness'
business carelessness coolness
cleanliness happiness meanness

38 Words ending 'al' and 'el'
accidental critical label
parallel towel vowel

39 Words ending 'ful'
awful cupful peaceful powerful
sorrowful tearful

40 Words ending 'edge'
edge dredge knowledge ledge
pledge wedge

41 Words with silent letters
bomb castle Christmas climb
column comb

42 More words with silent letters
exhausted ghost island listening
plumber tomb vehicle whistle

43 Words with silent 'w'
answer wrap wreck wrestle
wrist write wrong

44 Words with silent 'k'
knee knew know knife knob
knock knot know

45 Words with 'dge'
badge budget fidget gadget judge lodger

46 Words with 'ph'
autograph autobiography elephant
paragraph photograph telephone

47 Words with double consonants
battling bubbling happening
labelling occurring

48 More words with double consonants
recommendation referred running
sufficient wobbling wrapping

REVIEW

Which words do you find difficult and why?
How can you help yourself learn new
words? Brainstorm spelling strategies.

UNIT 1 A life in the day

AIMS

- To investigate autobiographical non-fiction writing.
- To produce your own version of an autobiographical piece of writing.

STARTER

1

Examine the topic sentences (first sentence) of the second and third paragraphs and write down the subject of each paragraph.

> An **autobiography** is a piece of writing in which someone writes about their own life.

INTRODUCTION

In this passage, Gary Gero writes about his whole life and fascinating occupation by focusing on the events of a typical day. It is a mixture of narrative, reminiscences and opinion about life and animals. What do you consider to be the most interesting thing that has happened to him?

2

Find evidence in the text that shows:

- the writer's love of animals
- his respect for the welfare and happiness of animals
- his admiration of animal intelligence.

A Life in the Day of Gary Gero

Gary Gero, 55, was the chief animal trainer for the Harry Potter film. He and his wife, Barbara, live on the San Juan Islands, Washington.

If there's a seven o'clock call I get up at six, throw on some warm clothes, and make toast and real coffee.

I visit the animal compound before going on set. Owls have a distinctive   5
warm, musky aroma which hits you as you walk in. And then there are the sounds. The babies say: 'Mom, feed me!' Some of the older ones hoot territorially.

Hedwig is a snowy owl with a couple of   10
flying doubles to help him out. I can pick him out because he has a deeper, silly hoot, like he didn't really get the hang of it . [. . .]

Owls have very small brains, but each of   15
the species is different. Barn owls are moderately intelligent, snowy owls are real dim. [...] We teach them to fly to and from a trainer, and to fly with things in their beaks. For one scene, a snowy owl   20
has to fly on the spot in front of a big fan. A snowy doesn't rely too much on flight

ability, so you're talking thousands of hours of training, thousands of treats.

Everyone meets with the director on set to work out the first sequence. Then we have a couple of hours while the shot is lit to get the animals fed and groomed. [...] Then they come up in the truck, nice and quiet, when it's time to work. Sometimes the animals get it right and the actors don't; sometimes everyone gets it right and the cameraman slips the focus.

Everyone has bad days, but with animals it's mostly down to preparation. Rats are great animals. They retrieve well, they fetch and carry. You never need tell a rat a thing twice – they learn quicker than dogs. It's a huge adjustment to then have to get your head around owls.

We spent months trying to work out how we could get Hedwig to fly with a broomstick. We had to get the broomstick light enough, [...] then work out a way for him to land without dropping it. Nobody thought we could pull it off, so everybody clapped and got real excited when we did it.

Animal stress is counterproductive. A stressed owl has flattened feathers, big eyes, and he may pant a little. We don't go there. If there's stress, we quit. I have a cool chest containing treats, mostly chicken and beef, with a bit of fur and bone. These owls have never eaten live food. Hell, can you imagine the problems we'd have with the toads and the rats?

Lunch is from the canteen. I stick to baked potato and tuna. [...] I had a job one time which involved making a bull talk. The only thing that bull would open his mouth for was Marmite.

When you're working with an animal, you're his partner. My best memories are of working with birds. Crows, ravens and jackdaws are so intelligent. They have strong monogamous bonds, and some mate for life. Once, a bird I raised chose me for its mate. Poor old girl. I took her somewhere she could breed with her own kind. Probably broke her heart. [...]

I love wolves and have a weak spot for primates. [...] They're great fun and they give out so much love. [...] But boy, a little monkey can wreck a house in no time. [...]

Most evenings, I say goodnight to everybody at the compound, then drive over to the pub for a drink and a meal. [...]

I'm real dirty at the end of the day – greasy from the meat and covered in owl poo – so I shower before bed. The ups are so up and the downs so down, the pressure is enough to chase a stone man out, but I love this job. Who cares if no one knows who I am? You saw Hedwig fly. You saw Fang follow Hagrid into the wood. Then you know my work.

Interview by Caroline Scott in *The Sunday Times Magazine*

DEVELOPMENT

3 Language

The writer's use of adjectives is very effective. Examine the line 'Owls have a distinctive warm, musky aroma which hits you as you walk in'. Rewrite this sentence in your own words.

4 Language

Look at the paragraph beginning on line 49. Find an example of:

a using commas for lists

b using a comma for a pause mid-sentence

c using a comma to bracket off an exclamation at the beginning of a sentence.

5 Reading

What makes Hedwig stand out from the other owls?

6 Reading

List two things that can go wrong when filming a scene with animals.

7 Reading

How did the writer get the bull to open his mouth?

8 Reading

What difficulties did Gary Gero encounter once when working with a female bird?

9 Reading

Write a short paragraph explaining whether you think Gary Gero is good at his job.

10 Speaking and listening

Tell your partner about one of your interests, hobbies or passions. Try and make your account interesting and entertaining.

11 Writing

Write your own article called 'A Life in the Day'. Comment on:

- what you do
- your interests
- your lifestyle
- your friends and family
- any areas or issues you feel strongly about.

12 Writing

Write the imaginary 'Life in the Day' of a famous person. You may have to do some research before you begin.

13 Writing

Write a spoof 'Life in the Day' from the viewpoint of one of Gary Gero's animals. Make it amusing and entertaining – what do you really think of your trainer?

REVIEW

Why do people enjoy reading autobiographical writing? What advice would you give someone about to begin writing their own autobiography? Read each other's 'Life in the Day' accounts, sharing any interesting or unusual passages.

UNIT 2 Lifestyles

STARTER

1

Look at the article below. Pick out the headline, the subheading and bullet points.

> A **broadsheet** newspaper generally has a more formal and serious tone than popular tabloid papers. Articles are often long, detailed and analytical. Daily broadsheet papers include The Daily Telegraph, The Times, The Guardian and The Independent.

INTRODUCTION

According to the writer of this article children are becoming obsessed with themselves. Do you agree with what he has to say?

2

Look at paragraph 6. What does it tell us about:

- children today
- children in the past
- the writer's opinion of children today?

Seven-year-olds put down toys in favour of hair gel

Children 'obsessed with fashion and fame'

BY MARTIN BENTHAM
Social Affairs Correspondent

He wears deodorant, likes perfumed body sprays and uses hair gel to get the right look: meet today's seven-year-old boy.

A survey of the pastimes, likes and dislikes of modern children reveals a widespread use of beauty products by primary school pupils of both sexes and an obsession with fashion and fame.

The report, by Mintel, the consumer research company, shows that youngsters are picking up 'adult' habits at ever younger ages. It found that a third of seven and eight-year-olds used deodorant and hair gel to improve their attractiveness, with the proportion rising to more than half for nine and 10-year-olds.

Eight out of 10 girls in the older age group wore perfume and lipstick and there was increasing fashion-consciousness among both sexes, with more than two-thirds of young children choosing their own clothes.

The findings were compiled from answers given by nearly 2,000 children aged between seven and 10.

Angela Hughes, Mintel's consumer research manager, said that 'adult' attitudes and the growing preoccupation of boys with their personal appearance, were the most striking findings. [...]

'Their pastimes are also very different. They spend more time indoors playing computer games, listening to music and watching television, and less on the physical activities and traditional toys and games that children in the 1960s and 1970s would have enjoyed.' [. . .]

Mary Llewellin, a 38-year-old mother from Bristol, [. . .] said the findings mirrored her experiences. [. . .] 'My children watch a lot more television than I did, have a wider social circle and are a lot more "grown up" in general. I was still playing with dolls at nine and was much more naive. In some ways, it is better now, although nostalgia makes me think that, in other respects, it is worse.'

Sonia Livingstone, a professor of social psychology at the London School of Economics, agreed that children's lives had changed greatly in the past 30 or 40 years. [. . .] 'A bedroom culture has also developed, with children seeing it as their right to spend time in their own bedroom, and parents sitting downstairs wondering whether their child will deign to come and see them. [. . .] Childhood has changed.'

The 21st-Century Child

- Eight out of 10 said that they liked spending time with their family, although a fifth also wanted more privacy.
- 63% of girls say they enjoy books, compared with 40% of boys.
- School is an increasing pressure. Eight out of 10 youngsters say that it is important to work hard, and only 42% report that they enjoy going to school

The Sunday Telegraph

DEVELOPMENT

3 Language

In the opening sentence, why does the writer begin by describing today's seven-year-old boy as 'He'? Think about:

- why he doesn't give this imaginary boy a name
- what image of young boys he is trying to create
- the effect on the reader.

4 Language

Pick out four facts and two opinions.

5 Language/Reading

Pick out two differences in lifestyle between Mary Llewellin as a child and her own children.

6 Reading

Look at the section 'The 21st-Century Child'. Comment on attitudes to:

- spending time with their family
- reading
- school.

7 Speaking and listening

Imagine one of you is a presenter on a TV chat show. You have invited children from your school onto the programme to talk about fashion and lifestyles. Act out the conversation.

8 Writing

Write an article for a teenage magazine about fashion and lifestyle. Think about:

- keeping language simple and relevant
- avoiding over-long paragraphs
- using headings and sub-headings
- organising your article into sections.

9 Writing

You have won a competition to have a makeover. Write a magazine article about it, commenting on your choice of image, hairstyle and clothes.

REVIEW

Compare the newspaper article and your own magazine article. What did you have to change to make your version more relevant and enjoyable for young people?

UNIT 3 — Teenage diaries

AIMS

- To look at the conventions of diary writing.
- To examine how characters can be developed in a humorous and imaginative way.

STARTER

1

Come up with five 'resolutions' to help you improve the quality of your English work.

 The **first person singular** is used when writing a diary or autobiography. It involves the use of the pronouns 'I', 'me', 'my', 'myself'.

INTRODUCTION

Read this extract from Adrian Mole's diary. What does Adrian think of his parents? Do you feel the same way about yours?

2

What advice would you give to Adrian?

The Secret Diary of Adrian Mole Aged 13 $\frac{3}{4}$

Thursday January 1st
Bank Holiday in England, Ireland, Scotland and Wales

These are my New Year's resolutions:
1. I will help the blind across the road.
2. I will hang my trousers up.
3. I will put the sleeves back on my records.
4. I will not start smoking.
5. I will stop squeezing my spots.
6. I will be kind to the dog.
7. I will help the poor and ignorant.
8. After hearing the disgusting noises from downstairs last night, I have also vowed never to drink alcohol.

My father got the dog drunk on cherry brandy at the party last night. If the RSPCA hear about it he could get done. Eight days have gone by since Christmas Day but my mother still hasn't worn the green lurex apron I bought her for Christmas! She will get bathcubes next year.

Just my luck, I've got a spot on my chin for the first day of the New Year!

Friday January 2nd
Bank Holiday in Scotland. Full moon

I felt rotten today. It's my mother's fault for singing 'My Way' at two o'clock in the morning at the top of the stairs. Just my luck to have a mother like her. There is a chance my parents could be alcoholics. Next year I could be in a children's home.

The dog got its own back on my father. It jumped up and knocked down his model ship, then ran into the garden with the rigging tangled in its feet. My father kept saying, 'Three months' work down the drain', over and over again.

The spot on my chin is getting bigger. It's my mother's fault for not knowing about vitamins.

Saturday January 3rd

I shall go mad through lack of sleep! My father has banned the dog from the house so it barked outside my window all night. Just my luck! My father shouted a swear-word at it. If he's not careful he will get done by the police for obscene language.

I think the spot is a boil. Just my luck to have it where everybody can see it. I pointed out to my mother that I hadn't had any vitamin C today. She said, 'Go and buy an orange, then'. This is typical.

She still hasn't worn the lurex apron.

I will be glad to get back to school.

Sue Townsend

DEVELOPMENT

3 Language

How does the writer make the apron seem unappealing as a Christmas present? How is the humour added to by the statement 'She will get bathcubes next year'?

4 Language

Look closely at the entry for Friday January 2nd. Pick out an example of each of the following and explain its effect:

- exaggeration
- humour
- repetition.

5 Reading

What did Adrian's father do to the dog on New Year's Eve? How does Adrian feel about this? How does the dog get its own back?

6 Reading

Pick out two statements that show Adrian thinks his parents are irresponsible.

7 Reading

What does Adrian's mother's comment 'Go and buy an an orange, then' tell the reader about her attitude towards her son?

8 Speaking and listening

Imagine you are in Adrian's class at school. Act out a conversation in which you give him some advice.

9 Writing

Write your own diary for the last few days, or make up an imaginary teenager and write their diary. Think about:

- what happens
- problems you encounter
- friends and family
- thoughts, opinions and feelings
- making your diary interesting and exciting.

10 Writing

Imagine that you are Adrian Mole. Write a letter to an agony aunt explaining your problems. Swap your letter with a classmate and write a reply.

REVIEW

Successful diary writing is not just about describing the events of the day. What else does a successful diary writer need to do to make their writing more interesting? Is there anything you could do to improve your diary?

AIMS

- To build up your vocabulary by using a thesaurus.
- To consider how using different words can increase the accuracy and range of your language and expression.

STARTER

1

Find the word in each group of synonyms which is the odd one out.

a happy, ecstatic, merry, dejected
b crestfallen, elated, desolate, miserable
c beautiful, hideous, alluring, gorgeous
d palatable, delectable, delicious, unpalatable
e hostile, amiable, convivial, friendly

f marvellous, commendable, terrible, good
g kind, charitable, generous, miserly
h horrible, loathsome, revolting, delightful
i active, indolent, energetic, industrious
j lethargic, idle, conscientious, slothful
k menacing, sinister, threatening, auspicious
l strange, peculiar, weird, familiar

> A **synonym** is a word which has the same or similar meaning as another word (e.g. synonyms for 'neat' could be 'tidy', 'trim', 'smart' or 'spruce'). A **thesaurus** is a book which contains lots of synonyms and helps writers and students express themselves clearly and accurately.

DEVELOPMENT

2

Find the correct synonyms for the following words using a thesaurus and the word parts in the grid. The first one is done for you.

enormous	dangerous	difficult	easy	bright	clear
gigantic	_____	_____	_____	_____	_____
strong	brave	thin	wide	weak	small
_____	_____	_____	_____	_____	_____

~~gigan~~	trans	ful	cour	tri	sim	hazard	parent
min	ageous	ad	ute	ple	iant	fee	ous
cky	brill	~~tie~~	der	power	ble	bro	slen

3

Use each of the synonyms in a sentence of your own.

4

Sort the following words into fifteen pairs of synonyms (e.g. peculiar/strange).

~~peculiar~~	enthusiastic	despise	attractive	passion
considerate	fascinating	marvellous	gluttony	pernicious
inventive	distinguished	splendid	intriguing	easy
tranquil	careful	~~strange~~	meticulous	alluring
greed	eminent	straightforward	creative	thoughtful
malevolent	wholehearted	detest	peaceful	ardour

5

Using a thesaurus, find at least **two** synonyms for the following words.

calm big dirty dangerous polite sad brave afraid

6

Using a thesaurus, find as many spooky synonyms as you can for these words.

ghost scary dark cold weird

7

Write a paragraph describing a haunted house, including as many of the spooky synonyms as you can.

REVIEW

By now you should be able to use a thesaurus accurately. You should also have expanded your vocabulary, which will allow you to express your ideas more clearly. What difference could a thesaurus make to your writing?

Being bullied

AIMS

● To examine how a script is constructed and used to explore ideas.
● To present in writing your viewpoints and ideas about bullying.

STARTER

1

> An **interrogative sentence** asks a question, for example, 'Are you going on holiday this summer?' An **imperative sentence** gives orders or commands, for example, 'You are going on holiday this summer.'

Write down an interrogative sentence and an imperative sentence that your teacher might use about:

● your school uniform
● your written work
● your behaviour in class.

INTRODUCTION

This script makes us realise that it is not only the victim of bullying who needs help. Who do you feel sorry for at the end of this extract?

2

Has this script changed your thinking about bullying?

The Bully

Scene 7

Home at Christmas. Tree with new racing bike in front of it.

JIM Gosh! Thanks, Mum. A racing bike. Just what I wanted. Fantastic!

MUM That's all right, Jim. You've been a good lad and you've worked hard. You deserve it.

JIM Can't wait to ride it to school. Now I won't have to catch the bus any more.

MUM Why? What's wrong with catching the bus?

JIM Er … nuthin'. Save some money on the bus fare.

MUM Oh, yes. I hadn't thought of that. Good idea!

Scene 8

Riding home from school next term, Jim sees Houseman's gang up ahead of him.

GANG MEMBER Look who it is.

HOUSEMAN Shove him off his bike.

Jim pedals faster, trying to race past them. Houseman lashes out, catching him on the side of the head. Jim falls off the bike on to the pavement banging his knees. The bike goes flying.

GANG MEMBER He's not very good at it, is he?

HOUSEMAN He won't be riding that for a while.

They start kicking the bike, ripping off the chain, wheels and pedals, then they walk

away laughing. Dave comes along and finds Jim howling and trying to fix the busted bike.

DAVE What happened to you? Fall off your bike?

JIM *(Pause. Sobs before he speaks.)* Shoved off, more like. Guess who? Houseman and his thugs. I thought I was OK going to school like this. Now what?

DAVE You gonna tell your mum this time?

JIM Nah, don't think so.

DAVE Why not?

JIM No point, really. It won't be long before that lot leave school and they won't be around any more. Don't want to upset her.

DAVE She will be when she sees that bike.

Scene 9

Back at home.

MUM Oh, Jim. You're late. I was worried about you. Are you OK?

JIM Yes, Mum. I fell off my bike and grazed my knee, that's all.

MUM You've only had that bike for a month or so as well.

JIM I'm afraid it's going to have to be repaired. Got a bit damaged.

Mum sees the bike for the first time.

MUM *(indignant)* Jim, I wish you'd take better care! I'm hard up, you know. That bike cost a lot of money. Goodness knows how much it's going to cost to get it mended. I'm not sure I can trust you to ride it again.

JIM Sorry, Mum.

MUM Your tea's ready for you on the table. I'm going out!

Later.

MUM Is everything all right, Jim? You seem to be having quite a few accidents lately. Falling off bikes, cutting your lip, things like that. Sorry I grumbled so much. I wondered if …

JIM My luck's out at the moment, Mum. That's all.

Scene 10

Walking down the hill with Dave to catch the bus, Jim's on the alert looking out for the Houseman gang, but they come out of an alleyway and surprise him.

HOUSEMAN Get him.

Jim sprints away trying to escape. One of the gang knocks his bag out of his hands. He doesn't have time to pick it up. He hides round the corner from the bus stop. Dave arrives carrying the bag.

DAVE I'm afraid they got to your bag before I did. Take a look. I picked all of 'em up but they're all trashed.

Jim looks inside. They've ripped up all of his school books. He stifles sobs, then straightens up.

JIM That does it. I won't, I won't, I *won't* stand for it any more. I'm gonna stop them.

DAVE What'll you do?

JIM Tell Mum for a start. There was nearly a year's work in there.

Scene 11

Back home.

MUM Oh, Jim, why didn't you tell me before?

JIM I didn't want to worry you, Mum. I thought they might stop.

MUM Well, they didn't, did they? And now you've got a whole year's work to do again.

JIM I'll have to copy all that stuff out again. What a drag!

MUM They're not going to get away with this. I'll see to it. We'll get it sorted. I'm off to see your Headteacher!

Scene 12

Nearly empty classroom on second floor at lunch-time. Jim's busy copying out his schoolwork. Houseman and gang march in. Houseman comes over to Jim. He looks really mad.

HOUSEMAN You've had it. You grassed on me, you little sneak. Got me chucked out.

He starts hitting Jim, who gets to his feet, hands covering his head and tries to run, but Houseman's mates grab him, lifting Jim off his feet.

GANG MEMBER What shall we do to 'im, then? Give 'im a good kicking?

HOUSEMAN No! Let's chuck him out the window.

Jim struggles furiously. As they open the window and try to lift him out he hears the door open.

JIM Help! Save me! Help!

The door shuts again. They swing him out of the window, holding his legs. He sees the ground spinning around a long way down below and closes his eyes.

GANG MEMBER You'd better not drop 'im. It'll mean Borstal for us.

HOUSEMAN I don't care. I want to kill 'im.

The door opens again. Mr Tomkins appears with Dave and some classmates. Houseman drops Jim back in the classroom and rushes away. Mr Tomkins helps Jim up.

MR TOMKINS Are you all right?

Jim splutters, unable to reply.

MR TOMKINS You sure you're all right?

JIM *(stammering)* I thought … he was going … I … thought … he … was … going … to … kill … me …

Scene 13

Bus stop in first scene.

JIM THE NARRATOR That was the last time I'd seen him until today. The last years at school were better after he'd gone.

As I stared at Houseman in the bus queue he turned and looked at me. I tensed, wondering if he'd do anything, but he didn't seem to recognise me. His eyes were glazed over and he looked rather depressed and lifeless. Perhaps he was on drugs or something. He looked scruffy, a bit like a down-and-out.

He'd forgotten me, but I would never forget him. Never.

Gene Kemp

DEVELOPMENT

3 Language

Much of the language of this script is informal. Pick out:

- two examples of slang
- two examples of apostrophes showing how a character drops a 'h' or 'th' when speaking.

4 Language

Write down a sentence which shows:

- Jim's fear and anxiety
- a build up of tension
- Jim's emotions and feelings.

5 Language

When Jim stammers in Scene 12, why does the writer use ellipses (...)?

6 Reading

How does Jim show his excitement when he receives the bike for Christmas?

7 Reading

Why do you think Jim might want to cycle to school rather than catch the bus?

8 Reading

Why doesn't Jim tell his mum about the bullying?

9 Reading

Explore Dave's role in the play. Write about:

- his friendship with Jim
- the way he helps Jim.

10 Reading

Write about Jim's feelings toward Houseman when he sees him in the bus queue. Explain:

- how we know Jim still fears Houseman
- how Houseman has changed
- how Jim's attitude towards Houseman has changed.

11 Speaking and listening

Act out the scene in which Houseman is expelled by the headmaster. Think about:

- the different ways in which the headmaster and Houseman speak
- the headmaster's reasons for expelling Houseman.

12 Writing

Imagine you or a friend are being bullied. Write a script about the problem and how you deal with it.

13 Writing

Produce an anti-bullying poster for school. Consider:

- why bullies bully
- what type of person is a bully
- how they could be helped to stop
- how their victims feel
- what might happen to them if they don't stop bullying.

REVIEW

Act out some of your scripts for the rest of the class. Consider the performances, and how well they convey the characters' emotions. Think about how scenery, costumes, lighting and sound effects could help a staging of the performances.

Experiences of school

Schools in the past

AIMS

- To look closely at a piece of writing by a major nineteenth-century writer.
- To examine how complex sentences are constructed.
- To listen for a specified purpose.

STARTER

1

Match these words to the language they come from.

**donate annual gradual famine
bucket husband bungalow caravan**

*Latin French Old English
Hindi Persian*

Word derivation *is concerned with the origins of words. For instance, many English words come from Old English (e.g. 'drive' – Old English 'drifen'). Greek, Latin and French are also a major source of English words, for example 'autograph' – Greek 'graphus' (to write); 'festival' – Latin 'festum' (holiday); 'comprehension' – French 'comprendre' (to understand).*

INTRODUCTION

The following extract describes the misery and neglect of the boys boarding at Dotheboys Hall. What aspects of Dotheboys Hall do you find particularly appalling?

Dotheboys Hall

He could not but observe how silent and sad the boys all seemed to be. There was none of the noise and clamour of a schoolroom; none of its boisterous play or hearty mirth. The children sat crouching together, and shivering together, and seemed to lack the spirit to move about. The only pupil who evinced the slightest tendency towards locomotion or playfulness was Master   5
Squeers, and as his chief amusement was to tread upon the other boys' toes in his new boots, his flow of spirits was rather disagreeable than otherwise.

After some half-hour's delay, Mr Squeers reappeared, and the boys took their places and their books, of which latter commodity the average might be about one to eight learners. A few minutes having elapsed, during which Mr Squeers   10
looked very profound, as if he had a perfect apprehension of what was inside all the books, and could say every word of their content by heart if he only chose to take the trouble, that gentleman called up the first class.

Obedient to his summons there ranged themselves in front of the schoolmaster's desk, half a dozen scarecrows, out at knees and elbows, one of   15
whom placed a torn and filthy book beneath his learned eye.

'This is the first class in English spelling and philosophy, Nickleby,' said Squeers, beckoning Nicholas to stand beside him. 'We'll get up a Latin one,

and hand that over to you. Now then, where's the first boy?'

'Please, sir, he's cleaning the back parlour window,' said the temporary head of 20
the philosophical class.

'So he is, to be sure,' rejoined Squeers. 'We go upon the practical mode of
teaching, Nickleby; the regular education system. C-l-e-a-n, clean, verb active,
to make bright, to scour. W-i-n, win, d-e-r, der, winder, a casement. When the
boy knows this out of the book, he goes and does it. It's just the same 25
principle as the use of the globes. Where's the second boy?

'Please, sir, he's weeding the garden,' replied a small voice.

'To be sure,' said Squeers, by no means disconcerted. 'So he is. B-o-t, bot, t-i-n,
tin, bottin, n-e-y, ney, bottinney, noun substantive, a knowledge of plants.
When he has learned that bottinney means a knowledge of plants, he goes 30
and knows 'em. That's our system, Nickleby; what do you think of it?'

'It's a very useful one, at any rate,' answered Nicholas.

'I believe you,' rejoined Squeers, not remarking the emphasis of his usher.
'Third boy, what's a horse?'

'A beast, sir,' replied the boy. 35

'So it is,' said Squeers. 'Ain't it, Nickleby?'

'I believe there is no doubt of that, sir,' answered Nicholas.

'Of course there isn't,' said Squeers. 'A horse is a quadruped, and quadruped's
Latin for beast, as everybody that's gone through the grammar knows, or else
where's the use of having grammars at all?' 35

'Where indeed!' said Nicholas abstractedly.

'As you're perfect in that,' resumed Squeers, turning to the boy, 'go and look
after *my* horse, and rub him down well, or I'll rub you down. The rest of the
class go and draw water up, till somebody tells you to leave off, for it's
washing-day tomorrow, and they want the coppers filled.' 40

So saying, he dismissed the first class to their experiments in practical
philosophy, and eyed Nicholas with a look, half cunning and half doubtful, as
if he were not altogether certain what he might think of him by this time.

Charles Dickens

2

In your opinion, what does Nicholas think of Mr Squeers by the end of the extract?

DEVELOPMENT

3 Language

Write down a phrase or sentence which demonstrates old-fashioned language.

4 Language

Write down a list of the rules for the use of speech marks. Think about:

- where speech marks go
- where to use commas
- when to use capital letters
- when to start a new line.

5 Language

There are lots of descriptive words in the first paragraph. Find:

- two adjectives associated with a gloomy atmosphere
- two nouns associated with sound
- two words associated with a happy atmosphere.

6 Language

Look closely at the complex sentence beginning 'A few minutes' (lines 10–13). Rewrite it using four or five simple sentences. What are the advantages and disadvantages of complex sentences?

7 Reading

How did the classroom at Dotheboys Hall appear different from a usual schoolroom to Nicholas?

8 Reading

How do we know that Squeers knows very little about spelling?

9 Reading

List three jobs Squeers asks the boys to do.

10 Reading

What is your opinion of Squeers? Comment on:

- his treatment of the boys
- his teaching.

11 Speaking and listening

Think of a list of questions you could ask either a parent or grandparent about their school experiences. Focus on:

- lessons
- teachers
- subjects
- activities
- uniform
- discipline
- memories – good and bad.

12 Writing

Write a magazine article called 'Schools Past and Present'.

- Think of sections and headings to help you organise your ideas (e.g. teachers, punishments, classrooms).
- Try and write about your school and a past school in the same section so you can draw comparisons between the two.

13 Speaking and listening

Discuss the questions in your questionnaire with a parent or a grandparent. Listen carefully to their answers, and note down interesting points to report back to the class.

REVIEW

What was Dickens trying to tell people by writing about Dotheboys Hall? What do you consider to be the main differences between schools in the past and schools in the present? Is it better to be at school nowadays?

UNIT 7 Progress report

AIMS

- To think about different subjects at school and the specialist vocabulary that goes with them.
- To evaluate your own performance at school.

STARTER

1

See if you can match up these jargon words with their correct definitions.

cliché genre imagery singular tabloid

- a type of writing or literature
- a word or phrase that is used so much it has lost much of its original force
- the form of a word used to talk about one thing
- the format of a small popular newspaper
- vivid mental pictures created by metaphors and similes

Come up with five jargon words for two of the following subjects.

History Geography Science PE Maths Art

> **Jargon** is another word for the technical language used in a subject. For instance, in English lessons you will use words like 'paragraph', 'consonant', 'synonym', 'vowel', etc.

INTRODUCTION

Read the poem 'Progress Report'. The boy in this poem indulges in some wishful thinking.

2

Think about your next parents' evening. How are your parents going to feel when they arrive home?

DEVELOPMENT

3 Language

Find two examples of each of the following.
- alliteration
- end of line rhyme

4 Language

Find a line in the poem with:
- a comma
- speech marks
- a dash
- a semi-colon
- an exclamation mark.
- a question mark
- an ellipsis
- brackets

Explain why each punctuation mark is used.

5 Reading

What does Dad think of Mum's dress?

6 Reading

In the imaginary Progress Meeting what does the teacher think of the boy's performance at school?

7 Reading

What had the boy been doing while his parents were at the Progress Meeting?

8 Reading

How did the real Progress Meeting go?

9 Speaking and listening

Act out the next morning's conversation between the boy and one of his parents.

10 Writing

Imagine that in twenty years you are invited back to your school for a prize-giving because you have become very famous. Describe your evening. Think about:

- how you feel
- how the school has changed

Progress Report

'... and you can't go
In that scruffy jacket either –
You'll look a proper fool.'
Mum and Dad getting ready to go
To the Progress Meeting
At school.
Dad says, 'Come to that,
Is that the dress you're going to wear?
Lean forward with that neckline
And your bellybutton's bare!'
They did get gone eventually,
Both suitably dressed in black,
Gone to a big session of talk
About me –
Behind my blooming back.

'He's really had an excellent term.
The work's been very demanding –
But in English, Maths, History, Geog ...
In everything he's outstanding.
On the sports field too he's broken records –
Well, look at the trophies he's lifted ...
And in Music he just plays everything,
He's really wonderfully gifted.'
'No weaknesses anywhere at all!' gasps Dad.
(Mum's looking over the moon).
'Absolutely none,' Sir firmly states,
'I'm sure he'll be Head Boy soon.
And meeting you both this evening,
Well, it's not difficult to see
Where your son's brilliance comes from ...'
Says Mum (and Dad), 'From me!'

And that's where the dreaming ended.
'You've been asleep by the telly,' says Mum;
They were back from the Progress Meeting,
Both looking pretty glum.
'I had a bit of a dream ...' I said.
'That's your problem,' said Dad,
'Dreaming instead of doing,
You need to shape yourself, my lad.
Your teacher says in English and Maths
Your marks are very low,
And in Geography, History and all that stuff –
Well, you just don't want to know.
No interest in Games or Music,' he says,
'None in Art or Drama –'
'Save the rest for morning,' says Mum,
'By then you'll be feeling calmer.'

And I trailed off to bed
Heart heavy as lead,
Mind silently screaming,
'Better pack in the dreaming.'

Eric Finney

- how the teachers have changed
- whether the evening goes smoothly
- the atmosphere
- whether you enjoyed the evening
- what you might say in your speech.

11 Writing

Write a list of your strengths and weaknesses in English. Then write your own progress report. Be honest.

12 Writing

Think of ways to remember the spellings of these jargon words.

alliteration apostrophe consonant expression genre metaphor narrative onomatopoeia synonym

REVIEW

Write down any areas in English which you can improve. How can you go about making these improvements?

AIMS

- To build up your vocabulary by using a thesaurus.
- To consider how using different words can increase the accuracy and range of your language and expression.

STARTER

1

> An **antonym** is a word with the opposite meaning to another word (e.g. hot/cold, love/hate, big/small). Very often a thesaurus will list antonyms of words as well as synonyms.

Using a thesaurus find as many antonyms as you can for the following words.

easy wide sad small ugly

DEVELOPMENT

2

Find the antonyms for the following words using a thesaurus and the word parts in the grid. The first one is done for you.

optimistic - pessimistic

poor export vague weak hope arrive tiny deep friend clever fact

pessi	my	ene	llow	dep	weal	power	im
defi	art	thy	desp	port	ive	stu	nite
air	sha	mistic	fic	ful	pid	mass	tion

3

Put the following antonyms into pairs.

far long poor light cure fresh near stale injure heavy rich short

4

Sort the following words into fifteen pairs of antonyms (e.g. detest – admire).

detest	generous	fascinating	brave	enthusiastic
tedious	malevolent	difficult	feeble	peaceful
selfish	cowardly	slender	safe	considerate
miserly	powerful	admire	clear	broad
meticulous	knowledgeable	hazy	ignorant	hostile
apathetic	dangerous	straightforward	careless	benevolent

Use one word from each pair in a sentence of your own.

5

Sort the following list of words into pairs of antonyms, putting them side by side into two columns: **Positive** and **Negative**.

good smelly sociable calm evil hideous offensive kind innocent destructive lazy energetic constructive guilty violent mean fragrant unfriendly pleasant attractive

Now write a description of two characters from a book, TV programme or film.

a someone who is good, attractive or likeable
b someone who is evil, unpleasant and a rogue

6

Think of antonyms for the following words:

little wonderful sweet stupid wet tedious straight feminine friendship obstinate patient amusing refined smooth indecisive

REVIEW

When you are next working on a piece of writing make sure you equip yourself with a thesaurus and see what a difference it makes to your work. Why is it so important to vary your vocabulary and use words accurately? Make a note of any new words you have learnt in today's lesson.

UNIT 9 The *Titanic*

AIMS

- To recognise the differences between a formal and informal register.
- To experiment with using a formal writing style.
- To use the correct language register in role plays.

STARTER

1

Put these words into two groups according to their register: formal or informal.

Mum mother dad father mega superb lad boy bloke man brat kids posse gang geezer gentleman chick woman mate friend footy soccer nosh food

> **Register** is the level of formality within language. Register ranges from informal slang or colloquial language to more formal standard English.

INTRODUCTION

The following extract, written by a survivor of the *Titanic*, captures the personal horror and tragedy of those who sailed on that fateful voyage. How does the writer's emotional account create a strong sense of tragedy and sadness?

2

Write down two pieces of evidence that suggest that this extract is written in a formal register.

DEVELOPMENT

3 Language

Comment on the writer's use of verbs in the sentence 'He staggered away and lay down fainting with his head on a coil of rope'. What impression is the writer trying to convey?

4 Language

Look at lines 44–45. Explain how the repetition of the word 'fear' and the use of adjectives combine to create an image of horror.

5 Language

Look at the following phrases and describe the impressions created by the writer.

- This boat will sink like a stone …
- his face was as white as paper
- a bull-dog of a man

6 Reading

In your own words describe what the initial crash must have felt like.

7 Reading

The writer's attitude changes at different stages of the disaster. Find evidence to show:

- that she believed the *Titanic* would not sink
- her reaction to the cry 'women and children first'
- how she reacted to the stoker climbing up from below.

8 Reading

How does Charlotte show her admiration for the actions and bravery of First Officer Murdock?

Survivor's True Story

It must have been a little after ten o'clock when my husband came in and woke me up. He sat and talked to me for how long I do not know, before he began to make ready to go to bed. And then 5 the crash! The sensation to me was as if the ship had been seized by a giant hand and shaken once, twice then stopped dead in its course. That is to say there was a long backward jerk, followed 10 by a shorter one. I was not thrown out of my berth and my husband staggered on his feet only slightly. We heard no strange sounds, no rending of plates and woodwork, but we noticed that the 15 engines had stopped running. […]

I think my husband would have retired to his berth without asking any more questions about the accident but suddenly we heard hundreds of people 20 running along the passageway in front of our door. […] 'We had better go on deck and see what's wrong', he said. […]

When we reached the second cabin promenade deck we found a great many 25 people there. Some officers were walking up and down, but I want to say that at that time no-one was frightened. […]

Our party of three stood close together. […] Suddenly there was a commotion 30 near one of the gangways and we saw a stoker come climbing up from below. He stopped a few feet away from us. All of the fingers of one hand had been cut off. Blood was running from the stumps and 35 blood was spattered over his face and over his clothes. […] I asked him if there was any danger. 'Danger', he screamed at the top of his voice, 'I should just say

so! It's hell down below, look at me. This 40 boat will sink like a stone in ten minutes.' He staggered away and lay down fainting with his head on a coil of rope. At this moment I got my first grip of fear – awful sickening fear. That poor 45 man with his bleeding hand and his speckled face brought up a picture of smashed engines and mangled human bodies. I hung on to my husband's arm and although he was very brave, and 50 not trembling, I saw that his face was as white as paper. We realised that the accident was much worse than we had supposed, but even then I and all the others about me of whom I have any 55 knowledge did not believe that the *Titanic* would go down. I have no clear idea of what happened during the next quarter of an hour. […] I saw First Officer Murdock place guards by the gangways 60 to prevent others like the wounded stoker from coming on deck. […] He was a masterful man, astoundingly brave and cool. I had met him the day before when he was inspecting the second 65 cabin quarters, and thought him a bull-dog of a man who would not be afraid of anything. This proved to be true, he kept order to the last, and died at his post. They say he shot himself. I do not know. 70

Those in charge must have herded us toward the nearest boat deck for that is where I presently found myself, still clinging to my husband's arm, and with little Marjorie beside me. Many women 75 were standing with their husbands and there was no confusion. Then above the clamour of the people asking questions of each other, there came the terrible cry

'Lower the boats!' 'Women and 80
children first! [...] They struck utter
terror into my heart and now they will
ring in my ears until the day I die. They
meant my own safety but they also
meant the greatest loss I have ever 85
suffered – the life of my husband. [...]

The third boat was about half full when
a sailor caught Marjorie in his harms
and tore her away from me and threw
her into the boat. [...] The deck seemed 90
to be slipping under my feet. It was
leaning at a sharp angle for the ship
was then sinking fast, bows down. I
clung desperately to my husband. [...]
A man seized me by the arm then 95
another threw both his arms about my
waist and dragged me away by main
strength. I heard my husband say 'Go,
Lotty, for God's sake be brave and go!
I'll get a seat in another boat.' The men 100
who held me rushed me across the
deck and hurled me bodily into the
lifeboat. I landed on one shoulder and
bruised it badly.

Other women were crowding behind 105
me, but I stumbled to my feet and saw
over their heads my husband's back as
he walked steadily down the deck and
disappeared among the men. His face
was turned away so that I never saw it 110
again, but I know that he went unafraid
to his death.

From *Titanic Voices*

9 Reading

Read from line 87 to the end. How does Charlotte convey a sense of great sadness when she and her daughter are parted from her husband?

10 Speaking and listening

Act out a conversation between Charlotte and her daughter ten years later in which Charlotte describes what happened when the *Titanic* went down. Think about whether to use formal or informal language.

11 Speaking and listening

Present a TV or radio news report on the disaster. Remember to use formal language.

12 Writing

Imagine you are Charlotte's husband. Write a letter to a friend explaining your decision to emigrate to America on the *Titanic*. Write in a formal register.

13 Writing

Produce a poster advertising the *Titanic*'s maiden voyage, aimed at potential first class passengers.

14 Writing

Write a newspaper article from April 1912 describing the *Titanic* disaster. Describe what happened and give eyewitness accounts. Remember to include headlines, sub-headings, columns and short paragraphs.

REVIEW

How do newspaper writers make tragic events like the sinking of the *Titanic* appear real and shocking? Have you managed to convey a real sense of tragedy and horror in your newspaper report?

UNIT 10 Ellen MacArthur

AIMS

- To consider how to make a piece of writing exciting and interesting.
- To use persuasive language in a formal letter.

STARTER

1

> A **topic sentence** comes at the start of a paragraph and introduces the subject of the paragraph. A topic sentence is important in signposting the development of a piece of writing, thereby helping the reader to understand the text more easily.

Write a paragraph for one of the following topic sentences, developing the subject in a logical manner.

- The night descended like a black shadow.
- Vandalism is a major problem in my area.
- It was the most important goal ever scored by an England centre forward.

INTRODUCTION

Ellen MacArthur is a yachtswoman whose bravery, persistence and skill have made her a true heroine of our time. The following extract is very clearly developed and structured. Notice the writer's use of topic sentences.

TRUE GRIT OF FEARLESS MACARTHUR

There would be nothing remarkable in Derbyshire producing a Hill Walker of the Year or even a Potholer of the Year. But for this landlocked county to produce Yachtsman of the Year, and for that award to go to a 22-year-old, slip of a girl from Whatstandwell, is nothing short of miraculous.[...]

When Ellen was eight, an aunt took her sailing on the east coast, after which she was hooked. [...] At 18, she sailed single-handed round Britain and won the Young Sailor of the Year award for being the youngest person to pass the Yachtmaster Offshore Qualification, with the highest possible marks in theory and practical examinations. [...] She wrote 2,500 letters to potential sponsors – and received just two replies.

They looked at her in a new light when she undertook the Mini-Transat solo race from Brest in France to Martinique in the French Caribbean in 1997. With little money, no major sponsorship and not even a return ticket, she took the ferry to France, bought Le Poisson, a 21ft yacht, and refitted it on site. [...] Then she sailed 2,700 miles across the Atlantic; a race which she completed in 33 days. This achievement brought her first major sponsorship from Kingfisher, who believe in backing young people with an ambition to succeed. [...]

Thousands follow Ellen's race progress on the Internet. Messages and digital

There are moments of pure elation – sunrises and seascapes that take the breath away. But there are nightmare times when lone sailors must become engineers.

She describes a night and day that ran together, when 15 litres of fluid (resembling cooking oil) burst from the rams controlling the keel, the big steel fin that goes down through the boat. [...] Before she'd fixed the keel, a piece on one of the sails ripped, which meant taking down the sail and sewing for five hours through the night. Water came through the hatch and was swilling round the boat. And then later, when she'd dried all the compartments, a mighty bang threw the boat on to its side and all the electricity that powered the satcom communication system went off.

pictures from a boat in the middle of the Atlantic can be instantly relayed around the world from the on-board computer and updated every hour. Satellite phones mean contact on shore for weather routing and emergencies. Ellen's uncle. Dr Glyn MacArthur, a GP in Crich, was woken during one night to hear Ellen's voice asking his advice on a head injury she'd sustained during a severe gale in the Route du Rhum.

Exhausting racing conditions mean sleeping in ten-minute snatches, a survival suit that doesn't come off for a week at a time and hands and wrists covered in salt sores and cuts. Dehydrated food comes in packets: if they get wet, the labels peel off and she doesn't know if she'll be eating curry or pudding until she opens one. Sails, weighing twice as much as she does, may need changing a dozen times a day.

What keeps her going is sheer determination not to be beaten: 'When it's a race, you just can't stop. [...] It would be easy to say, "chill out", when you're tired but you never have to lose the goal of the finish line. That's what you set out to do and that's what you stick to. [...] If there's one thing I've learned in this past year, it's that deep down in your heart, if you have a dream, then you can and must make it happen.'

Pat Ashworth in *Derbyshire Life Magazine*

2

How does the writer develop a real sense of achievement and bravery on Ellen's part?

DEVELOPMENT

3 Language

Which two of the following adjectives best describe this article?

- exciting
- complimentary
- emotional
- descriptive
- factual

4 Language

Explain how the writer uses the following to build up a sense of excitement and anticipation in the first paragraph.

- contrasting images, ideas and arguments
- description and language
- facts

5 Reading

How does the writer develop the idea that Ellen's sport is dangerous and difficult?

6 Reading

Pick out a piece of evidence which shows:

- sailing can be wonderful
- sailing can be a nightmare.

7 Reading

How is Ellen MacArthur 'spurred on' when she is out at sea?

8 Reading

What is Ellen's advice to anyone who has a dream?

9 Speaking and listening

Imagine that one of you is the host of a children's chat show and the other is Ellen. Devise a list of questions and act out an interview.

10 Writing

Imagine that you are taking part in a round-the-world yacht race. Write a diary for one day of your journey. Write about:

- your feelings on being alone
- any dangers or problems you might encounter
- the weather and the environment
- communication.

Try to make your diary dramatic and exciting.

11 Writing

Write a letter to Ellen MacArthur trying the persuade her to let you accompany her on her next round-the-world trip. Mention any relevant personal qualities which could be useful. Be persuasive and convincing.

12 Writing

Think of something you would like to achieve. Write a persuasive letter asking for sponsorship in which you put your arguments across forcefully.

REVIEW

Look back at your diary entries. Have you managed to convey an element of excitement? What does a piece of adventure writing need to keep a reader on the edge of their seat?

UNIT 11 Survival guides

AIMS

- To understand the main features of two types of non-fiction writing – websites and survival guides.
- To produce a survival guide.

> A **non-fiction** text is a piece of writing which is usually based on facts. It includes autobiography, biography, diary writing, newspapers, magazines, leaflets, textbooks and websites.

STARTER

1

What are the key features of a website? How is a website different from other forms of writing? Write a list of rules for producing a website. Think about:

- layout
- language
- topics
- interactive features.

INTRODUCTION

The survival guide on page 121 gives you a few tips on how to survive being marooned on a desert island. Do you think this piece of writing could have been set out differently?

2

What do think is the worst thing that could happen to you on a Pacific beach? Give reasons for your answer.

DEVELOPMENT

3 Language

Which of the following words and phrases might be the most appropriate for a survival guide?

A	B
a don't	please refrain from
b dangerous	could be a teeny weeny bit nasty
c try and sort out a few little bits and pieces beforehand	take precautions
d be careful	make sure that you are reasonably cautious when possible
e have a look over your shoulder	beware
f avoid potential danger	stay away from nasty situations that might be a little bit tricky

4 Reading

What advice is given to help you avoid eels?

SEASHORE SURVIVAL DANGERS

Dangers

Moray eels may be found in shallow water. They have a savage bite and guard their holes tenaciously. Keep clear of any you see and do NOT put your hands into crevices!

Giant clams on tropical reefs can be big enough to trap a limb if they snap shut on it.

Fish with venomous spines often live in very shallow waters. Most common, and most dangerous, in the tropics, a few occur in temperate waters. Bottom-dwelling kinds are almost impossible to detect and are often superbly camouflaged. Zebra fish are easier to see, but equally dangerous to contact. Use a stick to stir up the sand and rocks in front of you.

Sea snakes often occur in some numbers close in shore in the Tropical Pacific and the Indian oceans. They are inoffensive and bites are rare – but their venom is most toxic of all snake venom. Keep clear of snakes in the water. Found on shore, pin them with a forked stick – they make a good meal.

Many corals are sharp and can easily cut you. Some, such as the fire corals, sting on contact. Always approach a reef with caution. Exploit other sites for food first. Both the reef and its inhabitants – which may include cone shells – can present dangers.

Sharks

Although most sharks feed mainly in deep waters, some species frequent shallow waters and swim up rivers and any might come onshore looking for an easy meal. Most shark attacks on humans occur in very shallow water. Be watchful!

Lagoons

Reefs are often formed around tropical islands or out from the shore, making a breakwater which leaves still waters in a lagoon. Fish in the lagoon are often of the poisonous varieties. Barracuda and Red snapper, which are edible in the open sea, should be avoided if caught in lagoons – their eating habits cause them to become toxic.

http://survivalx.searchking.com/sea6.htm

---

5 Reading

Why are bottom-dwelling fish often difficult to see?

6 Reading

Why might coral be dangerous?

7 Reading

Where do most shark attacks on humans occur?

8 Reading

Why should you avoid eating fish caught in a lagoon?

9 Writing

Moving into a new area can be an exciting but difficult time. Produce a survival guide for young people moving into your area. You might wish to comment on the following:

- location
- facilities/amenities
- things to do
- dos and don'ts
- dangers.

Before you start, consider how you are going to organise your writing into suitable paragraphs or sections. Don't forget to make your language direct and to the point!

10 Writing

Write a letter to a Year 6 pupil who is coming to your school in September, advising them of both the dangers and pleasures of coming to your school.

REVIEW

Read out some of the survival guides produced by your class. Is the advice use-ful and suitable for people in your age group? Is the language simple and direct?

UNIT 12 Apostrophes

AIMS

To review, consolidate and secure the use of apostrophes in contractions and to indicate possession.

STARTER

1

In dialogue, showing where letters have been omitted may help to indicate how a character speaks. The following words are spoken by the pirate Long John Silver in *Treasure Island*. Read them out in the way Long John may have said them.

v'yages
Cap'n Trelawney
Three goes o'rum
Don't rightly know
don't you
wasn't you cap'n
innocent bird o'mine
on'y where are they?

Now rewrite these words, putting in the missing letters.

> A **contraction** is when two words are shortened or joined together in speech or poetry. e.g. we are becomes we're.

DEVELOPMENT

Apostrophes in contractions
Apostrophes can be used to show where letters have been omitted.

2

Contract the words in italics.

a *I am* very happy *you have* completed your homework.

b *She is* lazy and *he is* hard working.
c *I will* give you my pen if *you will* give me your pencil.
d *He will* go to the cinema if *she will* go with him.
e *We are* going on holiday and *they are* coming with us.
f *We will* go swimming and *they will* go to the park.
g *We have* got some sweets and *they have* got some crisps.
h *I would* like to give you some money if only *you would* wash my car.
i *He would* like a cheeseburger and *she would* like a pizza.
j *We would* enjoy a day at the seaside and *they would* love a day in the countryside.

3

Expand the following contractions.

a don't   —   do not
b can't
c couldn't
d doesn't
e aren't
f hadn't
g haven't
h shan't
i weren't
j won't

4

Use these contractions in a sentence of your own.

hasn't there's could've
they'll o'clock

Apostrophes for possession

Apostrophes can be used to show possession (e.g. the cat's whiskers).

5

Rewrite these phrases using an apostrophe to show possession (e.g. 'the hat belonging to the boy' becomes 'the boy's hat').

a the gun belonging to the soldier
b the house belonging to the couple
c the pen belonging to the girl
d the diamond belonging to the woman
e the book belonging to the teacher

Plurals

In the plural form the apostrophe comes after the 's' (e.g. the dogs' tails wagged). When the plural doesn't end in 's' (e.g. children) you add an apostrophe and 's' (e.g. children's).

6

Rewrite these phrases using an apostrophe to show possession.

a the shirts belonging to the footballers
b the drinks belonging to the girls
c the lights belonging to the cars
d the flowers belonging to the plants
e the coats belonging to the guests

7

Put the apostrophe in the correct place in the following examples.

a the childrens books
b the ladies prizes
c the mens bags
d the princess tiara
e James money

REVIEW

It is very important not to mix up apostrophe 's' and plural 's'. Look out for examples of the misuse of apostrophes – you'll find lots of them on signs and notices if you look closely.

123

UNIT 13 The slaying of the Minotaur

AIMS

- To consider how a writer creates atmosphere and leaves us in no doubt about the hero's bravery.
- To present a story in the form of a storyboard or comic.

 A **myth** is an ancient story, which often involves the brave actions of heroes fighting against the forces of evil and tyranny. Greek myths also involve the influence of gods on the affairs of men and contain a range of fabulous and dangerous monsters.

A **legend** is a traditional story, which may be founded on some truth but cannot be proved.

STARTER

1

Put the following people, creatures, objects and places with their correct myth or legend.

**Ulysses (Odysseus)   Sheriff of Nottingham   King Arthur   Sir Galahad
Merlin   Sherwood Forest   Camelot   Troy   Guinevere   Sir Lancelot
Laertes   Little John   Friar Tuck   Sir Gawain   Poseidon   Maid Marion
Cyclops   Excalibur   Robin Hood   Round Table   Minotaur**

The Legend of King Arthur	The Legend of Robin Hood	The Odyssey (Greek myth)

INTRODUCTION

The Minotaur, a creature that was half bull and half human, was the offspring of King Minos of Crete and his wife Pasiphae. The creature was the result of a curse laid on the couple to punish Minos for sacrificing only his second best bull, rather than the very best, to Poseidon, the god of the sea. As soon as the Minotaur could walk it went wild, destroying most of Crete and its inhabitants. To stop this havoc, the Minotaur was concealed in a complex labyrinth.

When Minos's son Androgeus was murdered in Athens, Minos insisted that Athenian youths be sent into the labyrinth to be hunted by the Minotaur by way of revenge. Theseus was one of these youths, and the following passage describes how he is able to kill the Minotaur with the help of Ariadne, the daughter of King Minos. Consider how the writer creates a sense of tension and excitement in the passage.

The Slaying of the Minotaur

Taking the sword, Theseus followed Ariadne through the sleeping palace, dodging into the shadows whenever a guard appeared. He had been locked in a room on the second floor and now they descended two stairways, their path lit by low-burning lamps. At the bottom there was a bare corridor leading to a heavy, wooden door. Ariadne gave him the ball of wool, tying one end to the handle. 5

10

'This is where the labyrinth begins, my love,' she said. 'I must leave you here.' [...] 15

Then Theseus opened the door and stepped through.

It was cold on the other side. Far underneath the ground, where the sun had never shone, a damp chill hung in the air. The walls were built with huge stone blocks and even three paces away from the door, the corridor branched out in a dozen different directions. Unrolling the ball of thread, Theseus tiptoed forward. There were no lights but some freak property of the rock had filled the caverns with a ghostly green glow. 20

25

Theseus clasped his sword more tightly and continued forward. Despite himself, he could not but admire the cunning of Daedalus. But for the lifeline that connected him with the exit, he would already have been hopelessly lost. He turned left, then right, noticing with a half-smile that he was crossing his own path for he could see the thread snaking along the ground ahead of him. 30

35

40

'Where are you?' he whispered to himself. His breath formed a phosphorescent cloud in front of his mouth. The air smelt of seaweed. He shivered and went on, no longer caring which direction he took. 45

Every passage looked the same. Every corner he turned took him nowhere. Every archway he chose led only into another identical passage. Kicking something loose with his foot, he glanced down. A human skull rolled against the wall and lay still. He swallowed hard. The immense silence of the labyrinth seemed to bear down on him. 50

55

'Where are you?' he said again, more loudly this time. The words scuttled down the corridors, rebounding off the walls. 60

'Where are you ... where are you ... are you?'

Something stirred.

He heard its breathing, then the scrape of feet on sand. The breathing was slow, irregular; like an animal in pain. He turned another corner and found himself in an open arena, surrounded by open archways. Was this where the sound had come from? He could see nothing. No. There it was again. He spun round. A bulky figure stood in one of the archways. It grunted. Then moved towards him. 65

70

The Minotaur was horrible, far more horrible than he could ever have imagined. It was about the size of a man, but a large man. Stark naked it stood before him, its fists clenched, its legs slightly apart. The creature was filthy – with dirt and with dried blood. A blue moss clung to one side of its body like rust. 75

80

Despite the chill, sweat dripped from its shoulders, glistening on its skin.

It was human as far as the neck. Its head was that of a bull ... and grotesquely disproportionate to the rest of its body. So heavy was the head that its human neck was straining to support it, a pulse thudding next to its throat. Two horns curved out of its head above a pair of orange eyes. Saliva frothed around its muzzle and splashed onto the stone floor. Its teeth were not those of a bull but of a lion, jutting out of its mouth and gnashing constantly as if the creature were trying to make them fit more comfortably. The whole head was covered with white hair. It carried a piece of twisted iron, holding it like a club.

Theseus stood where he was in the centre of the arena while the Minotaur approached him. He didn't move as it raised its clumsy weapon. Only at the last moment, as the iron bar whistled down towards his head, did he raise his own sword. There was a deafening clash as metal struck metal. The Minotaur reeled away, bellowing with surprise, for none of its victims had ever carried a

weapon. Taking advantage of the moment, Theseus lashed forward, but the Minotaur was too fast. It twisted away, receiving nothing worse than a gash on one arm. Then it put its head down and charged. Many young men and women had ended their lives impaled on the points of its two horns. Their blood still clung to them in a thick coat. But Theseus had been fighting all his life. With the grace of a matador, he seemed to glide to one side, then whirled round, bringing the sword lashing through the air. The blade bit into the creature's neck, cutting through sinew and bone. The Minotaur shrieked. Then animal head fell away from human body. For a moment it stood, gushing blood, its arms flailing at the air. Then it collapsed.

It took Theseus a long time to find the strength to move, but then, pulling himself together, he found the end of the thread and followed it back the way he had come. At last he reached the door and with a grateful sigh, let himself out. He was soaked in the Minotaur's blood, bruised and exhausted. But he could not stop yet.

Retold by Anthony Horowitz

2

What are the qualities that make Theseus a hero?

DEVELOPMENT

3   Language

Explain the use of the verb 'snaking' in the phrase 'he could see the thread snaking along the ground ahead of him'.

4   Language

Describe the atmosphere created by the writer's use of adjectives in the following phrases.

- ghostly green glow
- a damp chill
- the immense silence

5   Reading

The writer creates an unpleasant and eerie atmosphere in the labyrinth. Pick out a piece of evidence from the text that suggests:

- it was dark
- it was cold and clammy
- the rocks gave out a strange light.

6   Reading

Look at lines 47–50. Why does the writer repeat the word 'every' at the beginning of each of those sentences?

7   Reading

Explore how the writer creates a terrifying impression of the Minotaur. Examine:

- use of descriptive detail
- choice of words.

8   Reading

Describe how Theseus kills the Minotaur. How does the writer create the impression that Theseus is brave and skilful?

9   Speaking and listening

Prepare a TV news report in which you describe the death of the Minotaur. Include in your report:

- the background to the incident (you may need to do some library or Internet research)
- the killing of the Minotaur
- interviews with key characters
- interesting questions

Perform your report for the class.

10   Writing

Produce a comic strip describing the events surrounding the death of the Minotaur. Break down the story into key incidents.

11   Writing

Invent a legend about the place where you live. Make your legend interesting and exciting, using language suitable for a teenage audience.

12   Reading and writing

Find out about another Greek myth. Organise your information under the following headings.

- Key characters
- Location (setting)
- Main events
- Strange creatures
- Atmosphere

REVIEW

How does Theseus fit into the category of a superhero? Can you think of any heroes from literature, TV or film who have similar qualities to Theseus? What can we learn from reading stories like *Theseus and the Minotaur?*

UNIT 14 On the trail of the man-beasts

AIMS

- To conduct some research of your own using the library and the Internet.
- To present findings in a report using appropriate vocabulary and techniques.
- To use talk to question, hypothesise, speculate and evaluate.

STARTER

1

Which of the following phrases might you find in a report?

a The aim of this investigation is …
b Moonlight shimmered on the rooftops …
c A survey of interested parties demonstrated …
d It is evident that …
e Great goal, son – well done!
f This indicates that …
g There are many examples of …
h This evidence is groovy …

> A **report** is a text written about an investigation or an event. It should begin by introducing the subject and stating the purpose of the report, then describe events, processes and findings, before ending with a conclusion.

INTRODUCTION

The following extract is about the many strange humanoid creatures which have been spotted around the world. After reading the article, do you believe that man-beasts really exist?

2

Gather together information, evidence and opinions from the text under the following headings.

- Evidence for the existence of Big Foot or Yeti.
- Evidence against the existence of Big Foot or Yeti.
- What the experts think.
- Opinions about the reality of Big Foot or Yeti.

DEVELOPMENT

3 Language

Add the suffix 'ly' to the following words.

marked virtual usual noticeable occasional notorious

Think of a rule for adding the 'ly' suffix. Now use three of the words in a sentence of your own.

4 Language

Match up each of these words with its correct definition.

a extinct   b expert   c theorise
d indigenous e entity   f tangible
g fabrication h sceptic   i opinion

- a specialist in a given subject
- having totally died out
- a belief that cannot be proved to be factually correct
- to speculate
- definite, can be touched or seen
- a creature or being
- something which is made up
- someone who doesn't believe
- natural or belonging to that region

On the Trail of Man-Beasts

Cryptozoologist Dr Karl Shuker takes a fresh look at the search for Big Foot

On 20 October 1967, Roger Patterson shot a piece of amateur film that would be seen around the world. He and his rancher companion, Bob Gimlin, were travelling on horseback around the bend of Bluff Creek, in northern California, when they spotted something large and hairy on the other side of the creek. The horses turned away, the creature stood up, and revealed itself to be a huge gorilla-like beast with well-defined breasts, dark brown fur, and a markedly pointed head.

The creature strode swiftly away on its hind legs, turning to look at its two astonished eyewitnesses before disappearing into the surrounding forest. But Patterson ran after it on foot, and was able to shoot some colour film of it with his cine-camera.

Elusive creature

The Big Foot has been reported from many parts of the USA and Canada. [...] Witnesses generally describe a very sturdy, ape-like creature, standing between two and four metres tall and walking virtually erect on its hind legs. It has dark skin, which is usually covered in deep brown or black fur, a sloping forehead and broad flattened nose, noticeably long arms that swing to and fro as it walks, powerful muscular legs, no tail, and very large feet that leave behind five-toed prints (though three- and four-toed prints have occasionally been reported) measuring up to 50 cm in length. It appears to eat all manner of plant material, including roots and berries, as well as animals such as deer. It inhabits dense woodlands, sometimes in family groups, and is notoriously shy and elusive.

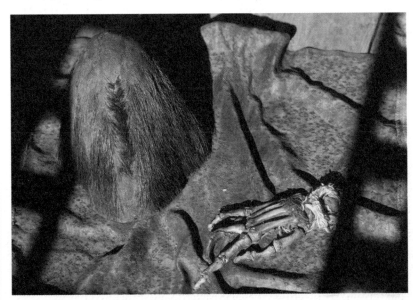

EXTINCT PRIMATE

A number of cryptozoologists believe that the North American Big Foot is a New World version of an extinct giant primate called *Gigantopithecus*. These experts theorize that a small number of these creatures may have survived, becoming known to Europeans and Asians today as the abominable snowman, or yeti.

For a long time, Western investigators assumed that there was only one type of yeti but, in 1960, renowned mountaineer and yeti hunter Sir Edmund Hillary revealed that the Nepalese people distinguish three separate creatures. The smallest is the *teh-lma*, just one metre in height, covered in red fur, with small feet. Inhabiting the warmer Nepalese and Tibetan Himalayan valleys, it seems to be a primitive form of pygmy human.

The 'true' yeti, which is the familiar type to which most reports refer, is the *meh-teh*. Although indigenous to the same geographical regions as the *teh-lma*, the *meh-teh* is a man-sized, cone-headed entity with reddish-brown fur, which mostly confines itself to dense mountain forests. [...]

The largest of the three yetis is the *dzu-teh*, also known as a *rimi*, and is said to stand up to three metres tall. It has shaggy dark fur, and very large feet with prints similar to humans'. [...] Researchers believe that this giant yeti could be a surviving form of *Gigantopithecus*.

Countless expeditions seeking the elusive yeti have been launched during this century[...] – but little tangible evidence has ever been gathered. Even the famous yeti 'scalp' brought back by Hillary to England in 1960, on loan from Nepal's Khumjung monastery, was later shown to have been made from the skin of a mountain-dwelling goat-like antelope called the serow. [...]

MAN'S RELATIVE?

Sceptics dismiss man-beast reports as misidentifications of bears or monkeys – or as complete fabrications on the part of their supposed eyewitnesses. To justify their opinion, they claim that if such creatures really did exist they would have been discovered by scientists many years ago.

However, this view fails to take into account that if such entities really do exist, they are almost certainly close relatives of modern man. As such, these men-beasts are undoubtedly the most intelligent mystery creatures – known as cryptids – presently awaiting discovery, and, in turn, the cryptids most able to avoid capture. Why, out of the many different species of hominid that have existed during the past few million years, should we assume that only one has survived to the present day? Perhaps these hairy men-beasts are living proof that we are not alone.

Dr Karl Shuker in *X Factor Magazine*

5 Reading

Describe the unusual creature seen by Roger Patterson and Bob Gimlin on 20th October 1967.

6 Reading

What do a number of researchers believe the North American Big Foot might be?

7 Reading

Look at the section 'Elusive Creature'. Describe the appearance, behaviour, diet and habitat of the creature.

8 Reading

What are the three separate creatures reportedly sighted by Nepalese peoples? Give their names and distinguishing features.

9 Reading

Why could the famous yeti scalp brought back to England by Edmund Hilary not be used as conclusive proof of the existence of the yeti?

10 Speaking and listening

Act out an interview in which you discuss the man-beast phenomenon with an explorer who has just returned from the Himalayas and has recently made a sighting of a man-beast. Consider:

- appropriate questions (e.g. 'Do you believe...?', 'Do you really feel that...?', 'Are you sure...?')

- responses that speculate on and explore the possible existence of man-beasts (using words such as 'probably', 'possibly', 'I'm convinced that')

- your conclusions about the man-beast phenomenon.

11 Writing

Now write a report with the title 'Man-beasts: Truth or Hoax?' Your report must include:

- an introduction – background to the Big Foot/Yeti phenomenon
- evidence for and against the existence of man-beasts
- expert opinion
- your own interpretation of the evidence
- a conclusion which may support or reject the existence of man-beasts.

Remember to think about ways of linking your points together. Search the Internet and your local library for additional information. Make notes!

12 Writing

There are regular reports of strange creatures from all around the world (e.g. large black cats in Britain, monkey men in India, the chupacabra in Central America). Write a newspaper report about the strange sighting of an imaginary weird creature where you live.

REVIEW

Why do you think people enjoy reading about amazing creatures? Can you think of any other strange creatures a cryptozoologist might be interested in? After writing your report, do you believe in the existence of man-beasts? Try to justify your opinion with any evidence you think is important.

UNIT 15 The sea-raiders

AIMS

- To work out meanings and develop strategies for learning the spelling of unfamiliar words.
- To think about the construction of complex sentences and examine ways of developing ideas in fluent and extended sentences.

STARTER

1

Complete a spider diagram of the key ingredients for two of these genres. Think of a book or story that fits into each genre.

**science fiction   horror
detective   adventure
romance   fantasy   thriller**

> **Signposting** a text means organising your writing so that the reader is directed through it clearly. It may be done by organising your work in sections and using certain connectives to make the sequence of ideas logical and clear.

INTRODUCTION

In the extract from one of H.G. Wells' popular short stories on page 133, Mr Fison makes a rather gruesome find whilst on holiday. What genre of story do you think the extract fits into?

2

Do you think Mr Fison did the right thing by flinging the rock at the sea-raiders?

DEVELOPMENT

3 Language

Work out the meaning of each of these words and think up some spelling strategies for them.

**rendered mark surmounted skerry
partially copiously excrescence**

4 Language

> **Fronting** is when you put an item you might normally expect to find in another position at the beginning of a sentence (e.g. 'Twenty yards beyond them, amid the surf of the now returning tide, two others were emerging from the sea').

Find another sentence from the extract where fronting is used and rewrite it in the order we would expect to see it in a modern text. Why do you think writers use fronting?

5 Language

Rewrite the complex sentence beginning 'Their bodies lay flatly on the rocks ...' as four simple sentences.

6 Language

Pick out the main clause in the final paragraph and comment on the writer's use of subordinate clauses.

7 Reading

How did taking his shoes and socks off save Mr Fison's life?

8 Reading

What was the pinkish object Mr Fison discovered as he came over the ridge?

The Sea-Raiders

Mr Fison, torn by curiosity, began picking his way across the wave-worn rocks, and, finding the wet seaweed that covered them thickly rendered them extremely slippery, he stopped, removed his shoes and socks, and coiled his trousers above his knees. His object was, of course, merely to avoid stumbling into the rocky pools about him, and perhaps he was rather glad, as all men are, of an excuse to resume, even for a moment, the sensations of his boyhood. At any rate, it is to this, no doubt, that he owes his life.

He approached his mark with all the assurance which the absolute security of this country against all forms of animal life gives it inhabitants. The round bodies moved to and fro, but it was only when he surmounted the skerry of boulders I have mentioned that he realised the horrible nature of the discovery. It came upon him with some suddenness.

The rounded bodies fell apart as he came into sight over the ridge, and displayed the pinkish object to be the partially devoured body of a human being, but whether of a man or woman he was unable to say. And the rounded bodies were new and ghastly-looking creatures, in shape somewhat resembling an octopus, and with huge and very long and flexible tentacles, coiled copiously on the ground. The skin had a glistening texture, unpleasant to see, like shiny leather. The downward bend of the tentacle-surrounded mouth, the curious excrescence at the bend, the tentacles, and the large intelligent eyes, gave the creatures a grotesque suggestion of a face. They were the size of a fair-sized swine about the body, and the tentacles seemed to him to be many feet in length. There were, he thinks, seven or eight at least of the creatures. Twenty yards beyond them, amid the surf of the now returning tide, two others were emerging from the sea.

Their bodies lay flatly on the rocks, and their eyes regarded him with evil interest; but it does not appear that Mr Fison was afraid, or that he realised that he was in any danger. Possibly his confidence is to be ascribed to the limpness of their attitudes. But he was horrified, of course, and intensely excited and indignant at such revolting creatures preying upon human flesh. He thought they had chanced upon a drowned body. He shouted to them, with the idea of driving them off, and, finding they did not budge, cast about him, picked up a big rounded lump of rock, and flung it at one.

And then, slowly uncoiling their tentacles, they all began moving towards him – creeping at first deliberately, and making a soft purring sound to each other.

H.G. Wells

9 Reading

Describe the sea-raiders. Comment on:

- their shape and general appearance
- suggestions that they are threatening and clever.

10 Reading

Why wasn't Mr Fison frightened of the sea-raiders? Pick out two reasons and explain them.

11 Reading

How did Mr Fison get the sea-raiders to move?

12 Speaking and listening

Imagine you are reporters called to a press conference with Mr Fison. Devise a list of questions for him.
Now present your questions and answers in a TV or radio broadcast.

13 Writing

Write a newspaper article about Mr Fison's gruesome discovery.

- Invent an eye-catching headline.
- Consider what, when, who, where, why and how.
- Include eyewitness accounts.
- Make your article sensational, entertaining and shocking.

14 Writing

Continue the story with about 200 words in the same style as the original. Think about:

- the word order and style of the original
- the use of fronting
- how complex sentences work
- vocabulary and descriptive language.

REVIEW

If you come across an older text, what can you do to help yourself to understand the meaning of unfamiliar words and complex sentences? Brainstorm some tips on things to do when responding to older writing.

UNIT 16 Link words and phrases

AIMS

- To group and develop sentences in paragraphs by using link words and phrases.
- To extend the use of connecting phrases when developing arguments and ideas.

STARTER

1

> **Link words and phrases** are used to link together sentences fluently in a paragraph. They signpost the development of ideas for the reader.

Describe one of the following processes using these link words – 'firstly', 'then', 'next', 'secondly', 'thirdly' and 'finally'.

- eating a hard-boiled egg
- brushing your teeth
- writing a postcard
- making your bed

DEVELOPMENT

Comparing and contrasting

2

Compare your bedroom with the bedroom of a friend, or a brother or sister, showing similarities and differences. Use some of the following link words and phrases.

Comparing words and phrases: similarly, compared with, in comparison to, equally, in the same way, as with

Contrasting words and phrases: but, yet, on the one hand, on the other hand, however, in contrast to, although, alternatively, in other words

3

Write a speech on one of these topics.

- the dangers of smoking
- the benefits of going to school
- the disadvantages of too much TV

Use some of these link words and phrases.

Opinion words and phrases: it appears that, it would seem, clearly, obviously, surely, certainly, it would appear, possibly, perhaps, probably, it is probable that, maybe, it is definitely true that, surely, on the whole, there is no doubt that

Extending words and phrases: so, because, therefore, thus, hence, as a result of, subsequently, consequently, accordingly

4

Write a letter to your headteacher persuading him or her to do one of the following. Use the link words and phrases below to join your sentences together.

- abolish school uniform
- cut down on homework

Show words and phrases: for example, such as, it appears, for instance, is shown by, the evidence is, is indicated by, is exhibited by, is suggested by, is manifested by, this implies

Restriction words and phrases (these express reservations and limit a point): although, if, only, only if, apart from, except for, excluding, unless, is limited by

REVIEW

Read out some of the work you have produced. Have you successfully used link words and phrases.

UNIT 17 The Pendle Witches

AIMS

- To think about the key features and style of non-fiction writing (e.g. a web page).
- To consider how to present information in a report after conducting your own research and considering a suitable format for presentation.

STARTER

1

Put these events in Shakespeare's life in chronological order.

1623 Anne Shakespeare died.
1616 Shakespeare died.
1609 Shakespeare's sonnets published.
1582 Shakespeare married Anne Hathaway.
1594 Shakespeare's first plays printed.
1599 The Globe Theatre opened.
1603 Death of Queen Elizabeth.
1564 Shakespeare was born.

> **Chronology** is the placing of events in their correct order of time or as they happen. The word 'chronology' comes from the Greek 'chronos' (time) and 'ology' (a science you might study).

INTRODUCTION

Possibly the most famous case of witchcraft in England involved the Pendle Witches of Lancashire. Read their story opposite. After considering the evidence, decide if they are guilty or innocent.

2

Why do you think the writer has chosen the present tense even when he/she is writing about events that happened nearly 400 years ago?

DEVELOPMENT

3 Language

Pick out three features that indicate that this is a web page. Consider both language and layout.

4 Reading

What did Alizon Device appear to do to a beggar?

5 Reading

What supposedly happened to the ale at the Inn at Higham?

6 Reading

What did Demdike claim happened to her which caused her to commit evil deeds?

7 Reading

What was found as a result of the investigation around Malkin Tower?

8 Speaking and listening

Interview one of the people involved in the Pendle Witches' story.

9 Writing

Imagine you go back in time and conduct your own investigation into the Pendle Witches, presenting your findings in a report. You might wish to adopt the following headings.

- Aims of the investigation
- Introduction (background to the story)

On the Broom

The Pendle Witches – were they malevolent people possessed by supernatural powers?

Or were they simple people, who, in a time of severe economic hardship, tried to make ends meet by begging and curing various ills?

The Pendle Witches' story revolves around two rival families led by two old women called Demdike and Chattox. Many local people lived in fear of the families, believing them to have special powers.

The Story of the Pendle Witches

18th March 1612 – Alizon Device, granddaughter of Demdike, is begging on the road to Colne. A pedlar refuses her some pins, she appears to paralyse him with a curse.

30th March 1612 – Alizon Device confesses to witchcraft. At the same time she incriminates Demdike and Chattox. She tells how the ale at the Inn at Higham was turned sour; also how the landlord's son was bewitched to death using a clay image.

2nd April 1612 – Demdike, Chattox and her daughter, Anne Redfearn, are ordered to the courts. Demdike confesses to evil deeds, claiming that the devil came into her and sucked her blood, leaving her stark mad.

3rd April 1612 – Demdike, Chattox and Redfearn are sent to Lancaster Castle charged with witchcraft.

Good Friday 1612 – A party of people gather at Malkin Tower, Demdike's home. They plot to kill the Keeper at Lancaster Castle and free the imprisoned women.

Late April – Investigations take place around Malkin Tower. Incriminating evidence found included human bones stolen from graves at Newchurch and a clay image used by James Device to cause the death of a neighbour. Three more of the Device family along with Alice Nutter, a gentlewoman from Roughlee, are taken away, questioned and imprisoned at Lancaster Castle to await trial. Demdike dies in prison before the trial begins.

17th Aug 1612 – The 'Witches Trial' begins at Lancaster Castle.

20th Aug 1612 – After being found guilty, the witches are hanged at Lancaster in front of huge crowds

http://www.pendle.gov.uk/tourism/witches.html

- People involved (the accused, witnesses)
- Events (crimes committed, evidence of witchcraft)
- Conclusion (your verdict – were the witches innocent or guilty?)

Avoid presenting your report in chronological order.

10 Writing

Write a report for a local history website. Your report can be about any local legends, interesting facts or stories.

Where are the best places to begin researching the place you live?

REVIEW

What conclusions have your class come to about the Pendle Witches' story? Why would any of the characters involved make up a story about their own or other people's involvement in witchcraft? Conduct a survey of people in your class to see whether they think the Pendle Witches are guilty or innocent.

UNIT 18 — Evil magic

AIMS

- To examine the differences between implicit writing, which only hints at meanings and actions, and explicit writing, which makes events clear and obvious.
- To experiment with both implicit and explicit writing.

STARTER

1

> The **root** of a word is its most basic form. Suffixes and prefixes can be added to the root to change it (e.g. we can add the prefix 'dis' or the suffix 'ing' to the root 'appear' to make 'disappear' or 'appearing').
> **Compound words** are made by joining two or more single words or roots (e.g. timetable, timeshare, timelag).

Write down the root words or stems in the following words from the passage.

bringing doubted children hitting happening demanded learned blackness movement dismissing vanished excitement dreadful drumming

INTRODUCTION

In the following horror story the violence is implicit or only hinted at. Nevertheless, it is a chilling tale. How does the writer build up a strong element of horror and suspense?

2

If the author was asked to write a sequel to this story, what might happen in it?

DEVELOPMENT

3 Language

Look at the Greek roots *micro, tele, scope* and *phone*. Find out what each means. How many words can you make from them?

4 Language

Break down these compound words into their component parts.

anybody everything backside sometimes anywhere something candleflames floorboards without

5 Reading

What is the effect of the first line on the reader?

6 Reading

Write down a piece of evidence from the text which shows:

- what people thought of Downing's children
- what Downing and his wife thought of their children.

7 Reading

How does the writer convey a sense of horror without going into explicit detail?

8 Reading

This story has a very clear message: 'you can't dine with the Devil without becoming the meal'. Explain this in your own words.

Feeding the Dog

This story's supposed to be true.

It's about a witch, one of the really bad kind, a man named Downing.

He'd spent years learning witchcraft, travelling all over the country, to meet other witches and be taught by them. He married a witch's daughter, and they had a horde of children. They kept a pack of cats too, who went out to steal for them, bringing back meat and fish from other people's tables. There were just as many children as there were cats, and some people said that the children *were* the cats; and the only people who doubted this were the people who thought that the children were worse than the cats. Downing and his wife cared just as much for all of them, and anybody who raised hand or stone against either children or cats had to spend the next few days in bed, aching all over, cursed by Witch Downing. [...] So, mostly, the little Downings, human and feline, got away with their thieving.

But a farmer named Hollis heard noises in his yard one night, and came out to find three of Downing's children tormenting the pigs in his sty by hitting them with sticks. He shouted at them and told them to go away, and they threw stones at him, and shouted names. Hollis was so angry then that he forgot about Witch Downing. [...] Hollis laid hold of the eldest and gave him the first hiding he'd ever had in his life. The other two ran away when they saw what was happening to their brother. They ran home and told their father.

Witch Downing went to see Farmer Hollis the next day, and demanded money in compensation for the terrible injuries inflicted on his poor boy. Farmer Hollis was afraid of what he had done, but he wouldn't back down now, and he said, 'What terrible injuries? I've done him no more harm than I've done my own sons – I've only given him the sore backside that he should have had a long time ago from you if you'd been any kind of a father!' [...]

'Don't preach at me!' Witch Downing said. He went home, thinking that no curse he'd ever set on anybody before was bad enough for Hollis.

So he made a thing. He killed a couple of his cats, and he caught a big dog, and he killed that too. He used poisons, and some of the worst magic he'd learned, and he made this thing that he called a dog – it looked something like a dog. But it was so black that you couldn't really see it, and its eyes shone all the time like a real dog's eyes do when light catches them – shone red, or green, and sometimes blue. It was big. At midnight Downing said to it, 'Hollis.' The thing went out, and it didn't come back that night. The next day Farmer Hollis was missing from his bed, and couldn't be found anywhere.

Witch Downing boasted that he knew what had happened to Hollis, and that people had better watch out! No one knew what he meant.

That night, Downing woke up and saw two bright green candleflames floating beside his bed. There was a shape around them, a blackness. Then the candle flames burned red, and teeth showed beneath them. It was the thing, the dog, come back. It sat beside Witch Downing's bed and looked at him. When he asked what it wanted, it made no movement or sound, but waited. When Downing tried to leave his bed, it growled, and he lay back quickly. He spoke incantations for dismissing spirits, but it stayed. At last he said, 'Farmer Hollis's wife.' Then the thing rose and went out.

People began to disappear. Farmer Hollis had vanished, and then his wife had disappeared the night after. The following day the Vicar couldn't be found; and then a market woman vanished. On the fifth night, the disappearance was of a woman who'd chased the witch's cats away with pepper, and on the sixth night, Farmer Hollis's little son.

But Downing no longer boasted. Now he slunk about and jumped if a dog barked. 95

People who had nothing much to stay for began to leave the town, and Downing began to run out of names. Night after night the thing came, sat by his bed, and waited. [...] Downing didn't want to find out what would happen if he kept the thing until morning, and he would gabble out, 'The boy who serves at the greengrocer's!' or 'The girl in the green skirt that I pass in 105 the lane!' And the thing would rise and go out. 100

Then came a night when Downing, worn out as he was, must have dozed. He woke with a great shock, and saw that the 110 sky was turning pink! And the thing was pacing up and down by his bed, whining with excitement. 'My wife!' Downing cried – and the thing leapt over him and on to his wife. There was a dreadful noise. Downing 115 jumped from the bed and ran away. There was not an eyelash left of his wife when he returned.

But the thing came to his bedside that night; and he could think of no one. When 120 the thing began to wave its tail, he said, 'The baby.' And there was no baby in its cot when Downing got up.

'My eldest son,' he said, the next night; and on nights after that, 'My eldest 125 daughter – Billy – Anne – Mary ...' And when the last of his children had gone, the thing still came, sat beside him, fixed its eyes on him, and waited.

Downing had nothing to say. Towards 130 dawn, the silence was filled with the drumming of the thing's tail on the floorboards, and a whine from its throat. The light increased – the thing couldn't stay any longer, and its master hadn't fed it. So it 135 ate its master before it left – and who knows where it went, or where it is now?

For all Downing's learning, he had never learned that you can't dine with the Devil without becoming the meal. 140

Susan Price

9 Speaking and listening 🗣️🗣️

Imagine you live in Downing's town, but decide to leave. Explain your reasons to your neighbour.

10 Writing ✏️

Look at lines 61–66. Imagine you are the writer and that your editor feels the extract lacks the graphic detail necessary for a modern horror story. Rewrite it so that it is full of gory details.

11 Writing 🏠

Write your own horror story, using a subtle approach with implicit horror. Concentrate on developing:

- plot
- setting
- characters
- atmosphere
- twists and turns
- imaginative ideas.

12 Writing ✳️

Swap the first draft of your story with a partner. Read your partner's story and write them a letter commenting on it.

REVIEW

What are the key ingredients of a good horror story? Why is 'Feeding the Dog' a good horror story? Now see if you have applied the same techniques in your writing.

Bewitched

AIMS

- To read one of Keats' complete longer poems.
- To write a review of a poem, closely examining some of the poetic techniques.

STARTER

1

Find as many English words as possible that originate from these French words.

ami (friend)   *mort* (dead)

chambre (room)   *terre* (earth)

femme (woman)

> **Derivation** is the study of where words originate from (e.g. 'gradual' originates from the Latin 'gradus', which means 'step' or 'degree').

INTRODUCTION

John Keats (1795–1821) was the youngest and possibly the most gifted of the great Romantic poets of the nineteenth century. This poem shows Keats' fascination with romance, mystery and the supernatural. These are all key elements of Romantic poetry, which sought to escape the real world of suffering, death and decay. See if you can spot any of these key elements.

> A **ballad** is a poem or song that tells a story (often including tales of bravery and adventure or love). A traditional ballad has many verses and can be very structured, with a regular rhyme scheme and fixed rhythm.

La Belle Dame Sans Merci

I

O, what can ail thee, knight-at-arms,
  Alone and palely loitering?
The sedge has wither'd from the lake,
  And no birds sing.

II

O, what can ail thee, knight-at-arms,
  So haggard and so woe-begone?
The squirrel's granary is full,
  And the harvest's done.

III

I see a lilly on thy brow,
  With anguish moist and fever dew;
And on thy cheeks a fading rose
  Fast withereth too.

IV

I met a lady in the meads,
  Full beautiful – a faery's child,
Her hair was long, her foot was light,
  And her eyes were wild.

V

I made a garland for her head,
  And bracelets too, and fragrant zone;
She look'd at me as she did love,
  And made sweet moan.

VI

I set her on my pacing steed,
  And nothing else saw all day long;
For sidelong she would bend, and sing
  A faery's song

continued

VII

She found me roots of relish sweet,
  And honey wild, and manna dew,
And sure in language strange she said –
  'I love thee true'.

VIII

She took me to her elfin grot,
  And there she wept and sigh'd full sore,
And there I shut her wild wild eyes
  With kisses four.

IX

And there she lulled me asleep
  And there I dream'd – Ah! woe betide!
The latest dream I ever dream'd
  On the cold hill side.

X

I saw pale kings and princes too,
  Pale warriors, death-pale were they all;
They cried – 'La Belle Dame sans Merci
  Hath thee in thrall!'

XI

I saw their starved lips in the gloam,
  With horrid warning gaped wide,
And I awoke and found me here,
  On the cold hill's side.

XII

And this is why I sojourn here
  Alone and palely loitering,
Though the sedge has wither'd from the lake,
  And no birds sing.

John Keats

2

Summarise the story of 'La Belle Dame Sans Merci' in the form of a storyboard.

DEVELOPMENT

3 Language

Using a dictionary, match up the words in List A with their modern equivalent from List B.

A	B
a **ail**	reeds
b **sedge**	trouble/bother
c **woe-begone**	storehouse for grain
d **granary**	dismal looking
e **steed**	horse
f **thrall**	short stay
g **gloam**	power
h **sojourn**	twilight/dusk

4 Language

Explain these two metaphors.

- fever dew
- on thy cheeks a fading rose

5 Language

Find two examples of alliteration in verse four.

6 Language

Rewrite one of the more old-fashioned lines in modern English.

7 Reading

Find as many words as you can in the first three verses which suggest a sad atmosphere.

8 Reading

By reading the first three verses what do we learn of the knight's appearance?

9 Reading

Pick out two examples of sensory language and explain which senses the poet is appealing to.

One of the many paintings inspired by 'La Belle Dame Sans Merci'. This painting is by Walter Crane (1865).

10 Reading

What was the warning given to the knight in his dream?

11 Reading

What effect has 'La Belle Dame Sans Merci' had on the knight?

12 Speaking and listening

Discuss this poem with a partner. Focus on:

- what happens
- what the poet is trying to say
- your impression of the poem.

13 Speaking and listening

Read the poem aloud, thinking about how to make your presentation entertaining and effective. Consider:

- who will read the parts of the narrator and the knight
- varying expression, pace and volume
- the possibility of choral speaking in parts.

14 Writing

Write a review of this poem. Concentrate on:

- what happens

- themes and messages
- imagery – simile and metaphors
- language
- sound effects (e.g. alliteration)
- structure – verses, rhyme scheme and rhythm
- atmosphere and mood
- your own impression.

15 Writing

Imagine you are either 'La Belle Dame Sans Merci' or the knight. Write the story of what happens from your point of view.

16 Writing

Produce a fact sheet about the poet John Keats. Use the library or the Internet to find facts about his life and work.

REVIEW

Why is it important to read poems and literature from long ago? What difficulties did your class experience in reading and understanding the poem? How can you help yourself understand texts like 'La Belle Dame Sans Merci'?

UNIT 20 Imagery: metaphors

AIMS

- To appreciate the impact of figurative language in texts by examining the use and function of metaphors.

STARTER

1

> A **metaphor** is a phrase which compares one thing to another without 'as' or 'like' (e.g. the surface of the lake was a mirror reflecting the sky). Metaphors often draw out striking and interesting features about the subject.

Think of a metaphor to describe two of the following.

- your school
- a computer
- a footballer
- the space under your bed
- the hair on your head

DEVELOPMENT

2

Read the following poem, then answer these questions.

a What is the blood compared to in the first verse?

b What impression of the blood does the phrase 'burst with a mild explosion' give the reader?

c How does the phrase 'bold as roses' add to the picture of the blood created by the poet? Think about what colour the roses might be and how they might look against the snow.

d Look at the second verse. What is the snow compared to?

January

The fox drags its wounded belly
Over the snow, the crimson seeds
Of blood burst with a mild explosion,
Soft as excrement, bold as roses.

Over the snow that feels no pity,
Whose white hands can give no
     healing,
The fox drags its wounded belly.

R.S. Thomas

3

Closely examine the following metaphors and pick out:

- the subject
- what the subject is being compared to
- the characteristics given to the subject in the comparison.

a

The swallow of summer ...
A blue-dark knot of glittering voltage,
A whiplash swimmer, a fish of the air.

b

My son aged three fell in the nettle bed.
'Bed' seemed a curious name for those green spears,
That regiment of spite behind the shed ...

c

... a pantomime
of damp, forgotten washing

on the washing line.
So, in the breeze:

the olé of a crimson towel,
the cancan of a ra ra skirt,

the monkey business of a shirt
pegged only by its sleeve ...

4

Look at the following metaphors from Shakespeare.

- What is the subject of each metaphor?
- What is the subject being compared to?
- What is the overall effect?

a

All the world's a stage,
And all the men and women merely
    players:
They have their exits and their
    entrances;
And one man in his time plays many
    parts,
His acts being seven ages.

b

Give me my Romeo: and, when he shall
    die,
Take him and cut him out in little stars,
And he will make the face of heaven so
    fine
That all the world will be in love with
    night,
And pay no worship to the garish sun.

c

But I am constant as the northern star,
Of whose true-fixed and resting quality
There is no fellow in the firmament.

5

Write your own poem using imaginative and striking metaphors. It could be about:

- a person you admire
- a special time of year
- an animal
- a place you enjoy going to.

REVIEW

How do metaphors help to bring a piece of writing to life? See if you can introduce new and startling metaphors into your writing. Share any interesting metaphors you have thought of with the rest of your class.

UNIT 21
An amazing word processor: the pen

AIMS

- To consider presentation and different font styles.
- To practise notemaking whilst undertaking research.

STARTER

1

Try and form as many words as you can by adding prefixes and suffixes to the following roots (e.g. 'nation' can be modified into 'national', 'international', 'nationality').

- act
- part
- script
- form
- press

INTRODUCTION

Despite the invention of computers the humble pen is still often the preferred way to word process your thoughts. The extract opposite traces the development of the pen. What difficulties might the calligraphers and students of long ago have encountered when writing?

2

Calligraphy is the art of producing beautiful and decorative handwriting. In China, Japan and the Islamic world the work of great calligraphers is respected in the same way people in the Western world respect great works of art.

Who might use calligraphy in today's world? When is it important for you to use neat and accurate handwriting?

DEVELOPMENT

3 Language

How can you tell that this extract comes from a reference book? Comment on:

- language (sentence structure and vocabulary)
- layout and presentational features.

4 Language

When did the development of written Arabic take place?

5 Reading

Describe two of the brushes a Chinese calligrapher might use.

6 Reading

Name two materials a European monk might have used instead of paper.

7 Speaking and listening

Look at the different styles of writing.

The quick brown fox jumped over the lazy dog
The quick brown fox jumped over the lazy dog
The quick brown fox jumped over the lazy dog
The quick brown fox jumped over the lazy dog
The quick brown fox jumped over the lazy dog
THE QUICK BROWN FOX JUMPED OVER THE LAZY DOG

Discuss suitable uses for each style (e.g. for a text in a particular genre or on the packaging for a specific type of product). Make notes on your discussion so that you can feed back to the class later.

8 Writing

Choose a piece of writing you really like (e.g. a poem, an extract from your favourite story or a song). Copy it down as quickly as you can, trying to make sure it's still legible. Then write it out as neatly as you can. Think carefully about

The Art of Calligraphy

SACRED WORDS

The development of written Arabic occurred at about the same time as the birth and spread of Islam in the 600s. To express the words of the Koran – the holy book of Islam – Arab calligraphers developed over the centuries a number of styles such as Kufic and Nashki. All of them are supremely elegant, making full use of the flowing forms of Arabic and the spaces that appear between them. Arab calligraphers used brushes and reed pens with carefully shaped nibs.

A BRUSH WITH GREAT ART

The Chinese brush was invented over 2,000 years ago. Calligraphers would keep a set of them, each a different length and thickness and each made of a fur selected for a specific purpose. For instance, a brush made of rabbit fur is ideal for a soft, curving line, while pig's bristles produce a harsh scratchy line. One great calligrapher, Wang Hsi Chih, who lived during the 300s, is said to have used a brush made from mouse whiskers! The hairs for each brush were carefully washed, grouped together to form the desired shape, then glued into a tube-shaped case usually made of bamboo or reed.

MIGHTER THAN THE SWORD

Some of the greatest European calligraphers were the medieval monks working in the monasteries. One of their tasks was to produce copies of the holy scriptures. They wrote out entire books, including the Bible, copying every word, line by line, onto sheets of parchment or vellum. The main tools of the medieval scribes were a quill pen, a sharp knife to trim the nib of the quill, and an inkhorn to hold the ink. After they had finished a page it might be passed onto an artist to be decorated with hand-painted illustrations known as illuminations.

from *The Story of Printmaking*

---

the style of handwriting you use and the spacing. You may wish to add your own illuminations.

9 Writing

Do some Internet research on one of the following topics.

- Chinese, Arab or European calligraphy
- modern font design
- how books are made now
- how books were made in the past

Make notes and feed your research back to the class.

REVIEW

Did you experience any difficulties when writing quickly? Why is it important to be able to produce legible handwriting under pressure? In what situations are you asked to write quickly and neatly? Come up with a list of advantages and disadvantages for:

- handwriting and pens
- computers and word processing.

UNIT 22 The arrival of printing

AIMS

- To look at how writing can be organised in a non-fiction text.
- To organise advice and instructions into a simple and easy-to-understand format.

STARTER

1

Match up the 'English' words with their European language of origin.

Words

yacht chauffeur dachshund graffiti mammoth tungsten cockroach cobra geyser fjord clan penguin kosher

Language of origin

Russian Swedish Yiddish Scottish (Gaelic) Welsh Spanish Portuguese German Norwegian Icelandic Italian Dutch French

> **Etymology** is the study of the origins of language. It is also concerned with the derivation (origins) and development of individual words.

INTRODUCTION

The arrival of printing in this country was one of the most significant events of the late medieval period. Read about how printing changed the world and consider what processes were speeded up by its arrival.

2

How do you think printing helped the world change over the last 500 years?

DEVELOPMENT

3 Language

Organise this extract into sections by giving each paragraph a title.

4 Language

Which of these words describe the language used in the passage?

simple complex formal informal factual descriptive informative vague direct clumsy

5 Language

Which age group is this article aimed at? What would you change to make it suitable for a teenage website?

6 Reading

Why were there so few books in the Middle Ages?

7 Reading

Who was the first person to make a printing press that used separate letters?

8 Reading

How did the arrival of printing change people's lives and the English language?

9 Speaking and listening

Design a website to encourage new Year 7 pupils to use the library. What different sections and features should you include?

10 Writing

Now produce your website. Think about:

- layout
- sections
- features – links, games, information, etc.
- language – is it clear and suitable?

William Caxton c. 1412 – 91

During the Middle Ages, few people in Britain could read and few ever saw a book. In any case, most books were written in Latin, the language of the Church, or French, which was spoken only by rich British people. Books were rare and expensive because they had to be copied by hand. It could take several months to finish a single volume.

By the 1400s, some printers were using wooden blocks to print books. The problem was that every letter of every page had to be carved separately – a very slow process. A great step forward was made in the 1440s by a German goldsmith called Johannes Gutenberg. He built a printing press that used separate metal letters. These could be quickly slotted into rows to make up a page. At last it was possible to make hundreds of copies of a book in a short time.

The new invention was brought to Britain by William Caxton. [...] The arrival of printing changed people's lives in many ways. It became easier for everyone to find out about new ideas and inventions. Printed Bibles helped people to make up their own minds about their religious beliefs, instead of just obeying the Catholic Church. Critics of the Church's teachings could spread their ideas in print. In the 1500s, this led to big areas of northern Europe setting up their own Protestant churches.

In the 1550s, one Protestant writer, John Foxe, summed up the changes printing had brought:

'Hereby languages are known, knowledge grows ... truth is discovered, falsehood detected. Through printing, the world begins now to have eyes to see and hearts to judge.'

Printed books even changed the English language. In the Middle Ages, there were big differences between the types of English spoken in different parts of the country. To a northerner, southern English was as hard to understand as French. Caxton helped to change this. Thanks to the new printed books, a standard version of written English was spread – one that could be understood all over the country.

from History Makers of the Middle Ages

If you don't have access to computers you might want to produce an advice leaflet about the school library instead.

11 Reading 🏠

Visit a library to find out about an author whose writing you have studied. Find out:

- how information about books and subjects can be found
- what help your librarian can give you
- how using a library compares with using the Internet.

REVIEW

How are libraries today different from the libraries of 20 years ago? Make a list of things all good libraries should have. How could libraries be improved to attract more young people?

UNIT 23 Books are a wonderful invention

AIMS

- To examine how ideas and opinions are conveyed in a formal piece of non-fiction writing.
- To write a discursive essay in which you put forward different viewpoints and analyse an issue.

STARTER

1

Match these English words with their language of origin.

Word

sofa trek canoe totem hassle boomerang chopstick karate gong yeti dungarees yoghurt

Language of origin

South African (Afrikaans) Haitian Turkish Hindi Tibetan Malayan Japanese Australian (Aboriginal) Chinese Modern American Arabic Native American

INTRODUCTION

Many students now go straight to the Internet if they want information, bypassing their nearest librarian. What do you think the writer of this article thinks about the emphasis on ICT in libraries?

> **Information and Communications Technology (ICT)** includes the use and study of new computer software and hardware, electronic communication, satellite communication, etc.

2

What is the first thing you will do when you next visit your library?

DEVELOPMENT

> **Superlative adjectives** (e.g. 'biggest', 'smallest', 'highest', 'lowest') state which object or person has the most of a particular quality. There are some unusual superlatives, which need the word 'most' in front of them (e.g. 'most beautiful', 'most difficult') and some irregular ones (e.g. 'best' and 'worst').

3 Language

Which does the writer think is more valuable – books or ICT resources? How does he make this opinion known?

4 Language

Pick out three superlative adjectives from the first paragraph. How do you make superlatives from these adjectives?

broad thin unusual tall wide childish

5 Language

Read the last three sentences. Comment on and explain:

- the use of commas in the first sentence
- the repetition of 'waited'
- the ideas about the best way to find information that the author wants to convey
- the use of the linking word 'meanwhile'.

6 Reading

According to Patrick Conway, what benefits does the Internet bring to the smallest library?

First Person

My column here last month about the advertisement for the new Durham Clayport Library which failed to mention the word 'books' has prompted a reply from the Director of Arts, Libraries and Museums at Durham County Council. 'Yes, slapped wrists all round', says Patrick Conway. 'Books should have a mention.' But, he argues, since libraries want to attract new users, they have to promote Information and Communications Technology (ICT) – it is thanks to the internet, he reminds me, that 'the smallest library can provide a not dissimilar range of information to the largest reference collections in the world's greatest cities.' Still, he concludes that 'first and foremost we believe that reading changes lives'.

This is encouraging: I want to believe that the library system is not giving up on books. Some readers of this column who work in libraries are not entirely convinced. One in Tower Hamlets, east London, tells me that all that borough's libraries are to be renamed 'idea stores', and includes an official description of the new idea store in Bow. The opening paragraph sets the scene. 'You step over the threshold and immediately smell the coffee from the café and see the bright moving images of idea store services on the video wall. [...] ' Books, even new books, are mentioned at one point, and I do not want to exaggerate the situation, but it is clear that technology is considered the main attraction.

Another reader who works in a library in the North-east says that she and her colleagues are fed up with being told to push the ICT side of the library. They are not against the technology ('a terrific tool') but are annoyed by the failure to recognise the worth of books. She mentions plans to scrap 'junior non-fiction', a category of books that are used for homework, on the grounds that the internet has made such books redundant. This is clearly not her experience, and she cites a typical recent example of some boys coming in to the library to find out some facts for their homework. They headed straight for the ICT area, even though only one of the computers was working. They logged on, waited, watched the machine crash, and then waited again. Meanwhile the staff had found the information for them in less than a minute by using an encyclopaedia. As she says, 'books are a wonderful invention'.

Ian Hislop

7 Reading

What new names are libraries to be given in Tower Hamlets?

8 Reading

Which part of the library did the boys who needed some facts for homework head straight for? Did they find the information they wanted?

9 Speaking and listening

Devise some instructions informing library users about the best way to find information.

10 Writing

Write an essay with the title 'Are Books Essential?'. Consider:

- how and why books are used
- the advantages and disadvantages of computers
- what you, your parents and teachers think about the value of books
- whether computers will ever replace books
- whether books have any advantages over computers.

11 Speaking and listening

Bring in one of your favourite books from home. Explain why you like it so much and try to persuade others to read it.

REVIEW

What pastimes have replaced reading in the last 50 years? What are the advantages of being a good reader? Discuss your essays – does your class believe that books are essential?

UNIT 24 Books make good pets

AIMS

- To appreciate the impact of figurative language.
- To experiment with figurative language.

STARTER

1

Which of these terms best fits each of the following phrases: simile, metaphor or personification?

- His fists were iron hammers.
- The cold air wrapped its clammy, icy fingers around me.
- Joe is as tall as a tree and laughs like a hyena.

> **Figurative language** involves the use of similes, metaphors and personification in an imaginative way which creates interest and impact.
> **Personification** is when an inanimate object is given human or animal qualities (e.g. the wind howled, the leaves danced in the breeze).

INTRODUCTION

The poem opposite is an excellent example of the use of personification, and cleverly compares a book to a pet. Which is your favourite example of personification?

2

What do you think were John Agard's reasons for writing this poem?

DEVELOPMENT

3 Language

> **Assonance** is the rhyming of vowels (e.g. 'Books make good pets') and is a device often used in poetry to create a particular mood.

Read the first verse again and listen to the sounds of the words. Find examples of the following types of rhyme.

- assonance
- rhyming words at the end of a line

4 Language

Explain the personification in lines 7–9. What feelings do these lines convey?

5 Language

Find two examples of alliteration.

6 Reading

Pick out five pets to which books are compared in the poem.

7 Reading

What does the verb 'burrow' suggest in lines 25–26?

8 Reading

Consider lines 56–57. What do you think the 'branches of yourself' might mean?

9 Reading

How might a book be 'as colourful as goldfish'?

10 Reading

Explain the line 'in the bowl of your imagination'. What idea is the poet trying to suggest?

11 Speaking and listening

Practise reading the poem aloud. Work on the volume, pace and expression of your voice. Now perform your version!

12 Writing

Write your own poem about something else that might make a good pet. Try using a spider diagram to brainstorm ideas.

Books Make Good Pets

Books make good pets
and don't need
going to the vet.

You don't have to keep
them on a lead   5
or throw them a stick.
They'll wag their tails
when you flick
their dog-eared pages.

Books make good pets   10
and don't need
going to the vet.

One curious look sets
them purring
on the cushion of your eyes   15
as if to say dear browser
you've picked me up before
and thrown me aside
but I have more than nine lives
and no need to keep twiddling 20
that piece of string.

Books make good pets
and don't need
going to the vet.

They'll burrow their way   25
through the dust of your mind
nibble at old ideas

to let in the new
and you don't have to empty
any droppings on a tray.   30
No thank you.

Books make good pets
and don't need
going to the vet.

They'll hibernate   35
in the shell of their covers
and patiently wait
as long as centuries
to be rediscovered
in their own good time   40
when some reader rolls them
over on their cracked spine.

Books make good pets
and don't need
going to the vet.   45

They're easier to care for
than tropical parakeets
and sometime come in pairs
but they prefer to breed
in stacks and piles.   50
You don't have to feed
them sunflower seed
and just about anywhere
will serve as a nesting site
and from the perch of a shelf   55
they'll help you take flight
among the branches of yourself.

Books make good pets
and don't need
going to the vet.   60

They're as colourful as goldfish
in all their stillness
and believe me this is no whim
books can glow and swim

in the bowl of your imagination. 65

John Agard

Consider the advantages of your objects and all the disadvantages of looking after and owning a real pet. What responsibilities would you have towards a real pet that wouldn't apply to your chosen object?
Use some of these techniques.

- imaginative, interesting vocabulary
- personification
- metaphors and similes
- repetition
- varied rhyme and rhythm

13 Reading

Look at the poem 'Books Make Good Pets' and find examples of similes, metaphors or personification.

REVIEW

Have you managed to incorporate personification successfully in your own writing? Look at the poems written by people in your class and read out any good examples.

UNIT 25 The fun they had

AIMS

- To write a text explaining how an invention works.
- To write a book review.

STARTER

1

Look at the following words which might be useful in a book review.

personality location friendly exciting technical entertaining tense slang incident action believable dialect comic spooky appearance dialogue speech trait happy sad place situation events depressing amusing complicated complex jargon witty interesting loyal secretive dark twists turns eerie likeable

Organise them into the following columns.

Plot	Setting	Atmosphere	Characters	Language

Here are some more useful words.

Word bank

genre	impression	suitability	ingredient
style	storyline	audience	favourite
strengths	relationships	messages	formal
weaknesses	beginning	feature	informal
opinion	ending	quality	register

INTRODUCTION

We take books for granted. But will books always be as commonplace as they are now? This story predicts a future without them. Do you think it is an accurate prediction?

2

Pick out all the technical language that helps you to understand how the mechanical teacher works.

The Fun They Had

Margie even wrote about it that night in her diary. On the page headed 17 May, 2155, she wrote, 'Today Tommy found a real book!'

It was a very old book. Margie's grandfather once said that when he was a little boy *his* grandfather told him that there was a time when all stories were printed on paper.

They turned the pages, which were yellow and crinkly, and it was awfully funny to read words that stood still instead of moving the way they were supposed to – on a screen, you know. And then, when they turned back to the page before, it had the same words on it that it had had when they read it the first time.

'Gee,' said Tommy, 'what a waste. When you're through with the book, you just throw it away, I guess. Our television screen must have had a million books on it and it's good for plenty more. I wouldn't throw *it* away.'

'Same with mine,' said Margie. She was eleven and hadn't seen as many telebooks as Tommy had. He was thirteen.

She said, 'Where did you find it?'

'In my house.' He pointed without looking, because he was busy reading. 'In the attic.'

'What's it about?'

'School.'

Margie was scornful. 'School? What's there to write about school? I hate school.' Margie always hated school, but now she hated it more than ever. The mechanical teacher had been giving her test after test in geography and she had been doing worse and worse until her mother had shaken her head sorrowfully and sent for the County Inspector.

He was a round little man with a red face and a whole box of tools with dials and wires. He smiled at her and gave her an apple, then took the teacher apart. Margie had hoped he wouldn't know how to put it together again, but he knew how all right and after an hour or so, there it was again, large and black and ugly with a big screen on which all the lessons were shown and the questions were asked. That wasn't so bad. The part she hated most was the slot where she had to put homework and test papers. She always had to write them out in a punch code they made her learn when she was six years old, and the mechanical teacher calculated the mark in no time.

The Inspector had smiled after he was finished and patted her head. He said to her mother, 'It's not the little girl's fault, Mrs Jones. I think the geography sector was geared a little too quick. Those things happen sometimes. I've slowed it up to an average ten-year level. Actually, the overall pattern of her progress is quite satisfactory.' And he patted Margie's head again.

Margie was disappointed. She had been hoping they would take the teacher away altogether. They had once taken Tommy's teacher away for nearly a month because the history sector had been blanked out completely.

So she said to Tommy, 'Why would anyone write about school?'

Tommy looked at her with very superior eyes. 'Because it's not our kind of school, stupid. This is the old kind of school that they had hundreds and hundreds of years ago.' He added loftily, pronouncing the word carefully, '*Centuries* ago.'

Margie was hurt. 'Well, I don't know what kind of school they had all that time ago.' She read the book over his shoulder for a while, then said, 'Anyway, they had a teacher.'

'Sure they had a teacher, but it wasn't a *regular* teacher. It was a man.'

'A man? How could a man be a teacher?'

'Well, he just told the boys and girls things and gave them homework and asked them questions.'

'A man isn't smart enough.'

'Sure he is. My father knows as much as my teacher.'

'He can't. A man can't know as much as a teacher.'

'He knows almost as much I betcha.'

Margie wasn't prepared to dispute that. She said, 'I wouldn't want a strange man in my house to teach me.'

Tommy screamed with laughter. 'You don't know much, Margie. The teachers didn't live in the house. They had a special building and all the kids went there.'

'And all the kids learned the same thing?'

'Sure, if they were the same age.'

'But my mother says a teacher had to be adjusted to fit the mind of each boy and girl it teaches and that each kid has to be taught differently.'

'Just the same they didn't do it that way then. If you don't like it, you don't have to read the book.'

'I didn't say I didn't like it,' Margie said quickly. She wanted to read about those funny schools.

They weren't even half finished when Margie's mother called, 'Margie! School!'

Margie looked up. 'Not yet, mamma.'

'Now,' said Mrs Jones. 'And it's probably time for Tommy, too.'

Margie said to Tommy, 'Can I read the book some more with you after school?'

'Maybe,' he said nonchalantly. He walked away whistling, the dusty old book tucked beneath his arm.

Margie went into the schoolroom. It was

right next to her bedroom, and the mechanical teacher was on and waiting for her. It was always on at the same time every day except Saturday and Sunday, because her mother said little girls learned better if they learned at regular hours.

The screen was lit up, and it said: 'Today's arithmetic lesson is on the addition of proper fractions. Please insert yesterday's homework in the proper slot.'

Margie did so with a sigh. She was thinking about the old schools they had when her grandfather's grandfather was a little boy. All the kids from the whole neighbourhood came, laughing and shouting in the school-yard, sitting together in the school-room, going home together at the end of the day. They learned the same things so they could help one another on the homework and talk about it.

And the teachers were people …

The mechanical teacher was flashing on the screen: 'When we add the fractions $\frac{1}{2}$ and $\frac{1}{4}$ –'

Margie was thinking about how the kids must have loved it in the old days. She was thinking about the fun they had.

Isaac Asimov

DEVELOPMENT

3 Language

Replace the adjectives in the following phrases with synonyms.

- a <u>very old</u> book
- <u>little</u> boy
- they turned the pages, which were <u>yellow</u> and <u>crinkly</u>

> A **thesaurus** lists synonyms or words with the same or similar meaning. Sometimes it is referred to as a dictionary of synonyms and antonyms (words of opposite meaning).

4 Language

Replace the verb 'hate' in these sentences with a synonym.

'I <u>hate</u> school.' Margie always <u>hated</u> school, but now she <u>hated</u> it more than ever.

5 Language

Rewrite the first two paragraphs as if you were Margie writing her diary. Write a third paragraph, summarising the rest of the story.

6 Reading

What type of books are Margie and Tommy used to?

7 Reading

What does Margie mean by 'school'?

8 Reading

Describe Margie's teacher. What is unusual about it?

9 Reading

What does Margie think of schools in the past by the end of the story?

10 Speaking and listening

Imagine that the government decides to ration books to one per person to save trees. Which book would you choose to have and why?

11 Writing

Choose a fiction book you have particularly enjoyed. Write a detailed review. Include a detailed paragraph on each of the following.

- plot – what happened, interesting twists and turns, beginning/ending
- characters – main characters, relationships, your favourite character
- setting – locations/places, time
- atmosphere – spooky, happy, sad, frightening/eerie
- key moments
- what the writer has to say
- your impressions.

12 Writing

Write the instruction booklet that goes with a mechanical teacher. Use the following headings:

- What is a mechanical teacher?
- The advantages of a mechanical teacher.
- What can your mechanical teacher do?
- How to make it work.
- Special features.

REVIEW

What conclusions have you and your classmates come to regarding the future of books? What pleasure can be gained from possessing and reading a book? Think about the key ingredients of a good book.

UNIT 26 Imagery: personification

AIMS

- To appreciate the impact of figurative language in texts by examining the use and function of personification.

STARTER

1

Give each of the following machines animal or human characteristics (e.g. aeroplane – 'the aeroplane lifted its wings away from the runway, a silver eagle soaring upwards').

- car
- TV
- train
- stapler
- computer printer
- lawnmower

DEVELOPMENT

2

Read the extract below from the poem 'In the Kitchen' by John Cotton.

> In the kitchen
> After the aimless
> Chatter of the plates,
> The murmuring of the gas,
> The chuckle of the water pipes
> And the sharp exchanges
> Of knives, forks and spoons,
> Comes the serious quiet,
> When the sink slowly clears its throat …

Explain the following examples of personification, commenting on the actions or sounds made by each object.

- the aimless / Chatter of the plates
- murmuring of the gas
- chuckle of the water pipes
- sharp exchanges / Of knives, forks and spoons
- the sink slowly clears its throat

Now write your own personification poem based on a room in your house or school.

3

Opposite are the first six verses of a poem.

a Describe how each month is personified. Comment on:
- the person or thing each month is compared to
- what each person or thing does
- the impression of each month the poet is trying to create.

b Now write a Cautionary Calendar for the remaining six months of the year.

4

Write a poem using the format of 'Cautionary Calendar' based on the days of the week. Make your poem amusing and use striking and unusual examples of personification.

Cautionary Calendar

Beware January,
His greeting is a grey chill.
Dark stranger. First in the kill.
Get out while you can.

Beware February,
Jolly snowman. But beneath the snow
A grinning skeleton, a scarecrow.
Don't be drawn into that web.

Beware March,
Mad Piper in a many-coloured coat
Who will play a jig then rip your throat.
If you leave home, don't go far.

Beware April,
Who sucks eggs and tramples nests.
From the wind that molests
There is no escape.

Beware May,
Darling scalpel, gall and wormwood.
Scented blossom hides the smell
Of blood. Keep away.

Beware June,
Black lipstick, bruise coloured rouge,
Sirensong and subterfuge.
The wide-eyed crazed hypnotic moon.

Roger McGough

REVIEW

Read out your favourite verse from your own Cautionary Calendar to the rest of the class. Are there any memorable examples of personification? Your teacher will now read the other verses of Roger McGough's 'Cautionary Calendar'. How do they compare with your versions?

UNIT 27 Gangs

AIMS

- To develop your ability as a speaker in a range of contexts.
- To develop atmosphere and tone by using a variety of descriptive techniques.

STARTER

1

Examine the following adjectives which could be used to describe tone in a passage.

desperate frightening angry pleading romantic funny sarcastic

Improvise one of the following situations, adopting one of these tones.

- Ask a classmate to borrow a pencil.
- You are in a restaurant and there is an insect in your milkshake. Take it back.

> **Tone** is the mood or atmosphere of a piece of writing (e.g. happy, sad, angry, comic). Very often the tone of a passage will change through a text to maintain the interest of the reader.

INTRODUCTION

In the passage opposite Chas McGill is determined to protect the unfortunate Nicky from Boddser Brown's gang of bullies. The story is set in 1940. Notice how the writer cleverly alters the mood of the passage by changing the characters' speech and actions. How can you tell whose side the writer is on?

2

What should now happen to Chas?

DEVELOPMENT

3 Language

Write down a sentence or phrase from the passage which shows each of the following tones.

- mockery (making fun of someone)
- anger
- determination

4 Language

Explain the meaning of the similes in lines 38 and 124–126. What tone or atmosphere is produced?

5 Language

> An **exclamatory** sentence is abrupt and emphatic. It expresses emotions such as anger or happiness (e.g. 'You stupid boy!' or 'Absolutely fabulous!').

Explain what emotions are being expressed in the following exclamatory sentences.

- 'You're bloody mad. Stop it!'
- 'Right McGill, you've asked for this.'

6 Reading

Explain the writer's use of the terms 'pack-leader' and 'wolf-gang'. What atmosphere does this create?

7 Reading

How does Chas poke fun at Boddser? What impression of Boddser is he trying to create?

The Machine Gunners

The wolf-gang was waiting just beyond the school gate; nine of them, including pack-leader Boddser Brown. Chas kept up his flow of rudeness, but watched Boddser out of the corner of his eye. Boddser was looking worried; he didn't like anything unusual.

'Gerraway, McGill; he's *ours*,' said Boddser.

'I beg your pardon, O Mighty One, O Star of the East, O Moon of my Delight. Your beauty is dazzling, especially your hair-cut, Four-eyes!' There was a titter even among the wolf-pack.

Boddser reddened. He looked uneasily at Clogger. He didn't like the new confidence in Chas's voice.

'Gerraway, McGill. I'm warning you. I've got no quarrel with you, for now.'

'Oh thank you, thank you, worshipful lord,' said Chas, making low salaams. 'May Allah bless your luscious toenails.' The smaller group moved past the larger one. So far, so good. They went on down Hawkey's Lane, not hurrying. Hurrying would be fatal. [...]

'Pull him out,' said Boddser to two of his minions. The minions dived for Nicky, who was between Chas and Cem.

Clogger moved like greased lightning. His steel toecap caught the first minion on the knee, leaving him writhing in the gutter. His fist caught the second full on the nose, drawing a satisfying stream of blood. The wolf-gang drew back and looked pointedly at Boddser. It was up to him, now, and the main road, full of people who might telephone the school, was only forty yards away.

'Get past them,' shouted Boddser. The wolf-gang streamed past, well clear of Clogger's boots, and blocked the end of the lane, solid. [...]

Boddser stepped out in front.

'Right McGill, you've asked for this.' His bluster was gone. He had made up his mind, as a man might decide to nail up a fence he'd watched sagging all winter. [...] Boddser didn't even sound cruel or gloating as he did when he tortured Nicky; just determined. The time for talk, Chas decided, was over. It was time for action. But what? Chas was quick, and not soft, but no one he knew could stand up long to the pounding of

Boddser's fists, except perhaps Clogger, and it wasn't Clogger's fight.

He could dive, head down, for Boddser's midriff, slide down 75 and pinion Boddser's legs and hope to push him over. But that would end, inevitably, with Boddser sitting on his chest, banging his head against the 80 pavement.

Boddser took off his gasmask haversack, then his schoolbag, his school raincoat, his blazer. He rolled up his sleeves slowly, 85 one after the other. Chas could think of nothing but to do likewise. He took off his gasmask case. [...] It was a circular tin, twice the size of a 90 large tin of beans and nearly as heavy. It swung from a long thin leather strap.

And then the idea came to Chas. It set him aghast. But it 95 was maim or be maimed now. He put the case down carefully and took off his schoolbag and coat and blazer, laying them in the fine gravel of the gutter. He 100 came up with his fists clenched, ready. Boddser advanced without hurry.

'Take your specs off,' shouted Chas. 'I don't want your mum 105 complaining to me dad if I break them!'

'Playing for time, McGill,' jeered Boddser. [...] But he took off his spectacles and handed them to 110 a minion, and advanced again. Chas saw the first blow coming, and ducked it.

Then he swung his right fist wildly, a yard from Boddser's 115 face and opened his hand. Fine gravel sprayed into Boddser's eyes. The huge menacing figure was suddenly crouched up helpless, tears streaming down 120 his face.

Calmly, full of murder, Chas picked up his gasmask case and swung it. It hit the side of Boddser's head with a sound like 125 a splitting pumpkin. Boddser screamed but did not fall. Chas swung at him again. The gasmask case dented dramatically. Boddser crashed into the 130 corrugated-iron fence. Chas raised his tin a third time. All the hate of all the years, infant school, junior school, boiled up in him. 135

It was as well that Cem snatched the gasmask from his hand.

'You're bloody mad. Stop it, stop it!' Cem yelled. 140

Robert Westall

8 Reading

Look at the paragraph beginning on line 57. What does Boddser decide to do and how is he going to approach it?

9 Reading

Pick out any words or phrases which show Chas's hatred of Boddser.

10 Speaking and listening

Act out two of the following situations, creating a different atmosphere in each one.

- Chas explaining his actions to his parents.
- Chas telling his friends about the encounter with Boddser's gang.
- Chas being sent to the headmaster the next day.
- Chas's interview with the police.

Consider:

- the different tone each role play would have
- the language register used by Chas when talking to different people.

11 Writing

Write a story in which you and your friends come face to face with a rival gang. Think about:

- descriptive words – adjectives and adverbs
- imagery – metaphors and similes
- realistic dialogue and a variety of reporting clauses (e.g. shouted aggressively, jeered mockingly, etc.)
- using a variety of tones.

12 Writing

Imagine you are the headteacher of Chas's school. Write a letter home to Chas's parents informing them that you have excluded him from school and explaining your reasons.

REVIEW

Have people in your class managed to produce an exciting and tense atmosphere in their stories? What emotions should you be trying to convey in a story in which you are describing a dangerous situation? Have you created the right tone?

UNIT 28 Rebels without a cause

AIMS

- To present, develop and signpost an argument in speech and writing.
- To write a magazine article presenting two conflicting viewpoints.

STARTER

1

One of you puts forward an argument supporting each of the issues below. The other puts forward a counter-argument opposing that point of view. Then swap roles.

- eating meat
- wearing school uniform
- body piercing
- homework

An **argument** is when you put forward a point of view in support of a particular belief. Argumentative writing considers different ideas and opinions on an issue.

INTRODUCTION

Disagreements with parents are part of growing up. Whose side are you on in the disagreements described in the extract opposite?

2

How might these issues be presented differently in a teenage magazine?

DEVELOPMENT

3 Language

Most of this article is written in the first person. Rewrite the paragraph beginning on line 4 in the third person.

4 Language

Expand the following contractions.

don't   it's   isn't   I'm

Now contract the following words

had not   have not   should not shall not

5 Language

The writer of this article uses dashes instead of colons and semicolons to break up sentences. Look at the examples in lines 4–5, 31–32, 37 and 41. Comment on:

- why a dash has been used in each example
- the two ideas in each sentence
- the advantage of using dashes instead of colons and semicolons.

6 Reading

Why has Byron shaved his head?

7 Reading

Give two disadvantages of shaving your head according to Byron.

8 Reading

Why doesn't Deirdre like Byron's shaved head?

9 Reading

How do we know that tongue piercing hurts after it is done?

10 Reading

What do Ivana's friends think about her pierced tongue?

11 Speaking and listening

Improvise a discussion with your parents about something you disagree about. You may wish to develop your discussion into a full-blown argument!

Rebels Without A Cause

Fancy a shaved head or a pierced tongue?
You can always rely on teenagers to find ways of annoying their parents.

Fourteen-year-old Byron Taylor shaves his head. Mum, Deirdre, 46, thinks he looks a prat.

Byron: I don't shave my head to look hard – it's just practical. I don't need to worry 5 about what my hair looks like when I get out of bed. I admit you might think I was menacing if you didn't know me. I'm more likely to get singled out if there's trouble. [...] 10
I love the feeling of not having hair. My head feels lovely and smooth. Girls don't like it much, though. They prefer lots of long flowing hair which must be a nightmare to look after. 15

Deirdre: It was such a shock to see Byron with his head shaved. Apart from looking a prat, he appeared so threatening. I don't want my son wandering around looking like a thug. [...] 20
The school was furious, which worried me. It's a shame because I know he isn't really a troublemaker. He just looks like one.

When Ivana Lawrence, 18, had her tongue pierced, her mum, Ingrid, 47, threatened to 25 throw her out of the house.

Ivana: I got my tongue pierced when I was 16. Mum and Dad said I was out if I went ahead. Whey they found out they were hurt but I'm still living at home! 30
The piercing isn't painful – a spray numbs your tongue – but it does hurt afterwards. For a week I lived on baby food and mashed bananas.
Most of my friends think it's cute. [...] 35

Ingrid: I felt hurt Ivana had it done. But the teens are a selfish stage – no matter what you say they'll do what they want. I've brought Ivana up to think things through and make her own 40 decisions – so I suppose I'll just have to live with this one.

Woman's Own

---

12 Writing 🇪

Write an article for a teenage magazine using the same format as 'Rebels Without A Cause'. Choose two issues where children and parents strongly disagree. Remember:

- use the first person
- be persuasive
- make notes before you begin.

13 Writing 🏠

Imagine your mum or dad comes home having had something drastic done to their appearance. Write a spoof magazine article entitled 'Rebel Without a Cause' in which your parents explain their outrageous actions and you express your strong disapproval.

REVIEW

Read out some extracts from your articles. Now make a list of areas where parents and teenage children might disagree. Draw up a teenagers' or parents' charter with a list of rules which could stop any further conflict.

Conflict

The trouble with parents

AIMS

- To investigate how English has changed since Shakespeare's day.
- To examine different attitudes towards issues in your own writing.
- To collaborate in, and evaluate, the presentation of a scripted dramatic performance.

STARTER

1

Look at the following haiku poem.

> *Lazing through hot days*
> *A leopard stretching sharp claws*
> *My cat dreams of nights.*

- Count how many syllables there are in each line.
- Rewrite each line, increasing it to ten syllables by adding extra words.

> **Blank verse** *is a type of non-rhyming poetic writing in which every line has ten syllables. Most of Shakespeare's plays are written in blank verse.*

INTRODUCTION

Read the following extract from *A Midsummer Night's Dream*. Egeus has brought his daughter Hermia to see Theseus, the Duke of Athens. Egeus asks Theseus for permission to kill Hermia because she had refused to follow his wishes and marry Demetrius. Hermia is in love with Lysander, who Egeus claims has enchanted his daughter. How do the other characters respond to Egeus's request?

DEVELOPMENT

2

How would Egeus be treated nowadays?

3 Language

Using a dictionary and thesaurus, find a modern equivalent for each of these words.

hath   aye   betwixt   gauds   filch'd

4 Language

Rewrite lines 5–6 as they would appear in modern English.

5 Language

Egeus's speech beginning on line 3 has many breaks in the middle of each line. How does Shakespeare's use of punctuation help us to understand how Egeus feels?

> A **caesura** *is a break in the middle of a line of verse which is used to break up rhythm or emphasise a point (e.g. 'Stand forth Demetrius. My noble lord').*

6 Reading

What gifts has Lysander given to Hermia?

7 Reading

By law, what can Egeus do if Hermia refuses to follow his wishes?

8 Reading

What does Theseus say will happen to Hermia if she doesn't marry Demetrius?

9 Reading

Find evidence which shows that:

- Egeus is angry and wishes to punish Hermia

A Midsummer Night's Dream

Enter EGEUS and his daughter HERMIA, and LYSANDER
and DEMETRIUS.

EGEUS Happy be Theseus, our renowned Duke!

THESEUS Thanks, good Egeus. What's the news with thee?

EGEUS Full of vexation come I, with complaint

Against my child, my daughter Hermia.

Stand forth Demetrius. My noble lord, 5

This man hath my consent to marry her.

Stand forth Lysander. And my gracious Duke,

This hath bewitch'd the bosom of my child.

Thou, thou, Lysander, thou hast given her rhymes,

And interchang'd love-tokens with my child: 10

Thou hast by moonlight at her window sung

With faining voice verses of feigning love,

And stol'n the impression of her fantasy

With bracelets of thy hair, rings, gauds, conceits,

Knacks, trifles, nosegays, sweetmeets (messengers 15

Of strong prevailment in unharden'd youth):

With cunning hast thou filch'd my daughter's heart,

Turn'd her obedience (which is due to me)

To stubborn harshness. And, my gracious Duke,

Be it so she will not here, before your Grace, 20

Consent to marry with Demetrius,

I beg the ancient privilege of Athens:

As she is mine, I may dispose of her;

Which shall be either to this gentleman,

Or to her death, according to our law 25

Immediately provided in that case.

THESEUS What say you, Hermia? Be advis'd, fair maid.

To you your father should be as a god:

One that compos'd your beauties, yea, and one

To whom you are but as a form in wax 30

By him imprinted, and within his power

To leave the figure, or disfigure it.

Demetrius is a worthy gentleman.

HERMIA So is Lysander.

THESEUS   In himself he is;

But in this kind, wanting your father's voice, 35

The other must be held the worthier.

HERMIA I would my father look'd but with my eyes.

THESEUS Rather your eyes must with his judgement look.

HERMIA I do entreat your Grace to pardon me.

I know not by what power I am made bold, 40

Nor how it may concern my modesty

In such a presence here to plead my thoughts,

But I beseech your Grace that I may know

The worst that may befall me in this case,

If I refuse to wed Demetrius. 45

THESEUS Either to die the death, or to abjure

For ever the society of men.

Therefore, fair Hermia, question your desires,

Know of your youth, examine well your blood,

Whether, if you yield not to your father's choice, 50

You can endure the livery of a nun,

For aye to be in shady cloister mew'd,

To live a barren sister all your life,

Chanting faint hymns to the cold fruitless moon.

Thrice blessed they that master so their blood 55

To undergo such maiden pilgrimage;

But earthlier happy is the rose distill'd

Than that which, withering on the virgin thorn,

Grows, lives, and dies, in single blessedness.

HERMIA So will I grow, so live, so die, my lord, 60

Ere I will yield my virgin patent up

Unto his lordship whose unwished yoke

My soul consents not to give sovereignty.

THESEUS Take time to pause; and by the next new moon,

The sealing-day betwixt my love and me   65

For everlasting bond of fellowship,

Upon that day either prepare to die

For disobedience to your father's will,

Or else to wed Demetrius, as he would,

Or on Diana's altar to protest,   70

For aye, austerity and single life.

DEMETRIUS Relent, sweet Hermia; and Lysander, yield

Thy crazed title to my certain right.

LYSANDER You have her father's love, Demetrius:

Let me have Hermia's; do you marry him.   75

EGEUS Scornful Lysander, true, he hath my love;

And what is mine my love shall render him:

And she is mine, and all my right of her

I do estate unto Demetrius.

William Shakespeare

- Egeus doesn't trust Lysander
- Theseus thinks highly of Demetrius.

10 Speaking and listening

Improvise a phone conversation in which Hermia or Egeus asks a friend for advice about their problems.

11 Speaking and listening

Act out this scene, using appropriate expression, pace and volume in your reading. What stage directions might help the actors?

How could your performance be improved? Consider:

- actions and movement
- speech style
- ability to work together.

12 Writing

Imagine you are Egeus or Hermia. Write a letter to the problem page of the *Athenian Times* explaining your problem and asking for advice.

13 Writing

Swap your letter with a partner. Imagine you are an Athenian agony aunt and reply to each other's letters.

REVIEW

How are modern parents' attitudes different to those expressed in *A Midsummer Night's Dream*? What are the main areas of conflict between parents and children nowadays?

UNIT 30 Imagery: similes

AIMS

● To appreciate the impact of figurative language in texts by examining the use and function of similes.

STARTER

1

Work out whether the following images are examples of similes, metaphors or personification.

a I wandered lonely as a cloud
b the merciless iced east winds that knive us
c mad gusts tugging on the wire
d misery of dawn
e the water mirrors a still sky
f emotion working in their veins like gentle blood
g she was an exploding fireworks factory

Make up a simile, a metaphor and an example of personification of your own.

> *Imagery* is the use of words to create striking and vivid pictures in a reader's or listener's imagination. Imagery involves the use of similes, metaphors and personification.

DEVELOPMENT

2

Complete the common similes using a word from the box.

> **boots feather ice ox beetroot butter owl fox water sheet**

a The orange squash was as weak as _____ .

b The new tennis racket was as light as a _____ .

c The boy who nearly fell off the climbing frame was as white as a _____ .

d The candle had been left in the sun and was as soft as _____ .

e The card player was as cunning as a _____ .

f My grandad is as wise as an _____ .

g I was so embarrassed my cheeks were as red as a _____ .

h The meat was as tough as old _____ .

i The weightlifter was as strong as an _____ .

j The vampire's breath was as cold as _____ .

3

Now finish off the following sentences with unusual and interesting similes of your own.

a The girl was as beautiful as a _____ .

b The footballer was so clumsy he looked like a _____ .

c That lesson was as interesting as _____ .

d When my dad sings he sounds like _____ .

e My brother's bedroom looks like
_____ .

4

Write down as many similes as you can find in the following extract from the poem 'Yes' by Frank Flynn.

> YES is a green word,
> It grows like grass
> It's as crinkly as cabbage,
> It's as lush as lime
> As springy as sprouts,
> It's as lollopy as lettuce
> As playful as peas
> As artistic as apples,
> Yes is as lazy as summer leaves …

Now see if you can write your own simile poem about a word of your choice.

5

Look at the following lines from the poem 'Timothy Winters' by Charles Causeley.

> Ears like bombs and teeth like splinters,
> A blitz of a boy is Timothy Winters.

a What does the simile 'Ears like bombs' suggest about Timothy's ears?
b Describe Timothy's teeth?

6

Look closely at the following poem.

Fireworks

> Like buds too wonderful to name,
> Each miracle unfolds,
> And catherine-wheels begin to flame
> Like whirring marigolds.
>
> *James Reeves*

Now fill in the gaps with your own words to describe a firework of your choice.

> Like _____ too wonderful to name,
> Each miracle unfolds,
> And _____ begin to flame
> Like _____ .

7

Finish off the following poem.

My Friend

> My friend _____
> Looks like a _____
> And acts like a _____ .
>
> My friend _____
> Moves like a _____
> And sounds like a _____.
>
> My friend _____
> Is as funny as a _____
> And as loyal as a _____.

You may wish to change some of the words (e.g. *looks*, *acts*, *moves*, *sounds*, *funny*, *loyal*) to suit your own ideas.

REVIEW

By comparing one thing with another, similes draw out striking features, interesting characteristics and unusual ideas which help the reader. Read out any interesting or unusual similes you invented whilst working on the activities in this unit.

UNIT 31 Magazine covers

AIMS

- To understand how information is presented on magazine covers.
- To use your knowledge of magazine contents to formulate and present a proposal for a new magazine.

STARTER

1

Write down all the features you would expect to find on a magazine front cover.

> The **readership** of a magazine or newspaper are those people who buy and read it. The readership of Sneak magazine, for instance, is teenage girls.

INTRODUCTION

The magazine front covers on page 172 are all from teenage magazines. What features do they have in common? Which one would you find interesting, if any?

2

What type of people are likely to read these magazines? Give reasons for your answer?

DEVELOPMENT

3 Language

Look at each magazine cover carefully. Copy and fill out the following chart based on your observations.

	Title or masthead	Main image	Tasters – what what you might find inside	Key lines and article headlines	Readership	Special features
Shout						
Sneak						
Top of the Pops						
Match						

4 Language

Pick out four examples of alliteration from the cover of *Shout* magazine.
Why is alliteration a popular feature of magazine headlines?

5 Language

Pick out an example of bullet points from one of the covers. Why are bullet points such a popular feature on magazine covers and in non-fiction writing generally? How do bullets help you organise information?

6 Reading

Look closely at the main picture on the cover of *Shout* magazine. Now answer these questions.

- Describe the appearance of the boy and the girl.
- What impression do the two young people give about their lifestyle and relationship?
- How might this picture attract readers to buy this magazine?
- What do think the publishers are trying to suggest about people who buy this magazine?

7 Reading

On the front cover of *Match* magazine explain the key line: 'England eat Danish for breakfast and now they FEAR NO-ONE!' Comment on:

- any element of humour
- whether it makes you want to open and read the magazine.

8 Speaking and listening

Choose one of the magazine titles. Invent a contents list for a new issue of your chosen magazine. Think about the regular features and articles you might find in a magazine of this type.

9 Writing

Imagine you have been invited to put forward a proposal for a new teenage magazine. Complete the following tasks.

- Form an editorial team to make decisions about your magazine and produce material for it.
- Think of a title.
- Write a contents list for the first issue.
- Design the front cover, outlining style, content and regular features.

Now write a proposal to your publisher, describing:

- the look of your magazine
- your potential readership
- special and unique features of your new magazine.

Now work on writing articles for your magazine. Give each other specific tasks which reflect your interests and special talents. Decide how many pages you will need and give yourselves deadlines – be realistic!

10 Writing

Write one of the magazine articles mentioned on one of the magazine covers on page 172.

11 Writing

Write an article that is going to appear in your own magazine. Make it original and interesting. Try to base your article on subjects or experiences relevant to you and your friends – avoid using material which is not your own.

REVIEW

What are the essential ingredients of a successful magazine cover? Look at the covers produced by people in your class. Are these covers appealing in terms of their presentation and content? Would you buy one of these magazines?

UNIT 32 Real life articles

AIMS

- To understand how themes, values and ideas are developed in a teenage magazine article.
- To use the key ideas and ingredients of a magazine article in your own writing.

STARTER

1

> 🎵 A **moral** is a message about how we should behave which we learn from reading a story such as a fairy tale or fable.

What is the moral of two of the following fairy tales?

- Little Red Riding Hood
- Three Little Pigs
- Goldilocks and the Three Bears
- The Tortoise and the Hare

INTRODUCTION

Sometimes we have very difficult decisions to make. The piece opposite is about one girl's decision to meet her real dad. See if you agree with her decision.

2

How have Jennifer's actions changed her life?

DEVELOPMENT

3 Language

Look at the paragraph beginning on line 26. What feelings is Jennifer trying to emphasise by asking all these questions?

4 Language

Pick out any words or phrases that suggest an informal register.

5 Language

Write down the following from the article.

- main heading
- introduction
- pull quote

6 Reading

How does Jennifer feel about her dad at the start of the article?

7 Reading

What is the main message of this article? Explain your answer by referring to the article closely.

8 Reading

In what ways was meeting her real dad a shock for Jennifer?

9 Reading

How does Jennifer feel about her real dad and her new family by the end of the article?

10 Speaking and listening

Describe either a difficult decision you have had to make or a challenge you have had to face.

11 Writing

Write an article for a teenage magazine about a difficult decision. Keep your language simple, lively and varied with an informal register (e.g. use slang).

- Use columns and short paragraphs.
- Have headings, sub-headings and pull quotes.

"I've met my real dad at last!"

Jennifer Tom, 12, from Scotland, didn't expect to be happy when she met her real dad – she'd rather have shoved him off a cliff – but it turned out to be a very special moment. 5

'Dad had left my mum before I was born so I didn't even have a clue what he looked like. Mum never spoke about him, he never wrote or phoned and I suppose I just thought he had abandoned me.

'But sometimes I would stop and think about him, especially when my friends spoke about their dads. Where was he? What did he think about me? Did he even know that I existed? I'd always 15 thought of Mum's boyfriend, Jerry, as my "father" but I still knew he wasn't my "real" dad .

'It's funny, but I wasn't thinking about him at all when my Mum suddenly asked me "Do 20 you want to meet your real dad?" Mum said he lived near and she'd stayed in touch. She told me some more about him too. He was married and had two boys aged four and seven. He had said he wanted to meet me! 25

'So, he obviously knew I existed. I could hardly believe it. My first thought was "Great!", but then I started to get anxious. What if we didn't like each other? Why didn't he want mum and me before but wanted me 30 now? Why did he leave? Was it because Mum was pregnant? Would his wife like me? And what about Jerry? Would I betray him if I liked my real father?

'Well, I agreed to meet him and a couple of 35 weeks later he came round one night after school. I was so nervous, as my friends, who helped me, will tell you. I was worried and excited at the same time.

'When he came in I just stood there in the 40 kitchen, unable to say much. It was weird seeing him. We looked quite alike and he had hair just like mine. He got on very well with my Mum. There were no arguments or anything. It all 45 seemed odd really.

'Actually it was a great relief to get this meeting over with. No one mentioned the past and that was cool with me. We seemed to decide – without speaking about it 50 – to start again. My dad asked me about school, sport, loads of stuff. He wanted to know everything. He also wanted me to meet his new family and showed me a picture of my "new" brothers. I really wanted to meet 55 them.

'Two days later I went to visit his family. I was very nervous all over again but need not have worried. I suppose they must have been nervous too. But it was great. 60

'Now we are all friends. Sometimes I stay over with my dad (and give Mum and Jerry a break!). We have done loads of catching up but we have never spoken about why Dad left. Perhaps one day, but I won't ask him yet, 65 I don't think.

'I'm really pleased to have met him and sometimes wish I had met him sooner. I certainly don't want to shove him off a cliff any more!' 70

> No one mentioned the past and that was cool with me.

- Use photographs and captions.
- Think about fonts and colour.

12 Writing

Redraft your article, either on a computer or by hand, introducing interesting presentational features to make your article more attractive to the reader.

REVIEW

Think about the five most important ingredients of a successful magazine article. Has your magazine article got all the ingredients needed to appeal to a teenage audience?

UNIT 33 England defy group of death

AIMS

- To examine the different ways a magazine article can be written and presented.
- To recognise bias and slant in a magazine article.

STARTER

1

> An **objective statement** relies on fact and truth. A **subjective statement** is based on opinions, feelings and personal preferences. **Bias** is the favouring of one side or viewpoint over another when reporting or talking about an event.

Put the following statements into two columns: objective and subjective.

a London is a big city.
b Rap music is cool.
c School dinners are excellent.
d There are lots of hills in the Lake District.
e Eating meat is wrong.
f January has 31 days.

Think of one subjective and one objective comment of your own.

INTRODUCTION

For some people football is an obsession. How does the article opposite make football appear almost a matter of life and death?

2

This is quite an unusual and interesting way to present a football match analysis. Can you suggest a more typical way of presenting a sports report?

DEVELOPMENT

3 Language

Explain why the following are used in the headline.

- alliteration
- tall, bold letters

4 Language

Examine lines 7–20 and pick out:

- an objective statement
- a subjective statement
- a fact
- an opinion
- a word connected with fighting.

5 Reading

On what positive note does David Beckham finish his assessment of the Sweden game?

6 Reading

Would you describe Sven Goran Eriksson assessment of the Argentina game as biased, balanced or a mixture of both?

7 Reading

According to Rio Ferdinand, what difficulties did the England players face in the Nigeria game?

8 Speaking and listening

Improvise a chat show interview with a famous person.

9 Writing

Write a magazine article about a concert, TV programme or sporting event you have seen recently. Write about:

- what happens
- key characters, actors, players, etc.
- your own interpretation of what happened.

ENGLAND DEFY
THE GROUP OF DEATH!

England's draw for the World Cup couldn't have been much worse. But we made it, nicking the runners-up spot with five points in three matches to make the second round.

So here's how England battled their way out of the Group of Death.

ENGLAND 1 SWEDEN 1

The first game of England's World Cup campaign, and the team started brightly. But in the second half, England lost their way and fell apart. Not good, not bad, just distinctly average.

BECKS: 'We didn't start as well as we should have, but credit to Sweden – they carried on going and kept on fighting, got the goal and then towards the end they had a few chances and David Seaman kept us in the game. A lot of the lads are down in the changing room right now… there's no need to be. At the end of the day we've not lost, but we felt in the first half we played some really good football. We're pleasantly pleased really, because we could have ended up losing the game.'

ENGLAND 1 ARGENTINA 0

This was the big one and England, with Beckham looking more like his usual self, gradually got a grip on the game.

SVEN: 'I am very pleased, of course. It was very hard in the last minutes, we were tired and they attacked a lot but we deserved to win the game and we played very good football for 70–75 minutes. In the last ten to 15 minutes we had big problems. Argentina played very well, they came forward with a lot of players and we were a little bit too tired. But we defended with big, big hearts and that's very important in football sometimes. It was an extremely important victory, especially after the way we played in the second half against Sweden last Sunday.'

ENGLAND 1 NIGERIA 0

A point was all that was needed to progress to the second round and England got it, but it was far from comfortable in a match played in very hot conditions.

RIO: 'We knew they would come out and try to cause us problems because they were playing for pride. We knew we were in for a tough game and they didn't surprise us. There was 'nuff pressure, because everybody was getting really excited after the Argentina game. We knew Nigeria were going to be really difficult to play against and we had to be fully concentrated, mentally and physically. There was some hot stuff out there, man, it was just crazy! It was the hottest conditions I've played in, as soon as I came off the pitch my feet were burning, but that's part and parcel of playing in the World Cup and you've got to get used to that.'

Match magazine

Try to capture the mood of the event.

10 Reading and writing

Find an interesting magazine article. Make notes on what you found particularly appealing about it. Was the article objective or subjective?

REVIEW

Share some of your articles with the class. Does your writing include the features, attractive presentation and imaginative content necessary for entertaining and interesting teenage magazine articles?

UNIT 34 Imagery: figures of speech

AIM

- To appreciate the impact of figurative language in texts by examining the use and function of figures of speech and idioms.

STARTER

1

> A **dead metaphor** is one which is so common or uninteresting we stop thinking of it as a metaphor (e.g. the leg of a table).

See if you can put these dead metaphors together correctly by matching up the words in the columns (e.g. leg + table).

teeth	table
foot	shoe
mouth	state
arm	chair
head	hill
tongue	tunnel
eye	mountain
brow	cog
leg	needle

Can you think of any dead metaphors of your own?

DEVELOPMENT

> A **figure of speech** is a type of metaphor in which a speaker or writer compares their subject to something else, often in an imaginative way which creates interest and impact. Figures of speech such as 'to kick up dust', which means 'to cause trouble', are commonly used.

2

Write out all the figures of speech you can find in the following passage.

The English teacher walked into the classroom like a bear with a sore head. His nerves were frayed. The exploding Christmas card had been the last straw and had sent him over the edge. To cap it all, it was raining cats and dogs and he was in his wife's black books. To put the tin lid on it, the Head had dropped a bombshell: she'd told him that he was too long in the tooth and should have been put out to grass along time ago. The final nail in his coffin, though, was a pupil going walkabout on the school trip. Then, the rough diamond, bold as brass, even made waves about losing his Nike trainers, crying crocodile tears. That was a major spanner in the works. He hoped his Head of Department would pull a few strings and save his skin.

3

Write down the meaning of five of these figures of speech.

4

Use five of the figures of speech in a paragraph of your own.

5

> An **idiom** is an expression which uses very unusual figures of speech to put ideas across. For example, 'a different kettle of fish' means 'a different matter altogether'; 'to play second fiddle' means 'to take a less important role'. Idioms generally only have meaning in the language of their origin.

Explain the following idioms.

a water off a duck's back
b to change one's tune
c rags to riches
d the pot calling the kettle black
e to pay through the nose
f a needle in a haystack
g light at the end of the tunnel
h the tip of the iceberg
i to eat humble pie

6

The following idioms have been translated literally from French. What do you think are the equivalent idioms in English?

a I've got a cat in my throat.
b I'm soaked to the bone.

7

Try and find another five common idioms not featured in this unit.

REVIEW

Why do people use idioms? Compare any new idioms you have found with those found by your classmates. Has anyone found any unusual idioms?

UNIT 35 Coping with parents

AIMS

- To look at how sentences and paragraphs can be structured and varied to create different effects.
- To analyse and discuss an emotional issue in order to find a solution.
- To trace the development of themes, values and ideas in a text

STARTER

1

> **Emotive language** creates an emotional response in the reader.

Look at this emotive sentence from the text you are about to read.

'When he leaned forward, the tears ran down his nose and splattered on to his shoes'.

Which of the following emotions is the writer trying to convey?

sadness happiness despair embarrassment anger pity

Write a sentence conveying one of these emotions.

INTRODUCTION

Six months ago Buddy Clark's mum left home after constant rows with his dad. To make matters worse, Buddy's dad lost his job and appears to be pursuing a career on the wrong side of the law. In the extract opposite Buddy's mum turns up unexpectedly. How do Buddy's thoughts and feelings change through the passage?

2

In this extract the writer uses short sentences, short paragraphs and punctuation within sentences to help create a variety of emotions and effects. Look at the following sentences.

- 'He leaned against the door-frame and swung the door wider so that she could come in, but she shook her head and glanced down the road as if she wanted to go.'
- 'How could he love his dad and be ashamed of him at the same time?'

What feelings is the writer trying to convey at each of these points in the text?

DEVELOPMENT

3 Language

Explain how the following sentences make you feel and how the writer achieves the desired effect.

- 'His mum wasn't coming home; she still hated him for stealing.'
- 'Her voice was accusing, almost angry.'
- 'He repeated it, louder.'

4 Language

Very often a writer will use concrete detail – objects you can see – to create a feeling of reality. Read the paragraph beginning on line 50.

- List the concrete details mentioned.
- Which senses is the writer appealing to? Find evidence to support your answer.

Buddy

He didn't know what to do or say. He hadn't seen her for nearly six months – was he still allowed to hug her like the old days? He thought of shaking hands but that was ridiculous. He leaned against the door-frame and swung the door wider so that she could come in, but she shook her head and glanced down the road as if she wanted to go. His heart sank. His mum wasn't coming home; she still hated him for stealing. She turned to him but he looked at the ground and began playing with the catch on the door.

'You don't seem very pleased to see me.' Her voice was accusing, almost angry.

He shrugged and flicked the catch a couple of times to cover up the silence.

'I'd better go, then.'

'You can come in if you want.' He tried to make it sound friendly but it came out as a mumble.

'No, I'd better go.'

Tears began to well up in his eyes and he pressed his thumb hard against the sharp edge of the catch to hurt himself.

'You're all right, are you?'

He nodded and clenched his teeth tightly to stop a tear from sliding out of his eye.

'Why are you all in the dark?'

He turned and looked into the house, pretending that he hadn't noticed that the lights were off.

'I thought you were someone else,' he said, keeping his face turned away.

'What?'

He repeated it, louder.

'Oh. You're not in trouble are you?'

He shook his head and the first tear splashed against his nose as he did so.

'Sure?'

He nodded and kept staring towards the kitchen until he heard her shoes scrape on the doorstep as she started to walk away. He listened as her footsteps faded away, then closed the door and sat down on the bottom step of the stairs. When he leaned forward, the tears ran down his nose and splattered on to his shoes.

He rubbed his eyes fiercely with the sleeve of his pullover, glad that the rough texture made his skin sore. It was always the same. Whenever he started crying he found himself wishing that someone could see him. Like now – he wanted his mum to see him and feel sorry for him. Not even his tears were real.

Yes, he wanted her back. Well, then – wasn't that why he was crying? Partly. But there were other things, too. Why hadn't he told her he was sorry? Because he was a phoney – that's why. It was the same with his dad. If he really loved him, he wouldn't care what other people thought about him or the clothes he wore.

He was crying because he hated himself. He was crying because he was scared. And because he felt sorry for himself. And because all these feelings jumbled around inside him until he didn't know what was what.

How could he love his dad and be ashamed of him at the same time? How could he love his mum and hate her for leaving? Or want to be part of 3E and yet despise it? If he really thought stealing was wrong, why did he do it? Why couldn't he be simple, instead of having all these opposite things in him? 85 90

He stood up and went to the kitchen, bumping against the wall. He ran the cold water and splashed it on his face. He was drying himself on the towel when the bell rang. This time it probably was the Beast, but he didn't care. 95 100

He opened the door. It was his mum again.

'Buddy, I don't want to stay here in case your dad comes back. Come for a walk, will you? Please.' 105

Nigel Hinton

5 Reading

Why do you think Buddy's mum shook her head when he opened the door to let her in?

6 Reading

What evidence is there to suggest that Buddy feels awkward and uncomfortable? Look at:

- his actions
- his speech.

7 Reading

How does Buddy feel when his mum leaves?

8 Reading

List three things Buddy is confused about.

9 Speaking and listening

Act out the conversation Buddy has with his mum when they go for a walk.

10 Speaking and listening

Imagine you work for an organisation which takes phone calls from children with emotional problems. Improvise the conversation when someone asks for advice about a problem (e.g. bullying, committing a crime, running away from home).

11 Writing

Imagine you are Buddy. Write a letter to a friend describing your meeting with your mum. Write about:

- what happened
- how you felt
- what you are going to do in the future.

12 Writing

Write a diary entry for a day you fell out with your best friend. Write about:

- the events leading up to your disagreement
- reasons for falling out
- whether or not you manage to resolve your differences.

REVIEW

Sometimes it is easier to make sense of emotional problems by writing down your thoughts on paper. Why do some people find discussing their problems and emotions difficult?

UNIT 36 Smoking campaign

- To develop a variety of drama techniques to help you use language persuasively.
- To look at different ways of conveying important information, both in speech and in writing.
- To use formal and informal language in appropriate situations.

STARTER

1

Think of three arguments for each of the following.

- giving up smoking
- eating fewer sweets
- not talking in class

 An **argument** is a strong viewpoint which is put forward in a discussion. For instance, a strong argument for cycling to work or school is that it is good for your health.

INTRODUCTION

The following poem by Trevor Millum expresses a number of arguments for and against smoking.

2

Read this poem aloud using a range of appropriate speech styles to suit each different verse. You may wish to include some suitable actions.

The Fags on Which They Drag

There's one secret smoker
In the bogs at break
Says the fags on which she drags
Are keeping her awake.

There's two secret smokers
By the sheds at dinner
Say the fags on which they drag
Help to keep them thinner.

There's three secret smokers
During Art & Craft
Say the fags on which they drag
Save them going daft.

There's four swaggering smokers
Going home from school
Feel the fags on which they drag
Will show that they're no fools.

There's five desperate smokers
In the staffroom after lessons
Wish the fags
On which they drag
Had never
  Been
    Invented!

Trevor Millum

DEVELOPMENT

3 Language

Look at the way this poem is written. Examine:

- layout
- poetic techniques
- language.

4 Reading

Why do the smokers by the sheds smoke?

5 Reading

What reason do the smokers in Art and Craft give for continuing to smoke?

6 Reading

What image do you think the smokers on the way home from school want to give out?

7 Reading

How do the smokers in the staff room feel about smoking?

8 Speaking and listening

Discuss as many reasons as you can for not smoking.

9 Speaking and listening

Imagine you are in the toilets at break and a couple of your friends start smoking. Act out a conversation in which you try to persuade them to stop smoking. Try to:

- convey persuasive arguments for not smoking
- be forceful in your approach
- use a variety of techniques (e.g. rhetorical language, emotive language, sarcasm)
- vary your mannerisms and speech style.

10 Speaking and listening

Imagine that you are going to produce a public information film aimed at young people explaining the dangers of smoking. Include the following in your film:

- interviews with smokers and ex-smokers of different ages
- information about the dangers of smoking
- what you can do to stop yourself from starting to smoke
- how you can help older children to give up smoking.

You can act your film out in front of the class if you don't have access to a video camera.

11 Writing

Produce an advice leaflet for young people about a health issue of your choice. Think about:

- appropriate sections and layout
- relevant information
- messages you might want to put across
- impact – is your presentation of the message effective?

12 Writing

Design a poster warning children about the dangers of smoking.

REVIEW

What have you learnt about putting across information and messages in either speech or writing? What are the advantages of conveying messages through film as opposed to writing and pictures? Which did you enjoy producing the most – the film or the advice leaflet? Do you work better in a pair, in a group situation or on your own?

UNIT 37 | Theme park project

- To develop ideas through group discussion.
- To make a formal presentation using a variety of devices to successfully engage the audience.

STARTER

1

> A **modal verb** is placed in front of another verb to modify it (e.g. 'can', 'could', 'may', 'might', 'must', 'ought', 'should', 'would'). When these verbs express a condition (e.g. She would go to the cinema if she knew you were going as well) they are also known as **conditional verbs**.

Put a modal verb in each of these sentences.

a She _____ like ham in her sandwich.

b He _____ score a goal with this penalty.

c My parents _____ buy me a computer for my birthday.

Now think of three sentences using modal verbs, including one conditional verb.

INTRODUCTION

Camelot theme park in Lancashire is inspired by the legend of King Arthur and the knights of the Round Table. Look at the extract from the park's web page on page 186. Which of the attractions do you think you would enjoy the most?

2

How have the designers of this website tried to make Camelot appealing to young people? What techniques have they used?

DEVELOPMENT

3 Language
Pick out all the words you can find associated with knights and the legend of the Round Table.

4 Language
Find a synonym for 'bravery' in the text.

5 Language
Pick out any words associated with magic.

6 Reading
Give two reasons why jousting tournaments were held in medieval times.

7 Reading
How did the knights show off in jousting tournaments?

8 Reading
How does 'Mad Edgar' entertain the crowds?

Shows

Jousting Tournament – *Avalon Arena*

King Arthur commands all his loyal subjects to witness this spectacular show of chivalry and valour as his brave knights of the Round Table do battle for king and country.

Jousting was part of the tournaments in medieval times which were used to train the knights. These tournaments were a popular form of entertainment. This involved two knights charging at one another on horseback in an effort to knock one another off. Jousting was very popular in these times and the knights often showed off by pretending to rescue damsels in distress.

The Camelot Jousting Show, hosted by Mad Edgar, can be seen in the 'Avalon Arena' daily. See our intrepid knights do battle with each other and marvel at their skill!

30 minute shows.

Merlin's New Magic Show – *King Arthur's Castle*

You'll be amazed and enthralled before you can say abracadabra, with the wise old wizard's brand new display of magic and trickery.

20 minute shows. Daily.

Mad Edgar's Juggling Show – *King Arthur's Castle*

Every court needs a fool and Camelot is no exception. Our jester is called Mad Edgar and he certainly lives up to his name. Watch Edgar juggle everything from clubs to ping pong balls using his hands, arms and sometimes even his mouth!

20 minute shows. Daily.

Edgar can also be found meandering around the park, providing on the spot entertainment and antics and entertaining the crowds at the jousting tournament in the Avalon Jousting Arena.

9 Reading

How does the writer create the impression that Camelot will be an amazing experience? Pick out:

- words which suggest pleasure, wonder and excitement
- amazing exploits and events that will take place.

10 Speaking and listening

You have been invited by your local council to enter a competition to design a theme park. Before you start making detailed plans, discuss:

- themes (e.g. a legend, myth, historical period, place)
- attractions (e.g. rides, shows, events, special features, food and retail outlets).

To get some more ideas you could look at some theme park websites on the Internet.

11 Writing

Make a map of your theme park. Next to each attraction write a brief description, making it sound appealing and fun. At some point write a detailed paragraph about the park as a whole, explaining why your ideas are so wonderful and how they would work.

12 Writing

Imagine you are a teacher organising a class trip to your theme park.
Write a letter to parents informing them of the arrangements.

13 Speaking and listening

Present your theme park proposal to the rest of the class. Decide:

- how you are going to make your presentation interesting and eye-catching
- what key points you are going to emphasise
- what presentation techniques you are going to employ.

Plan carefully and decide what everybody is going to say in advance.

You may wish to use the whiteboard, music, props, handouts, an overhead projector or a computer.

14 Speaking and listening

Now assess your presentations.

15 Writing

Write an article for the school magazine describing a class day trip to your new theme park. Try to convey a sense of fun and excitement. Make up some amusing incidents involving your classmates and your teachers.

REVIEW

Decide as a class which presentation was the best. Why were some presentations better than others? What can you do in the future to make your presentations more successful, interesting and entertaining?

UNIT 38 Onomatopoeia

AIMS

- To understand onomatopoeia, considering why and when writers might use it.
- To use some examples of onomatopoeia accurately in your own writing.

STARTER

1

> **Onomatopoeia** is an effect in speech or writing when words sound like the noise they describe. (e.g. The firework exploded with a loud **bang**. The angry driver made the car horn **honk** loudly.)

Pick out the onomatopoeic words from the beginning of Jessie Pope's poem 'Noise'.

> I like noise.
> The whoop of a boy, the thud of a hoof,
> The rattle of rain on a galvanized roof,
> The hubbub of traffic, the roar of a train,
> The throb of machinery numbing the
> brain ...

Write two more lines of your own.

DEVELOPMENT

2

What might the following onomatopoeic words describe?

cheep chime crackle creak gush hiss peal twang

3

Complete the following sentences with a suitable onomatopoeic word from the list below.

wailing crunched crackled screeched fizzed squawked hissed plopped chirped splashed

a The speeding car _____ to an abrupt halt.

b The firework's fuse _____ .

c The chicks _____ in their nest.

d The jam _____ into the rice pudding.

e A large stone _____ into the large still pool.

f The turkey _____ as the farmer chased it around the field.

g Small twigs _____ in the fire.

h Gravel _____ under his heavy boots.

i The snake _____ in the grass.

j The _____ of the baby attracted the attention of his mother.

4

Find a word in the list below which best describes each of the following sounds.

baa rumble echo creaking scream snap crying gargle spluttering clunk

a a metal gate closing
b the noise of a sheep
c breaking a biscuit
d a sound of terror

e a swinging door with a rusty hinge

f the sound of a car engine failing to start properly

g the sound of thunder

h the sound you might get when you shout in a large enclosed space

i the sound when you rinse your mouth out after brushing your teeth

j what babies are good at when they are hungry

5

Match up the following noises with their makers.

howl	someone with a cold
clatter	a pig
clash	the wind
hum	horses' hooves
jangle	bee
giggle	cymbals
grunt	amused children
boom	a laughing witch
cackle	a distant cannon
sniff	shaking keys

6

Use five of the following onomatopoeic words in a sentence.

babbling clang clicked clunked creaked hoot jangled meow moo neigh oink quack rattled squeak tinkle roar whistled whoosh

7

Write a poem or short paragraph with lots of onomatopoeic words describing one of the following.

- animals
- a winter's day
- a derelict house
- a school playground

REVIEW

How does the use of onomatopoeia help to bring a piece of writing to life? Read out to the class any good examples of onomatopoeia you have either learned or invented.

UNIT 1 — My future

AIMS

- To write a formal and accurate essay in a specified time using standard English.
- To experiment with presentational devices when word processing a CV.

STARTER

1

Try reading out loud the following extract in a Glaswegian accent.

Unrelated Incidents

this is thi
six a clock
news thi
man said n
thi reason
a talk wia
BBC accent
iz coz yi
widny wahnt
mi ti talk
aboot thi
trooth wia
voice lik
wanna yoo
scruff

Tom Leonard

2

Now rewrite the extract in standard English.

> **Standard English** is the kind of English used in formal situations. It is the English of the media (e.g. news broadcasters and writers) and the majority of literary writing.

INTRODUCTION

In the following extract we learn something about the background and education of the comedian and entertainer Sacha Baron Cohen, made famous by his creation Ali G. Is there any indication from his essay that the young Sacha Baron Cohen would turn into Ali G?

The polite little swot who grew into Ali G

Ali G, the drug dealing bad boy who has based an entire television career on the premise that he is seriously *fick*, is the owner of a dark secret.

It turns out that far from being a child of the ghetto who couldn't string two *sillubles togevva*, his creator was actually a precocious little swot who once won an award for an essay on the importance of good English. What's worse, he actually liked *maffs*.

G's early academic career came to light when the *Times Educational Supplement* unearthed his entry for an essay competition held in 1980. Then he was an eight-year-old schoolboy known as Sacha Baron Cohen, and he didn't go to 'da Matthew Arnold Skool in Staines' as he pretended, but to Haberdashers' Aske's School, a seriously posh place in Borehamwood, Herts.

In his entry, one of 11 published in the *TES*, he wrote that 'school is a wonderful thing'.

He explained: 'My first lesson on Monday morning is English. This reminds us of the correct way to speak and write English. This is very important as most of the boys have been watching television and speaking with their parents all weekend.'

Curriculum Vitae

Name:
Ali G

Date of Birth:
Me woz born in da heart off da Staines ghetto.

Address:
Me nan's. I has lived wiv me Nan in Staines from da day me woz born, coz wiv both me parents havin been smoked, der werent no one else around to look afta her.

Education:
Englefield Green Playgroup (1979–87), Da Matthew Arnold Skool (1988–91). Me woz failed by the skool system and hated every minute me spent in da classroom. In fact added together, dat time woz probably da most borin three hours of me life.

Qualifications:
3 E' levels (all grade O). GNVQ Food Hygiene

Work History:
As well as bein unemployed I iz also got a lot of well important careers.

Gangsta:
as head of da West Staines Massive.

Telly Presenta:
afta happearrin on some crap programme it werent long before me ad me own show. Dis meant me was able to take a in depf look at a lot off serious issues.

Aufor: Check dis – I iz just read me very first book. It iz called Da Gospel ... Da Gospel Acc ... somefin or ovver ... to Ali G.

Curriculum Vitae

Name:
Sacha Baron Cohen

Date of Birth:
1972. Second of three sons. Father, Gerald, owns menswear shop in Piccadilly and House of Baron, Golders Green. Strict Jewish mother, Daniella, from Israel.

Address:
Hampstead, north London.

Education:
Haberdashers' Aske's (1980–1989)

Rosh Hanikra kibbutz, Israel (1989)

Christ's College, Cambridge (1990–1993)

Qualifications:
History degree 2:1. Focused on American Civil Rights Movement.

Work History:
Member of Habonim, the Jewish youth movement.

Cambridge Footlights.

Ran own comedy club in Hampstead with his brother.

Paramount Comedy Channel.

Character on Channel 4's
11 o'clock Show, 1998.

The Ali G Show, 2000.

The Gospel According to Ali G, 2001.

Daily Telegraph – Saturday, March 9, 2002

3

How does Ali G show us in his CV that he may be 'seriously fick'?

DEVELOPMENT

*A **relative clause** adds meaning and expands the main clause of a sentence (e.g. Joanne, <u>who is an excellent organiser</u>, often uses a computer to plan her busy schedule). In this case 'who is an excellent organiser' is the relative clause. It is separated from the main clause by commas before and after it.*

4 Language

Write the following words in standard English.

- sillubles togevva
- maffs

5 Language

Pick out one relative clause from the first four paragraphs. How does the clause add extra information?

6 Reading

How did Ali G's early academic career come to light?

7 Reading

According to his essay, what did the young Baron Cohen think about school?

8 Reading

What does Ali G think about school? What happened to his parents?

9 Speaking and listening

Discuss what you would like to be in ten years' time, if you could be anything you liked. Conduct an interview with your future self on an imaginary TV breakfast talk show. Act out your interview for your classmates.

10 Writing

Write a timed essay, in about half an hour, using one of the following titles.

- Is school a wonderful thing?
- Are school holidays absolutely necessary?

Before you begin:

- devise a plan
- think carefully about your chosen topic and jot down any ideas, arguments and evidence.

Be sure to use standard English, and try to include some relative clauses too.

11 Writing

Write your own CV. Use the following headings.

- Personal details
- Education
- Work history
- Hobbies and interests

If you have access to a computer, word process your CV, setting it out carefully. Experiment with presentational features such as headings, bullet points, indentations, font sizes and styles, bold and italic fonts, and colour.

12 Writing

Write a CV for yourself at the age of thirty.

REVIEW

What difficulties did you encounter when writing your timed essay? What tips could you give students who may have to write under timed conditions in their Key Stage 3 SATs? As a class, read out some extracts from your essays and look at how they might be improved.

UNIT 2 — The place where I come from

AIMS

- Produce a piece of personal writing, focusing on structure.
- To examine the features of a non-fiction text which help to convey information and ideas in an amusing or entertaining way.

STARTER

1

The following words are commonly misspelled. Write down the correct spelling of each.

reccommendation enviroment badmington analises proffessor developement excercise suprise surposing

Think of a mnemonic to help you remember how to spell one of the words (e.g. 'one **c**ollar two **s**leeves' for 'necessary').

INTRODUCTION

 A **travelogue** is an account of a person's experiences and observations whilst travelling. It is often exciting and amusing.

The American writer Bill Bryson is probably the most famous travel writer of recent times. His travelogues are hugely popular because of their sharp observations and humorous descriptions. Bill Bryson comes from Des Moines, Iowa – how does he feel about his home town? What does the opening sentence suggest about his attitude?

The Lost Continent: Travels in Small Town America

I come from Des Moines. Somebody had to.

When you come from Des Moines you either accept the fact without question and settle down with a local girl named Bobbi and get a job at the Firestone factory and live there for ever and ever, or you spend your adolescence moaning about what a dump it is and how you can't wait to get out, and then you settle down with a local girl named Bobbi and get a job at the Firestone factory and live there for ever and ever.

Hardly anyone ever leaves. This is because Des Moines is the most powerful hypnotic known to man. Outside town there is a big sign that says WELCOME TO DES MOINES. THIS IS WHAT DEATH IS LIKE. There isn't really. I just made that up. But the place does get a grip on you. People who have nothing to do with Des Moines drive in off the interstate, looking for gas or hamburgers, and stay for ever. There's a New Jersey couple up the street from my parents' house whom you see wandering around from time to time looking faintly puzzled but strangely serene. Everybody in Des Moines is strangely serene.

The only person I ever knew in Des Moines who wasn't serene was Mr Piper. Mr Piper was my parents' neighbour, a leering cherry-faced idiot who was forever getting drunk and crashing his car into telephone poles. Everywhere you went you encountered telephone poles and road signs leaning dangerously in testimony to Mr Piper's driving habits. He distributed them all over the west side of town, rather in the way dogs mark trees. Mr Piper was the nearest possible human equivalent to Fred Flintstone, but less charming.

Bill Bryson

2

What techniques does Bill Bryson use to create an amusing picture of Mr Piper?

DEVELOPMENT

3 Language

Pick out one example of repetition from the text. How does Bill Bryson's use of repetition reinforce his feelings about Des Moines?

4 Language

There are very few facts in this extract. Can you find two?

5 Language

Find two opinions in this extract.

6 Reading

Bill Bryson's strength as a travel writer revolves around his ability to make people laugh by including interesting facts and personal anecdotes in his descriptions. His almost conversational style creates a strong bond between author and reader. Examine how he makes his description of Des Moines amusing and entertaining. Think about:

- style, language and comparisons
- personal opinions
- humour
- interesting anecdotes and observations.

7 Speaking and listening

Take turns talking about the place where you were born or the place you live in now for one minute. Include:

- interesting facts and observations
- humorous and entertaining anecdotes
- descriptions of buildings, attractions and people.

8 Writing

Write a short description of either the place you come from or the place you live in now. Make it humorous and entertaining. Think about:

- how to open your description, perhaps with an introduction of the place
- how to end your description, perhaps with an apt anecdote or a summing up of how you feel about the place
- organising your ideas clearly into sentences and paragraphs
- the effect of your writing on the reader – is it entertaining, interesting and amusing?
- your descriptions – do they include lively and varied vocabulary?

9 Writing

Imagine you go to live in your favourite holiday destination. Write a letter to a friend, persuading him/her to come and visit you.

REVIEW

Read through your description. Have you managed to make your writing entertaining and lively by including interesting vocabulary and amusing anecdotes? Look at each other's efforts and read out any particularly striking work to the whole class.

UNIT 3 Stereotypes

- To comment on how writers from another culture view their community and other people's perceptions of that community.
- To examine how the cultural background of a writer influences language, style and themes.

STARTER

1

Write down the irregular plural forms for the following words.

foot deer tooth fungus stimulus analysis salmon axis goose curriculum sheep cactus

Can you think of any other words which either don't change in their plural form or have an unusual ending?

2

Look at the final verse. How does this verse undermine the stereotypical image of West Indians outlined earlier in the poem?

INTRODUCTION

John Agard was born in British Guyana in the West Indies in 1949 and came to live in Britain in 1977. In the following poem he attacks some British people's perceptions of West Indians. How many stereotypical images of a West Indian can you find in this poem?

Stereotype

I'm a fullblooded
West Indian stereotype
See me straw hat?
Watch it good

I'm a fullblooded
West Indian stereotype
You ask
if I got riddum
in me blood
You going ask!
Man just beat de drum
and don't forget
to pour de rum

I'm a fullblooded
West Indian stereotype
You say
I suppose you can show
us the limbo, can't you?
How you know!
How you know!
You sure
you don't want me
sing you a calypso too
How about that

I'm a fullblooded
West Indian stereotype
You call me
happy-go-lucky

Yes that's me
dressing fancy
and chasing woman
if you think ah lie
bring yuh sister

I'm a fullblooded
West Indian stereotype
You wonder
where do you people
get such riddum
could it be the sunshine
My goodness
just listen to that steelband

Isn't there one thing
you forgot to ask
go on man ask
This native will answer anything
How about cricket?
I suppose you're good at it?
Hear this man
good at it!
Put de willow
in me hand
and watch me stripe
de boundary

Yes I'm a fullblooded
West Indian stereotype

that's why I
graduated from Oxford University
with a degree
in anthropology

John Agard

Morphology is the study of words and their form and structure. Often it involves the study of prefixes, suffixes and inflections (words which have changed, such as verbs which have added 'ed' or 'ing').

DEVELOPMENT

Accent is the way a speaker pronounces words. **Dialect** is a regional variety of language which has its own words, grammar and expressions.

3 Language

Find one example of a Caribbean dialect phrase.

4 Language

Rewrite the following words and phrases in standard English.

- if I got riddum in me blood
- if you think I lie bring yuh sister
- Put de willow in me hand

5 Language

Find three compound words in the poem.

6 Language

Find an example of each of the following and comment on its effect on the reader.

- repetition
- rhythm

7 Reading

In your own words describe the stereotypical West Indian portrayed in this poem. Think about:

- appearance
- behaviour
- hobbies, pastimes and sport
- people's attitudes towards West Indians.

8 Reading

How do you think John Agard feels about people's attitudes towards West Indians? Refer closely to the text.

9 Speaking and listening

Choose two of the following people.

a teacher a policeman an American a Japanese person an Australian

Come up with a stereotypical image of your chosen person. Think about appearance, behaviour, speech, pastimes, etc.

10 Writing

Do you consider yourself to be a Northerner, Southerner, Cockney, Geordie, Lancastrian, Brummie, etc.? Or do you belong to an ethnic group from outside Britain (e.g. Bangladeshi, Eastern European, African, etc.)?

Write your own 'stereotype' poem, beginning each verse 'I'm a full-blooded ...', substituting John Agard's West Indian for your own ethnic, cultural or regional group. Try to use some dialect words or phrases.

11 Writing

 *A person's **culture** is defined by their values, beliefs, traditions and lifestyle.*

Use the Internet, CD-Roms or your library to find out about another culture. Organise your findings under these headings for a classroom display.

- Language
- Traditions, pastimes, festivals
- Religion
- Food, clothes, music
- Similarities to and differences from my culture
- Popular stories, songs and poems

REVIEW

Read through each other's 'stereotype' poems and consider whether you have captured the speech patterns and culture of your chosen group. Read out loud any particularly successful poems. Think about the appropriate accent and speech style when reading.

UNIT 4 Common spelling errors

AIMS

- To recognise strengths and weaknesses when spelling.
- To spell high-frequency words accurately.

STARTER

1

Write down any of the following words which you think are spelled correctly. Then write down the correct version of each misspelled word.

**adition almighty arguement
brakeing developement excersise
forty freind fulfil inattentive
independant jelous misellaneous
permenent pysical prioritize
skillful stomache teecher wierd**

DEVELOPMENT

2

Use each of the following commonly confused words in a sentence of your own.

**affect/effect
advise/advice
aloud/allowed
bath/bathe
childish/childlike
coarse/course
check/cheque
past/passed
quiet/quite
threw/through**

3

Spot the spelling mistake in each of the following sentences and write the misspelled word out correctly.

a Our holiday accomodation was terrific.
b There is an introduction at the begining of this book.
c There is a huge busness park on the edge of town.
d The Prime Minister was very definate about his decision to change the law.
e I write in my dairy every day.
f You look very disapointed.
g The man looked very embarased when his hat was blown off.
h Vandalism damages the enviroment.
i Please don't interupt me when I'm talking.
j Is it necesary to wear make-up to school?
k Those lines are paralel.
l That tie is outragous.
m To make a meringue you should seperate the egg white from the yolk.
n The keys are in my possesion.
o I'm going to send round a questionaire.

4

One word in each of the following sentences has been used incorrectly. Write down the word which should have been used in each case.

a The train is stationery.
b This building has two stories.

c Wednesday is proceeded by Tuesday.

d The principle character of *The Wizard of Oz* is Dorothy.

e I went to the bank yesterday to enquire about a lend.

f Netball practise is on Wednesday.

g My uncle immigrated to New Zealand.

h The new housing estate is intensive.

i I herd laughter in the distance.

j Daffodils are my favourite flours.

k The patient was conscience after his operation.

l I love the piece of the countryside.

m The police sent out a plead for information about the robbery.

n The mountaineer began his dissent.

o The professor is very intelligible.

5

The following words are often spelled incorrectly. Use a dictionary to find the missing vowels.

a aud_ble
b auxil_ary
c b_oyant
d expl_nation
e hyg_enic
f imag_nary
g mant_lpiece
h orig_nal
i potent_al
j prep_ration
k prior_tise
l qu_ue
m rest_urant
n sincer_ly
o second_ry
p unfortun_tely

6

Use a dictionary to find the missing consonants.

a autum_
b campai_n
c colum_
d con_uer
e cons_ience
f desi_n
g ex_aust
h Feb_uary
i knowle_ge
j lis_en
k meanw_ile
l obstac_e
m ras_berry
n reco_nise
o tec_nique
p te_ture

7

Learn the spelling of some of the following words for homework.

a achievement actually aggressive changeable committee courteous

b descendant diarrhoea dilemma dissatisfied exaggerate

c government harass immediately jewellery medieval

d mischievous perceive permanent predominant primitive

e propeller quarrelling receipt schedule subtlety

REVIEW

By now you should have a grasp of easily confused and commonly misspelled words. Which of the words in this unit do you have trouble spelling? Make a point of writing down any words you find tricky to spell or confusing.

UNIT 5 Do we need school uniform?

AIMS

- To examine how connectives are used to formally develop and structure ideas.
- To gather together and synthesise information from a variety of sources.
- To organise ideas coherently into a formal essay written in standard English.

STARTER

1

Describe one of the following processes to your partner using the link words below.

- Getting ready for school.
- Making the perfect cup of tea.
- Asking someone out for a date.

firstly secondly furthermore subsequently consequently eventually finally alternatively however

> A **connective** is a word which joins together parts of a sentence (e.g. 'and' or 'but').
> **Link words or phrases** help join together all the ideas, opinions and arguments in a piece of writing (e.g. 'therefore', 'however', 'in other words', etc.).

INTRODUCTION

In this unit you are going to look at how an argument is developed in a magazine article. Look at the extract opposite and locate the arguments for and against school uniform.

2

Using a thesaurus, match up each of the following words with their correct synonym.

rebellion	equals
comply	conform
peers	imposing
enforcing	revolt
indication	condition
regulation	concession
proviso	suggestion
compromise	lawful

> A **synonym** is a word which has the same or similar meaning as another word (e.g. big – large; small – tiny; clever – intelligent).

DEVELOPMENT

3 Language

Pick out any connectives and link words or phrases from the passage. Can you suggest any alternatives?

4 Reading

From the article pick out two arguments for having school uniform.

5 Reading

Pick out one argument against wearing school uniform.

6 Reading

Give two reasons why one Cambridge headteacher disagrees with school uniform.

7 Reading

In your own words, sum up the arguments of the writer in the final paragraph.

SHOULD SCHOOL UNIFORM STILL BE AROUND?

THE ISSUES

School uniform is a controversial subject, since there are arguments both for and against it. The subject of school uniform has caused problems both in school and in the home!

UNIFORM: THE FACTS

School uniform is a fairly cheap way of dressing your child in school hours. The argument for uniform is that it means all the children are dressed in the same way, so there's no indication of a family's financial situation. Any tension which may arise from this is therefore reduced. It also removes problems related to choosing what to wear every day.

The case against occurs when the school's rules on uniform spark other forms of rebellion in terms of appearance. For example, the pupils may add extra items like jewellery and hair ornaments, or fail to wear things like belts and regulation shoes.

WEAR WHAT YOU LIKE

Generally, before children hit their teenage years, they are happy to wear uniform. If there isn't one, they tend to go to school in the same kind of clothes as their peers. It is after this age, when parents have less influence over what is worn, that school clothes may become a serious issue.

While some teenagers are happy to comply with school regulations and wear uniform, others are eager to follow the ever-changing trends, in a search for identity which costs parents considerably more than a uniform would, and in many cases results in cupboards full of clothes that will never be worn again.

So should children wear uniform? One Cambridge headteacher, whose own children are not in uniform, says girls in secondary school hate it. They devote far too much time and energy to breaking the rules, while staff have to spend an equal amount of time enforcing them. 'In any case,' he adds, 'it is good for girls to express their individuality through appearance and to learn to do so without feeling they have to rebel.'

My own view is that schools should aim for a compromise, meeting the children half way. Having a uniform up to secondary school age and imposing it strictly could solve many of these problems. After that, let them wear what they want, perhaps with the proviso of some kind of colour coding – perhaps blue or black. As for hair, jewellery and make-up, it's probably not the most important issue when it comes to education.

Editorial in a woman's magazine

---

8 Speaking and listening

Devise a questionnaire asking people what they think of school uniform, and use it to interview your classmates, teachers and parents.

9 Writing

Write an article about school uniform which is suitable for a teenage magazine. Use the results of your questionnaire.

10 Writing

Write a formal essay in 30 minutes with one of the following titles.

- School uniform: do we need it?
- Animal exploitation: a necessary evil?
- Global warming: myth or fact?

When writing you should:

- capture the reader's interest with a good opening paragraph
- use data from questionnaires and quote from any information you have found.
- use lively, imaginative language whilst still keeping it formal
- use link words when necessary
- avoid over-long sentences
- include a conclusion to round things off.

REVIEW

Discuss the arguments for and against school uniform. Did you use link words and phrases successfully in your essay? Could anything be improved?

UNIT 6 Segregation

AIMS

- To examine how an author portrays life in a different historical and social context.
- To recognise layers of meaning in the writer's choice of words.

STARTER

1

> *American English* is a variety of English which includes different words and spellings from British English. Whereas a British English speaker would say 'autumn', and 'crisps', an American English speaker would use 'fall', and 'potato chips'.

Find the British English equivalent for the following American English words.

hood (of car) **trunk** (of car)
**intersection checkers thumbtack
garbage movie apartment sneakers
vacation elevator gasoline attorney
cookies flashlight hobo**

How many other American English words can you think of?

INTRODUCTION

The following extract is taken from *Roll of Thunder, Hear My Cry*. The story, published in 1976, centres around Cassie Logan, a young black girl who grows up in the tense atmosphere of racial prejudice and segregation in 1930s Mississippi. This passage describes her first day back at school after the summer holidays, which is sadly overshadowed by news of the burning of the Berrys, a local black family. How does the writer make it clear that Miss Crocker has very little time for Cassie?

2

Why is Cassie disappointed by the end of the passage, despite the promise of a new book? Why do you think the children have not been given brand new books?

DEVELOPMENT

3 Language

Pick out any words which indicate that this passage is set in America.

4 Language

> An *adverb* is a word or phrase that gives you more information about the verb of a sentence (e.g. He walked **quickly**).

What do the following adverbs suggest about Cassie's mood?

- I sighed <u>heavily</u>.
- I jumped up <u>quickly</u> to face Miss Crocker.
- We <u>eagerly</u> awaited the unveiling.

5 Language

How is Cassie's dislike of Miss Crocker implied throughout this passage? Look closely at:

- Miss Crocker's speech and actions
- the writer's choice of words to describe Miss Crocker.

Roll of Thunder, Hear My Cry

The chiming of the second bell began. I stood up dusting my bottom as the first, second, third, and fourth graders crowded up the stairs into the hallway. Little Man flashed proudly past, his face and hands clean and his black shoes shining again. I glanced down at my own shoes powdered red and, raising my right foot, rubbed it against the back of my left leg, then reversed the procedure. As the last gong of the bell reverberated across the compound, I swooped up my pencils and notebook and ran inside.

A hallway extended from the front to the back door of the building. On either side of the hallway were two doorways, both leading into the same large room which was divided into two classrooms by a heavy canvas curtain. The second and third grades were on the left, the first and fourth grades on the right. I hurried to the rear of the building, turned to the right, and slid into a third-row bench occupied by Gracey Pearson and Alma Scott.

'You can't sit here,' objected Gracey. 'I'm saving it for Mary Lou.'

I glanced back at Mary Lou Wellever, depositing her lunch pail on a shelf in the back of the room and said, 'Not any more you ain't.'

Miss Daisy Crocker, yellow and buckeyed, glared down at me from the middle of the room with a look that said, 'Soooooooo, it's you, Cassie Logan.' Then she pursed her lips and drew the curtain along the rusted iron rod and tucked it into a wide loop in the back wall. With the curtain drawn back, the first graders gazed quizzically at us. Little Man sat by a window, his hands folded, patiently waiting for Miss Crocker to speak.

Mary Lou nudged me. 'That's my seat, Cassie Logan.'

'Mary Lou Wellever,' Miss Crocker called primly, 'have a seat.'

'Yes, ma'am,' said Mary Lou, eyeing me with a look of pure hate before turning away.

Miss Crocker walked stiffly to her desk, which was set on a tiny platform and piled high with bulky objects covered by a tarpaulin. She rapped the desk with a ruler, although the room was perfectly still, and said, 'Welcome, children, to Great Faith Elementary School.' Turning slightly so that she stared squarely at the left side of the room, she continued, 'To all of you fourth graders, it's good to have you in my class. I'll be expecting many good and wonderful things from you.' Then addressing the right side of the room, she said, 'And to all our little first grade friends only today starting on the road to knowledge and education, may your tiny feet find the pathways of learning steady and forever before you.'

Already bored, I stretched my right arm on the desk and rested my head in my upraised hand.

Miss Crocker smiled mechanically, then rapped on her desk again. 'Now, little ones,' she said, still talking to the first grade, 'your teacher, Miss Davis, has been held up in

Jackson for a few days so I'll have the pleasure of sprinkling your little minds with the first rays of knowledge.' She beamed down upon them as if she expected to be applauded for this bit of news, then with a swoop of her large eyes to include the fourth graders, she went on.

'Now since there's only one of me, we shall have to sacrifice for the next few days. We shall work, work, work, but we shall have to work like little Christian boys and girls and share, share, share. Now are we willing to do that?'

'YES'M, MIZ CROCKER,' the children chorused.

But I remained silent. I never did approve of group responses. Adjusting my head in my hand, I sighed heavily, my mind on the burning of the Berrys.

'Cassie Logan?'

I looked up, startled.

'Cassie Logan!'

'Yes, ma'am?' I jumped up quickly to face Miss Crocker.

'Aren't you willing to work and share?'

'Yes'm.'

'Then say so!'

'Yes'm,' I murmured, sliding back into my seat as Mary Lou, Gracey, and Alma giggled. Here it was only five minutes into the new school year and already I was in trouble.

By ten o'clock Miss Crocker had rearranged our seating and written our names on her seating chart. I was still sitting beside Gracey and Alma but we had been moved from the third to the first row in front of a small potbellied stove. Although being eyeball to eyeball with Miss Crocker was nothing to look forward to, the prospect of being warm once the cold weather set in was nothing to be sneezed at either, so I resolved to make the best of my rather dubious position.

Now Miss Crocker made a startling announcement: This year we would all have books.

Everyone gasped, for most of the students had never handled a book at all besides the family Bible. I admit that even I was somewhat excited. Although Mama had several books, I had never had one of my very own.

'Now we're very fortunate to get these readers,' Miss Crocker explained while we eagerly awaited the unveiling. 'The county superintendent of schools himself brought these books down here for our use and we must take extra-good care of them.' She moved toward her desk. 'So let's all promise that we'll take the best care possible of these new books.' She stared down, expecting our response. 'All right, all together, let's repeat, "We promise to take good care of our new books."' She looked sharply at me as she spoke.

'WE PROMISE TO TAKE GOOD CARE OF OUR NEW BOOKS!'

'Fine,' Miss Crocker beamed, then proudly threw back the tarpaulin.

Sitting so close to the desk, I could see that the covers of the books, a motley red, were badly worn and that the gray edges of the pages had been marred by pencils, crayons, and ink. My anticipation at having my own book ebbed to a sinking disappointment. But Miss Crocker continued to beam as she called each fourth grader to her desk and, recording a number in her roll book, handed him or her a book.

Mildred D. Taylor

---

6 Reading

How does Cassie feel about the school she goes to? Consider:

- her thoughts and feelings towards Miss Crocker
- the way the children are treated by Miss Crocker.

What do you think are Cassie's views about the society she lives in?

7 Reading

What is the reaction of the children when they are told that they will all have books?

8 Speaking and listening

Imagine that you are two of the children in Miss Crocker's class. Act out a conversation in which you discuss being given second-hand books from the local whites-only school.

9 Writing

Write an essay in which you compare and contrast the Great Faith Elementary School with your own school. You should write about:

- the behaviour and attitude of the pupils
- the teachers and their approach
- the facilities and resources
- the atmosphere.

10 Writing

Imagine you are either Cassie or her younger brother Little Man. Write a letter to a friend describing your first day back at school. Include your thoughts and feelings about Miss Crocker and receiving the second-hand books.

REVIEW

How would it have felt to be a black schoolchild in the southern states of 1930s America? What do you feel are the major differences between school in 1930s America and school in 21st-century Britain? What are the main ideas the author wants to convey?

UNIT 7 Schools long ago

AIMS

- To work out the meanings of difficult words by examining contexts and relationships with other words.
- To compare the work of two major writers from different times and cultural contexts.

STARTER

1

Put the following comments from an English report into non-standard English. The first one is done for you.

Standard English	Non-standard English
Overall, she is making satisfactory progress.	Mainly OK / lazy little so and so at times.
Needs to adopt a serious and consistent approach.	
Could improve the accuracy and presentation of handwriting.	
Written work often lacks detail and development.	

INTRODUCTION

Charlotte Brontë's *Jane Eyre* was first published in 1847. In this extract, we witness life at Lowood School, a boarding school where Jane was sent by her unkind aunt, Mrs Reid, to keep her out of the way. How does Charlotte Brontë create a picture of misery and cruelty at Lowood School?

2

Do you think it is acceptable for teachers to beat children? How do you think Helen Burns felt after being hit by Miss Scatcherd?

DEVELOPMENT

3 Language

Match up the words from the text (on the left) with a synonym (on the right).

commenced	required
obliged	untidy
dispense with	apron
slatternly	began
pinafore	abandon

Jane Eyre

The next day commenced as before, getting up and dressing by rush-light; but this morning we were obliged to dispense with the ceremony of washing: the water in the pitchers was frozen. A change had taken place in the weather the preceding evening, and a keen north-east wind, whistling through the crevices of our bed-room windows all night long, had made us shiver in our beds, and turned the contents of the ewers to ice. [...]

In the course of the day I was enrolled a member of the fourth class, and regular tasks and occupations were assigned me: hitherto, I had only been a spectator of the proceedings at Lowood, I was now to become an actor therein. At first, being little accustomed to learn by heart, the lessons appeared to me both long and difficult: the frequent change from task to task, too, bewildered me; and I was glad, when, about three o'clock in the afternoon, Miss Smith put into my hands a border of muslin two yards long, together with needle, thimble, &c., and sent me to sit in a quiet corner of the school-room, with directions to hem the same. At that hour most of the others were sewing likewise; but one class still stood round Miss Scatcherd's chair reading, and as all was quiet, the subject of their lessons could be heard, together with the manner in which each girl acquitted herself, and the animadversions or commendations of Miss Scatcherd on the performance. It was English history: among the readers, I observed my acquaintance of the verandah: at the commencement of the lesson, her place had been at the top of the class, but for some error of pronunciation or some inattention to stops, she was suddenly sent to the very bottom. Even in that obscure position, Miss Scatcherd continued to make her an object of constant notice: she was continually addressing to her such phrases as the following: –

'Burns' (such it seems was her name: the girls here were all called by their surnames, as boys are elsewhere), 'Burns, you are standing on the side of your shoe, turn your toes out immediately.' 'Burns, you poke your chin most unpleasantly, draw it in.' 'Burns, I insist on your holding your head up: I will not have you before me in that attitude,' &c. &c. [...]

My attention was now called off by Miss Smith desiring me to hold a skein of thread: while she was winding it, she talked to me from time to time, asking whether I had ever been at school before, whether I could mark, stitch, knit, &c.; till she dismissed me, I could not pursue my observations on Miss Scatcherd's movements. When I returned to my seat, that lady was just delivering an order, of which I did not catch the import; but Burns immediately left the class, and, going into the small inner room where the books were kept, returned in half a minute, carrying in her hand a bundle of twigs tied together at one end. This ominous tool she presented to Miss Scatcherd with a respectful courtesy; then she quietly, and without being told, unloosed her pinafore, and the teacher instantly and sharply inflicted on her neck a dozen strokes with the bunch of twigs. Not a tear rose to Burns' eye; and, while I paused from my sewing, because my fingers quivered at this spectacle with a sentiment of unavailing and impotent anger, not a feature of her pensive face altered its ordinary expression.

'Hardened girl!' exclaimed Miss Scatcherd; 'nothing can correct you of your slatternly habits: carry the rod away.'

Burns obeyed: I looked at her narrowly as she emerged from the book-closet; she was just putting back her handkerchief into her pocket, and the trace of a tear glistened on her thin cheek.

Charlotte Brontë

4 Language

See if you can work out the meaning of the following old-fashioned words merely by examining their context and relationship with other words in the text.

**acquitted animadversions
import book-closet**

5 Reading

In the first paragraph, how does the writer create a sense that the girls suffered?

6 Reading

What tasks had the girls to perform in the fourth class?

7 Reading

Describe Miss Scatcherd's treatment of Helen Burns.

8 Speaking and listening

Consider the differences and similarities between Lowood School in *Jane Eyre* and the Great Faith Elementary School in *Roll of Thunder, Hear My Cry*. Discuss:

- the facilities and organisation of each school
- the actions, speech and attitudes of the teachers
- rules and the way pupils are treated
- the behaviour, feelings and thoughts of the pupils
- relationships between teachers and pupils
- the atmosphere in each school.

9 Writing

Write an essay comparing and contrasting Lowood School and the Great Faith Elementary School. Refer closely to the text and include the topics you discussed in Activity 8.

10 Writing

Imagine you are Miss Scatcherd. Write your end of term report on Helen Burns using formal English.

REVIEW

What are the main things to remember when you are comparing writers from different times and cultures?

UNIT 8

Revising English-specific vocabulary

AIMS

- To spell words accurately from different subject areas.
- To know and use terms that are useful for analysing language.

STARTER

1

Quickly write down the following terms on individual pieces of paper and fold them up so you can't see the words.

accent allegory autobiography ballad biography blank verse cliché dialect ellipsis fiction idiom haiku myth narrative plot pun slang sonnet theme tone

Now take it in turns to choose a piece a paper and give an accurate definition of each word. Use the glossary to check your definitions. Keep a score of how many words you define correctly.

DEVELOPMENT

2

Pick out the three words that are spelled correctly in the following list. Then correct the misspelled words.

advertisment apostrophe commer consonent dialoge exspression figurative grammer narrater personification prepasition ryme subordinat vocabulery

3

Match up the following parts of speech with their correct definition.

a abstract noun	a word which denotes an action
b adjective	a word which replaces a noun in a sentence (e.g. 'he', 'she', 'it', 'we', etc.)
c adverb	a word which relates nouns or noun phrases to other words in a sentence (e.g. 'to', 'in', 'round', etc.)
d concrete noun	a word which names an emotion or concept that is not tangible
e compound sentence	a word which names a specific person or place, a title of a book, film, poem or play
f complex sentence	a sentence of two or more main clauses
g proper noun	a sentence of one main clause and one or more subordinate clauses
h preposition	a describing word
i pronoun	a word which describes or gives information about an action
j verb	a word which names an object

4

Write out the following technical terms in full and match them to their correct definition.

a	an_____m	a word of the same or similar meaning
b	al_____n	a fourteen-line poem
c	cl___e	another word for a verse of poetry
d	co_____e	when a word sounds like the sound it describes
e	con_____n	the first or primary meaning of a word
f	de_____n	an additional or secondary meaning of a word
g	ge___e	a comparison using 'as' or 'like'
h	on_____a	a type or category of writing
i	si_____e	a joining word
j	s___za	a part of a sentence
k	sy_____m	when a sequence of words begins with the same letter
l	so_____t	a word of opposite meaning

5

Read the passage.

The Kite Rider

The Jade Circus was an odd mixture of opposites. Parts were more putrid than the   1
foulest corners of the fish market, and parts were glimpses into the fabled City of
Gems. Elephants like drought-dead trees stood amid steaming piles of dung, and
stocky little horses with hogged manes ate out of crates of sweepings from the
market. A red panda sat listlessly scratching itself, and two camels, legs folded   5
under them, spat at anyone who passed by. There were pyramid piles of bird
cages, each with a different songbird inside, snared specifically so that they could
be freed at the end of each show.

Geraldine McCaughream

Pick out the following parts of speech and technical features.

a A proper noun in line 1.
b An adjective in line 2.
c A preposition in line 3.
d A simile in line 3.
e Two concrete nouns and two adjectives in line 4.

f A verb in line 6.
g An adverb in line 5.
h A pronoun in line 7.
i An example of alliteration in line 7.
j A modal verb in line 7.

REVIEW

You have now revised many difficult English-specific words which will come in very useful when you sit your KS3 English SATs. If you are still unsure about any terms, look them up in the glossary at the back of this book.

UNIT 9 Into the mists of the Lost World

AIMS

- To look at how ideas are shaped into cohesive paragraphs.
- To consider how descriptive detail is used to convey a sense of excitement.

STARTER

1

> The **denotation** of a word is its first or primary meaning – generally the first definition given by a dictionary.
> A **connotation** of a word is its secondary or alternative meaning.

Using a dictionary find the denotation of the following words and give at least one connotation.

soft bright dump roll hot

INTRODUCTION

In this extract from his book *Quest for the Lost World*, the actor Brian Blessed writes about his excitement in following in the footsteps of one of his childhood heroes, Professor Challenger from Arthur Conan Doyle's *The Lost World*. How does Blessed convey an increasing sense of excitement in this passage?

2

Work out whether the denotation or connotation of each of the following words is being used in the passage.

- corners
- chance
- top
- base
- mass
- mother
- burst
- wall
- break
- flooded

What is the meaning of each word in the context of this passage?

Into the Mists of the Lost World

A dream had come true. Ever since I was a boy, I've longed to explore the mysterious plateau of Mount Roraima in Venezuela – a primeval wilderness immortalised by Sir Arthur Conan Doyle in his book The Lost World.

This expanse of tropical rainforest is truly one of the world's forgotten corners, and Roraima is its forgotten mountain.

It's an extraordinary 9,000-ft plateau with vertical walls and a flat summit. It is also two billion years old and covered by impenetrable forest. In Conan Doyle's science fiction novel it was the last place on earth where dinosaurs still roamed.

I got the chance to visit Mount Roraima when a 22-day expedition was planned and a place suddenly became free.

I live for adventure. I've climbed the Matterhorn and Mont Blanc. I've been on Everest twice and reached 28,000ft without bottled oxygen. I've also climbed the mighty Aconcagua in Argentina, at 22,830-ft the highest mountain in the western hemisphere. Now I was ready for a new challenge.

Mount Roraima is nowhere near so high, but every bit as exciting. At 62, I was by far the oldest in the group, but I pride myself on being extremely fit. [...] Roraima, though, is no picnic. The weather is unpredictable and it's easy to get trapped between the dozens of fast-flowing rivers. Numerous expeditions have come unstuck upon reaching the top. A year before, a German woman was blown over the edge.

Our hike from the base of Roraima began at 10am. It was already 30C (86F). The landscape was a mass of flat-peaked mountains, ending with the mother of them all.

We stopped for lunch in a forest glade. Hummingbirds – darts of brilliant green and blue – visited one flower after another. A morpho butterfly whizzed past. It was azure blue and had a huge wing-span. [...]

The next morning we crossed the shallow Maturu Paru River and began our ascent to base camp. The heat was terrible, but then the heavens opened. Great black clouds enveloped Roraima until it faded from sight and waterfalls poured over the cliffs.

Just as suddenly the sun burst through and the precipices shone a deep red colour. At base camp that evening a helicopter circled overhead (a Brazilian film crew). I was reminded of my favourite passage from Conan Doyle's book – the point at which Professor Challenger sees his first pterodactyls. [...]

I looked up at the sheer wall of Roraima and saw it was half-covered in a mysterious mist. Was there no end to these wonders?

The end, in fact, was coming quite dramatically. I'd reached 9,000 ft and there was only a little further to go. I moved upwards, on to firmer ground, towards a break in the cliff and I saw Anthony ahead.

Memories flooded back ... I remembered Mr Brown, my old headmaster, who had caned me for skipping school to listen to The Lost World on the radio. [...]

Then, as I placed my feet on top of a boulder, Anthony whispered, 'Welcome to the Lost World.'

Brian Blessed

DEVELOPMENT

3 Language

Examine closely the following three topic sentences.

- A dream had come true.
- I live for adventure.
- The end, in fact, was coming quite dramatically.

Why are these sentences good openings for paragraphs?

4 Language

Pick out the following features in paragraph 5:

- the topic sentence
- a sentence developing the topic sentence
- connectives and link words
- detail or facts relevant to the topic.

5 Language

Look at the penultimate paragraph. What is the purpose of this paragraph? Comment on:

- suspense
- the author's thoughts and feelings.

6 Language

This article is constructed of paragraphs of varied length. What type of paragraphs are used to:

- give facts and describe actions
- convey thoughts and feelings
- describe landscape and weather?

7 Language

How does Brian Blessed create a sense of excitement and wonder in the passage? Comment on:

- the use of narrative detail, facts and information
- the use of descriptive detail and atmosphere
- his thoughts and feelings
- language and expression.

Does reading the extract make you want to buy the book?

8 Reading

Why was Brian Blessed a suitable person to go on the expedition to the summit of Mount Roraima?

9 Reading

What dangers might be encountered on such an expedition?

10 Speaking and listening

One of you plays Brian Blessed, the other plays an interviewer. Conduct an interview for a radio chat show. Try to convey:

- Blessed's inspiration for his expedition to Mount Roraima
- what Mount Roraima is like
- Blessed's excitement and sense of achievement.

11 Writing

You win a competition to visit Mount Roraima and are allowed to take two people with you. Unfortunately, things go wrong on your expedition. Write a personal account describing your

experiences. Develop a sense of mystery and excitement by using:

- interesting details and description
- varied vocabulary and expression
- the senses and emotions
- varied sentence and paragraph length
- emphatic sentences to open paragraphs.

12 Writing

Describe Mount Roraima as it might appear in an adventure holiday brochure.

REVIEW

How successfully have you conveyed excitement in your account? Have you varied your sentence and paragraph structure to create different atmospheres and effects? Look closely at each other's writing and comment on the use of sentences and paragraphs.

UNIT 10 — The Sentinel

AIMS

- To develop writing for a range of purposes and audiences.
- To further develop paragraphing and sentence structure in your own writing.
- To use compound and complex sentences in writing.

STARTER

1

> A **spelling rule** is a device to help you remember difficult or unusual spellings. One common rule is 'i before e except after c'.

See how many words you can find which obey the 'i before e' rule, then find some exceptions.

INTRODUCTION

In the extract opposite, a group of space explorers stumble upon a strange monolith placed on the summit of a lunar mountain by an advanced civilisation. Carefully consider how the writer gradually develops the awesome nature of the discovery.

2

What do you think might be the purpose of the strange monolith on the lunar mountain?

DEVELOPMENT

> A **complex sentence** is made up of a main clause and one or more subordinate clauses (e.g. Although I didn't want to spend so much, I still bought the bike).

> A **compound sentence** involves two or more clauses of equal importance (e.g. I had lots of money and I bought a bike).

3 Language

Pick out a complex sentence from the passage, specifying:

- the main clause
- at least one subordinate clause.

4 Language

Write out a compound sentence from the passage, underlining two clauses of equal importance.

5 Language

Look at the paragraph beginning on line 35. Write down:

- any connectives or link words
- emotions and thoughts linked to the topic sentence.

6 Reading

Describe the plateau on which the space explorer found himself.

7 Reading

Explain how the writer develops a sense of anticipation and excitement.

8 Speaking and listening

Perform a TV news report which announces the discovery of a pyramid-like structure on the Moon. One of you plays the TV reporter, the other plays the space explorer. Think of questions and answers that convey a sense of excitement and offer some explanation for the existence of the structure.

The Sentinel

Garnett looked at me anxiously. I could tell that he wanted to go first, but I smiled back at him through the glass of my helmet and shook my head. Slowly, taking my time, I began the final ascent. 5

Even with my space-suit, I weighed only forty pounds here, so I pulled myself up hand over hand without bothering to use my feet. At the rim I 10 paused and waved to my companion, then I scrambled over the edge and stood upright, staring ahead of me.

You must understand that until this 15 very moment I had been almost completely convinced that there could be nothing strange or unusual for me to find here. Almost, but not quite; it was that haunting doubt 20 that had driven me forward. Well, it was a doubt no longer, but the haunting had scarcely begun.

I was standing on a plateau perhaps a hundred feet across. It had once 25 been smooth – too smooth to be natural – but falling meteors had pitted and scored its surface through immeasurable eons. It had been levelled to support a glittering, 30 roughly pyramidal structure, twice as high as a man, that was set in the rock like a gigantic, many-faceted jewel.

Probably no emotion at all filled my 35 mind in those first few seconds. Then I felt a great lifting of my heart, and a strange, inexpressible joy. [...] The old, discredited dream of the first explorers was true. There had, 40 after all, been a lunar civilization – and I was the first to find it. [...]

My mind was beginning to function normally, to analyze and to ask questions. Was this a building, a 45 shrine – or something for which my language had no name? [...] I wondered if it might be a temple, and I could picture the adepts of some strange priesthood calling on 50 their gods to preserve them as the life of the Moon ebbed with the dying oceans, and calling on their gods in vain.

I took a dozen steps forward to 55 examine the thing more closely, but some sense of caution kept me from going too near. I knew a little of archaeology, and tried to guess the cultural level of the civilization that 60 must have smoothed this mountain and raised the glittering mirror surfaces that still dazzled my eyes. [...]

And then I noticed something that 65 set the scalp crawling at the back of my neck – something so trivial and so innocent that many would never have noticed it at all. I have said that the plateau was scarred by meteors; 70 it was also coated inches-deep with the cosmic dust that is always filtering down upon the surface of any world where there are no winds to disturb it. Yet the dust and the 75 meteor scratches ended quite abruptly in a wide circle enclosing the little pyramid, as though an invisible wall was protecting it from the ravages of time and the slow but ceaseless 80 bombardment from space. [...]

I picked up a fragment of splintered rock and tossed it gently toward the shining enigma. If the pebble had vanished at that invisible barrier I 85 should not have been surprised, but it seemed to hit a smooth, hemispherical surface and slide gently to the ground.

I knew then that I was looking at nothing that could be matched in the 90 antiquity of my own race.

Arthur C. Clarke

9 Writing

Now write a newspaper article describing the space explorer's discovery of a black pyramid on the Moon. Remember to:

- consider what, where, when, who, why and how
- include eyewitness accounts
- structure your report into logically ordered paragraphs that aren't too long.

10 Writing

Continue the story, trying to maintain the same style as the original. Answer these questions.

- What is the purpose of the black pyramid structure?
- What happens to the two space explorers?

Try to develop:

- interesting descriptive detail
- a range of imaginative vocabulary
- an exciting and tense atmosphere
- a sense of mystery
- sentences of varied length.

REVIEW

If an alien structure or alien life form was discovered on the Moon, how would it be reported by the media? Have your TV and newspaper reports managed to convey some of the excitement an amazing discovery like this would generate? In your story, did you use sentences of different lengths and varied vocabulary to create interesting effects?

UNIT 11 — The story of *Apollo 11*

AIMS

- To read a text and extract relevant factual information.
- To examine how a subject is treated differently in fiction and non-fiction texts.

STARTER

1

> **Memory aids** are useful ways of remembering spellings. Memory aids include using mnemonics, learning word families or breaking words down into separate syllables. Grouping words together and remembering letter patterns can also help.

See how many words you can make with the following letter patterns.

- ient
- ui
- here

INTRODUCTION

The lunar mission of *Apollo 11* is possibly one of the most famous and well-documented events of history. Neil Armstrong's first step on the moon's surface was an amazing achievement.

What are the limitations facing a writer of non-fiction who is trying to create a factually accurate account?

2

Do you get a strong sense of the importance of this event from the passage? Give reasons for your answer.

The Invasion of the Moon 1969

ARMSTRONG: *'We're going to try it … hatch coming open.'* Aldrin now guided Armstrong as he made his ungainly exit, on his knees and backwards through the narrow hatch, into an alien world.

ALDRIN: *'Neil, you're lined up nicely … Toward me a little bit … OK, down … roll to the left … put your left foot to the right a little bit … you're doing fine.'*

ARMSTRONG: *'OK, Houston, I'm on the porch.'* Unlike all the moon landing heroes of science fiction, Armstrong was crouching with his back to the moonscape on a platform just outside the hatch. Now he gingerly felt with his feet for the first rungs of the ladder.

PAO: Neil Armstrong on the porch at 109 hours, 19 minutes, 16 seconds [3.51 BST] … twenty-five minutes of PLSS time expended now.

The life support systems Armstrong and Aldrin were now living on had enough oxygen and water for up to four hours.

ALDRIN: *'OK, everything's nice and sunny in here.'*

ARMSTRONG: *'OK, can you pull the door open a little more?'*

ALDRIN: *'Did you get the MESA out?'* The MESA (modularized equipment stowage assembly) was a panel on the

descent stage to the left of the foot of the ladder which Armstrong opened by pulling a cord. As the flap came down, it revealed the television camera and some of the equipment which would be used by the astronauts to collect moon samples.

ARMSTRONG: *'I'm going to pull it now. Houston, the MESA came down all right.'*

MCC: *'Houston, roger, we copy and we're standing by for your TV. … Man, we're getting a picture on the TV.'* On the giant screen at Mission Control an obscure jumble of black and white images flickered into place.

MCC: *'There's a great deal of contrast in it and currently it's upside down on our monitor, but we can make out a fair amount of detail. … OK Neil, we can see you coming down the ladder now.'*

On the television screen the picture had now turned the right way up. The surface of the moon appeared as a sheet of white paper while the 'sky' was inky black. In the foreground the ladder could be made out, a grey form descending from top left of the screen. A shadowy grey figure could be seen coming down it.

ARMSTRONG: *'I'm at the foot of the ladder. The LM foot pads are only depressed in the surface about one or two inches. Although the surface appears to be very fine, fine grained, as you get close to it, it's almost like a powder. Now and then it's very fine.'* Armstrong was now standing with both feet on the three-foot diameter pad at the base of the landing leg.

ARMSTRONG: *'I'm going to step off the LM now.'* He lifted his left foot and, pushing it out a little, planted history's most witnessed footprint. *'That's one small step for man, one giant leap for mankind.'*

Peter Ryan

BST = British standard time
LM = lunar module
MCC = mission control centre (at Houston)

PAO = public affairs officer ('voice' of mission control)
PLSS = portable life support system

DEVELOPMENT

3 Language

The layout of this non-fiction passage is very unusual.

- Explain how it differs from a piece of prose or a script.
- What are its key features?
- Why are the dialogue and events set out in this original and peculiar way?

4 Language

How would you describe the language of this passage? Write about:

- vocabulary
- sentence structure.

5 Language

Find a synonym for the following words.

- ungainly
- obscure
- stowage

6 Language

What are the advantages of using so many abbreviations in a text of this type?

7 Reading

How long would Armstrong and Aldrin's oxygen last after landing on the moon?

8 Reading

How did Armstrong open the MESA?

9 Reading

What was wrong with the initial TV pictures?

10 Reading

How far were the LM pads depressed into the surface of the moon? What was the surface like?

11 Reading

What did Armstrong say when he stepped onto the moon's surface?

12 Speaking and listening

Imagine you are an alien landing on the surface of the Earth for the first time. You happen to land on a school field. Act out the conversation you have with your Mission Control. Think about:

- sights, sounds, smells
- the terrain and geography
- the reception you receive from the locals.

13 Writing

Compare and contrast the two extracts from 'The Sentinel' (Unit 10) and 'The Invasion of the Moon 1969'. Consider how each writer treats the subject of lunar exploration. Write about:

- similarities and differences
- content – facts, events, action and detail
- style, language and expression
- atmosphere and excitement
- your preference.

14 Reading and writing

Find out as much as you can about one of the planets in our solar system by using the Internet, the library or a CD-Rom encyclopaedia. Write a short paragraph describing what you would see if you landed on that planet. Try to convey your experience in a way which would interest both a group of scientists at Mission Control and a live world-wide audience!

REVIEW

What are the main differences between the writing styles found in the extracts from 'The Sentinel' and 'The Invasion of the Moon 1969'? What are the reasons for these differences? Which extract did you prefer and why?

UNIT 12 Revising subject-specific vocabulary

AIMS

- To spell words from different subject areas accurately.

STARTER

1

In which subject you would use the following words? Write each word with the answer.

acrylic broadsheet desert digestion dynasty harmony improvise multiplication nutrition particles password perspective quadriceps regional rehearsal spreadsheet symmetrical tabloid textile vocal

DEVELOPMENT

2

Many of the following words from school subjects are often spelled incorrectly. See if you can spell them correctly.

agilaty aproximately carbohidrate ceramony citisen climmate coresponding discipal dramatize evaparation exibition festaval forground inovation instumentle intenational interractive laboritory minral movment muscel palete parliment percusion perimetre playwrite procesor rythm scaner settlment temprature trator

3

Choose the correct word highlighted in bold.

a My dad painted an interesting **landscape/portrait** of my mum.

b I sketched an interesting **spectrum/perspective** of our school from my art classroom.

c I used lots of interesting **components/ingredients** when I baked a cake in Food Technology.

d My **design/recipe** for a new car was displayed on open evening.

e I played the **role/position** of an old man in Drama.

f The London Underground is a **tourist/transport** system.

g There are many people in southern Africa who suffer from **poverty/erosion**.

h The United Kingdom has a **chronological/constitutional** monarchy.

i The Romans created a great **civilisation/contradiction**.

j I wrote a simple **programme/program** in ICT.

k A scanner is a useful piece of **hardware/software**.

l The **ratio/radius** of a circle can be measured from its centre to its circumference.

m A **crotchet/quaver** is one beat long.

n I have got huge **hamstrings/biceps** on my arms.

o My PE teacher is very **gymnastic/athletic** and runs marathons.

p A mosque is a **Muslim/Hindu** temple.

q Catholicism is a Christian **symbol/faith**.

r Hydrogen is an **organism/element**.

s Shire horses are **mammals/predators**.

4

Use each of the following words in a sentence of your own.

**collage   portfolio   rehearsal   habitat   source   preview   virus
perpendicular   melody   tactic   frequency   condensation**

5

The following lists contain words you should know how to spell before you go into Year 10. Learn how to spell any unfamiliar words. Use a dictionary to check any meanings you don't know.

Art
collage dimension gallery illusion perspective portrait

Design and Technology
component design disassemble evaluation portfolio specification tension

Drama
characteristics director improvise rehearsal scenario theatrical

Geography
amenity contour erosion estuary habitat infrastructure pollution physical regional transportation

History
cathedral chronological colonisation constitutional dynasty imperialism propaganda rebellion republic revolution

ICT
database graphic interface justify multimedia sensor virus

Library
alphabetical anthology catalogue encyclopaedia genre glossary thesaurus

Mathematics
addition adjacent circumference co-ordinate denominator equilateral equation isosceles multiplication parallel symmetry vertices

Music
composition harmony melody percussion syncopation timbre

PE
athletic mobility quadriceps qualify tournament

RE
biblical celebration commandment commitment immorality pilgrimage prejudice religious spiritual

Science
alkaline amphibian circulation condensation frequency nutrient organism particles respiration vertebrate

REVIEW

You have now successfully revised many words which are often incorrectly spelled. Furthermore, you have revised many words from other subject areas which will come in very useful when you sit your KS3 SATs. Look up any words you are still unsure about in a dictionary or ask your subject teachers for an explanation.

UNIT 13 Freaks of nature

AIMS

- To explore how non-fiction texts can convey information in an amusing and entertaining way.
- To use a variety of creative features in a non-literary text.

STARTER

1

Write down five of the following words which best describe you.

bossy clever friendly handsome irresponsible kind lazy mean modest polite punctual reliable selfish sensitive sporty witty

Now write down five words to describe your partner. Compare your results – did you have any of the same words?

INTRODUCTION

*A **review** is is a piece of writing which expresses an opinion on the success of a TV programme, film, book, play or musical performance.*

People buy newspapers not only to be informed of the latest news but also to be entertained. The article that follows is an amusing and fascinating review of a wildlife programme. How does the writer make us want to read on, watch the TV programme or even read the book the series is based on?

2

Which example of animal behaviour did you find the most interesting and why?

DEVELOPMENT

3 Language

Anthropomorphism is when an animal or object is given human characteristics.

Pick out one example of anthropomorphism from the text. Consider:

- what human characteristics the animal is given
- how giving the animal human characteristics makes it more entertaining and interesting.

4 Language

The writer uses a French phrase – *promenade à deux* – which is a type of dance which people do side by side. Find out the meaning of these French phrases which are sometimes used in English.

*déjà vu   laissez faire   faux pas
fait accompli   tour de force*

5 Reading

To what does the writer compare the nest built by the bowerbirds of Australia?

6 Reading

How do the bowerbirds like to decorate their nest?

7 Reading

This article sets out to entertain people. Comment on the writer's use of:

- interesting facts about unusual animal behaviour

FREAKS of nature

Lobsters that conga their way across the ocean floor and elephants that trek miles to find leaves they know will help induce an overdue baby. A newly discovered species of octopus that can take the shape of a crab or fish, birds that build lawns outside their nests and chimps that know exactly what to eat if they have an upset stomach.

Welcome to the world of weird nature – the astonishing secret life of animals uncovered by film-maker and author John Downer. In his latest book, *Weird Nature*, […] Downer documents the hidden – and frequently bizarre – habits of the animal kingdom.

'Until recently, one of the greatest crimes in science was to be accused of ascribing human thoughts and emotions to animals,' says Downer. 'As we learn more about the complexities of animal behaviour, that position is beginning to appear untenable. The similarity in our behaviour and that of the rest of the animal kingdom is more than mere coincidence.'

Take, for example, the bowerbirds of Australia and New Guinea, whose strange behaviour reflects our practice of offering gifts during courtship. The male bird constructs a bachelor pad made out of twigs, leaves and moss in order to attract and seduce a mate. To add to his appeal, he tastefully adds ornaments of feathers, pebbles, berries or shells, and even steals human trinkets, such as shiny coins, pen caps, keys or jewellery to help create the perfect romantic mood. […]

'The showier species tend to spend less effort on their bowers, while the drab ones build flashy ones to compensate for their lack of sex appeal,' says Downer. […]

Like us, some birds go 'clubbing' to find a mate. The most sensational dance is performed by the red-capped manikin, whose routine is similar to Michael Jackson's 'moondance', complete with the steps that give the appearance of walking backwards while moving forwards.

Another unusual mover is the bushbaby, which can bounce around like a living rubber ball. A single leap can carry it two metres (seven feet) into the air, or six times its body length, which is equivalent to a human high jumper clearing two stacked double-decker buses. The Sifaka lemurs of Madagascar show a similar talent for jumping, but they progress in a series of vertical hops that makes them appear to pogo across the forest floor. […]

Mating scorpions move rather more slowly. In courtship, the male and female link claws and perform a strange *promenade à deux* as they mate. The ungrateful female sometimes ends the dance by eating her partner, so the male may take the precaution of drugging her first with a sting. […]

'As we researched the television series and the book, it became clear that we were not only uncovering some of the strangest examples of animal behaviour, we were also uncovering something about ourselves,' says Downer. […] 'The actions of animals seem weird when they are unfamiliar, but they are equally strange when they remind us of ourselves. Perhaps this is to be expected. The living embodiment of weird nature is closer than we think – it is us.'

Mail on Sunday

- comparisons to human beings
- language and style.

8 Speaking and listening

Produce and perform a TV documentary about your school in the style of a wildlife documentary. Include:

- descriptions of typical pupil and teacher behaviour
- descriptions of pupil and teacher habitat and plumage
- strange or bizarre characteristics.

Before you begin:

- decide what areas, people and activities you are going to focus on
- think of anything unusual about your school
- think about how to give teachers and pupils animal-like characteristics.

9 Writing

Write a review of the TV documentary you produced about your school in the style of the extract. Don't forget to make your review amusing and entertaining.

10 Writing

Write a review of a TV programme you enjoy watching. Consider:

- the audience – who the programme is aimed at
- the characters or presenters
- the content – what happens or what the programme is about
- what makes the programme so appealing.

REVIEW

What techniques did you learn to make non-fiction writing more entertaining? Were the class documentaries realistic and entertaining? What would you change in your own presentation after witnessing the performances of the rest of the class?

UNIT 14
Grendel the Monster

AIMS

- To extend knowledge of the literary heritage by examining an extract from an Anglo-Saxon work.
- To extend and apply knowledge of word origins.

STARTER

1

*Words of **Anglo-Saxon** or **Old English** origin are still used today in everyday conversation.*

Old English	Modern English
habban	to have
haelo	health
haer	hair
healf	half

Which modern English words have developed from these Old English roots?

seld (rare)	**hund (dog)**
wis (wise)	**mis (wrong)**
un (not)	**buc (pitcher)**

INTRODUCTION

The following extract is a translation of an Anglo-Saxon story. The tale is part of a strong oral tradition, in which stories were passed from generation to generation by word of mouth. The original author is unknown. Beowulf, the nephew of Hygelac, King of the Geats, defeats the monster Grendel in battle. How does the writer develop a sinister and frightening atmosphere?

2

How does the writer create the sense that a great battle is taking place?

Beowulf

Through the dark night a darker shape slid. A sinister figure shrithed down from the moors, over high shoulders, sopping tussocks, over sheep-runs, over gurgling streams. It shrithed towards the timbered hall, huge and hairy and slightly stooping. Its long arms swung loosely.

One man was snoring, one mumbling, one coughing; all the Geats guarding Heorot had fallen asleep – all except one, one man watching.

For a moment the shape waited outside the hall. It cocked an ear. It began to quiver. Its hair bristled. Then it grasped the great ring-handle and swung open the door, the mouth of Heorot. It lunged out of the darkness and into the circle of dim candlelight, it took a long stride across the patterned floor.

Through half-closed eyes Beowulf was watching, and through barred teeth he breathed one word. 'Grendel.' The name of the monster, the loathsome syllables.

Grendel saw the knot of sleeping warriors and his eyes shone with an unearthly light. He lurched towards the nearest man, a brave Geat called Leofric, scooped him up and, with one ghastly claw, choked the scream in his throat. Then the monster ripped him apart, bit into his body, drank the blood from his veins, devoured huge pieces; within one minute he had swallowed the whole man, even his feet and hands. […]

Grendel slobbered spittle and blood; his first taste of flesh only made him more ravenous. He wheeled round towards Beowulf, stooped, reached out for him, and Beowulf …

Beowulf leaped up and stayed the monster's outstretched arm. […]

Grendel tried to break free but Beowulf held him fast. The monster snorted and tugged, he could feel his fingers cracking in the Geat's grip.

Now the great room boomed. Clang and clatter shattered the night-silence as Beowulf and Grendel lurched to and fro in their deathly tug-of-war. Tables and mead-benches were overturned, Grendel roared and snarled, and in the outbuildings Danes woke and listened in the darkness. […]

Now Beowulf twisted Grendel's right arm behind his neck. He locked it and turned it, slowly he turned it, putting terrible pressure on Grendel's shoulder.

The monster bellowed and dropped to one knee. He jerked and his whole body shuddered and trembled. With superhuman strength he jerked again as he tried to escape Beowulf's grip, he jerked and all at once, his right shoulder ripped. A ghastly tearing of muscle and sinew and flesh; a spurting of hot blood: the monster's arm came apart from his body. Grendel howled. He staggered away from Beowulf, and reeled out of the hall.

Charles Keeping and Kevin Crossley-Holland

DEVELOPMENT

3 Language
Pick out adjectives which describe:
- Grendel the monster
- the landscape.

4 Language
How does the writer develop the sinister appearance of Grendel?

5 Reading
Explain how the writer creates a tense and sinister atmosphere at the start of the passage. Consider:
- Grendel's appearance and manner
- the description of the landscape and the hall
- the use of adjectives and concrete detail.

6 Reading
What techniques does the writer use to make the battle between Beowulf and Grendel realistic and vivid? Consider:
- actions and movement
- the senses – particularly sights and sounds
- language, imagery and expression.

7 Speaking and listening
Imagine that you are Beowulf. You return to the court of your uncle Hygelac and describe the night you fought Grendel at Heorot. Make your account exciting using some of the gory details in the extract.

8 Writing
After defeating Grendel, Beowulf decides to go and destroy Grendel's mother in her dismal lair at the bottom of the sea. Write a short passage describing the battle that takes place. Make your account as action-packed, violent and bloodthirsty as the one you have just read.

9 Writing
Write about something amazing you have done in a way which would captivate and entertain a reader. Think about:
- what you did – action and details are important
- atmosphere, thoughts and feelings
- sights and sounds
- interesting words and expressions.

REVIEW

Have you managed to create a sense of excitement in your account? What does a piece of action writing need to grip and entertain a reader? What type of things did audiences enjoy hearing about at the time *Beowulf* was written?

UNIT 15 Caliban

AIMS

- To analyse the language and the form of a scene from a Shakespeare play.
- To convey action, character, atmosphere and tension when scripting and performing a play.

> **Blank verse** is verse which doesn't have a regular rhyme. Shakespeare's plays are generally written in blank verse with a regular pattern of ten syllables with five stresses in each line.

STARTER

1

Mix and match the words in these Shakespearean insults to form your own new insults.

- Hang thee young baggage
- you green-sickness carrion
- mumbling fool
- princox
- tedious old fools
- bloody bawdy villain
- remorseless, treacherous, lecherous, kindless villain
- you juggler, you canker blossom

Think of some of your own imaginative and amusing modern English insults – keep them clean! Try your insults out on a friend.

INTRODUCTION

The Tempest centres around Prospero, the exiled Duke of Milan, who has magical powers. Prospero lives on a lovely island with his daughter Miranda and his slave Caliban. In this scene we hear about Prospero's failed attempts to educate Caliban. What is Prospero's and Miranda's opinion of Caliban?

2

Is Caliban grateful for what Prospero has done for him? Why had Prospero stopped being kind to Caliban?

The Tempest (from Act 1, Scene 2)

PROSPERO   – Thou poisonous Slave,
　　Got by the Divel himself upon thy Wicked
　　Dam, come forth.
　　[Enter Caliban]
CALIBAN   As wicked Dew as ere
　　My Mother brush'd with Raven's Feather from
5　Unwholesome Fen drop on your both: a Southwest
　　Blow on ye, and blister you all o'er.

PROSPERO For this, be sure, to night thou shalt have Cramps,
Side-stitches, that shall pen thy Breath up; Urchins
Shall, for that vast of Night that they may work,
10   All Exercise on thee; thou shalt be pinch'd
As thick as Honeycomb, each Pinch more stinging
Than Bees that made 'em.
CALIBAN   I must eat my Dinner.
This Island's mine by Sycorax my Mother,
Which thou tak'st from me. When thou cam'st first,
15   Thou strok'st me, and made much of me; would'st give me
Water with Berries in't and teach me how
To name the Bigger Light, and how the Less,
That burn by Day and Night; and then I lov'd thee
And shew'd thee all the Qualities o' th' Isle,
20   The fresh Springs, Brine-pits, Barren Place, and Fertile.
Curs'd be I that did so. All the Charms
Of Sycorax – Toads, Beetles, Bats, – light on you:
For I am all the Subjects that you have,
Which first was mine own King, and here you sty-me
25   In this hard Rock, whiles you do keep from me
The rest o' th' Island.
PROSPERO   Thou most lying Slave,
Whom Stripes may move, not Kindness: I have us'd thee,
Filth as thou art, with Humane Care; and lodg'd thee
In mine own Cell, till thou didst seek to violate
30   The Honour of my Child.
CALIBAN   Oh ho, Oh ho, would't had been done
Thou didst prevent me; I had peopl'd else
This Isle with Calibans.
MIRANDA   Abhorred Slave,
Which any Print of Goodness wilt not take,
Being capable of all Ill: I pitied thee,
35   Took Pains to make thee speak, taught thee each Hour
One thing or other, when thou didst not, Savage,
Know thine own Meaning, but wouldst gabble like
A Thing most Brutish, I endow'd thy Purposes
With Words that made them known. But thy vile Race,
40   (Though thou didst learn) had that in't which Good Natures
Could not abide to be with; therefore wast thou
Deservedly confin'd into this Rock,
Who hadst deserv'd more than a Prison.
CALIBAN You taught me Language, and my Profit on't
45   Is I know how to curse: the Red-plague rid you,
For learning me your Language.

William Shakespeare

DEVELOPMENT

3 **Language**

Rewrite the following lines as they would be written today.

- ... and then I lov'd thee/ And shew'd thee all the Qualities o' th' Isle
- When thou cam'st first, Thou strok'st me ...

4 **Language**

Pick out an example of each of the following.

- caesura (a punctuated pause in the middle of a line)
- enjambment (running on of lines)
- end-stopped line (a line of verse with punctuation at the end)

5 **Reading**

Write down two insults directed at Caliban by Prospero.

6 **Reading**

Explain the following in your own words.

- the curse aimed at Prospero by Caliban in lines 4–5
- the counter-curse placed on Caliban by Prospero in lines 7–12

7 **Reading**

How did Prospero treat Caliban when he first arrived on the island? What did Prospero teach Caliban?

8 **Reading**

How did Caliban betray Prospero's trust?

9 **Reading**

At the end of the passage, how does Caliban show his lack of appreciation for what Prospero has done for him?

10 **Reading**

Explain how Shakespeare creates and develops a feeling of intense and mutual dislike between Prospero and Caliban. Consider:

- what has happened before this scene takes place
- what they say about each other.

11 **Speaking and listening**

A new company called Monster Pet Incorporated has opened in your nearest town. You decide to buy a new bio-engineered monster pet. Act out two conversations with your new pet.

a adopting a pleasant and kind tone (as Prospero must have once talked to Caliban)

b in an aggressive, insulting tone (similar to the one adopted by Prospero towards Caliban in the passage)

12 **Writing**

Imagine you are Caliban. Write a diary entry describing the events in the passage. Describe how you feel about Prospero and Miranda. You may wish to include:

- details about where you now live
- your reaction to Prospero's treatment of you
- your plans and ambitions for your island.

13 **Writing**

Write a script based on one of the conversations you created in Activity 11. Make sure you adopt the correct tone and set the script out correctly.

REVIEW

Why is aggressive language and conflict often a feature of a successful script? Have you managed to incorporate sufficient insults and heated exchanges in your own writing? Perform your own script in front of the class, then discuss ways of improving drama skills.

UNIT 16 Vocabulary building: word formation

AIMS

- To apply knowledge of word origins and families to understand new words.
- To make use of a good etymological dictionary.

STARTER

1

*An **inflection** is a word ending which either changes a singular noun into a plural or alters a verb form. For example, the present tense of 'like' is changed to the past tense 'liked' by adding the inflection 'd'; the singular 'dog' is changed to the plural 'dogs' by adding the inflection 's'.*

See how many words you can make with the following roots by using inflections.

act   child   fall   live   man

DEVELOPMENT

2

*One of the commonest ways of creating new words in English is **compounding**. This is generally done by combining two nouns (e.g. 'bath' + 'room' = 'bathroom'), combining an adjective with a noun (e.g. 'green' + 'fly' = 'greenfly') and less commonly by combining a noun or adjective with a verb form (e.g. 'heartbroken' or 'easygoing').*

See how many compound words you can make with the following root words.

air   hand   head   house   light   motor paper   sea   table   water

3

*A **blend** is a word which is made up by combining parts of other words to form new words (e.g. 'smog' originates from 'smoke' and 'fog'). They are sometimes known as portmanteau words.*

Use your dictionary find out the original words from which the following blends were created.

bedsit   breathalyser   brunch electrocute   guesstimate   heliport hi-fi   moped   motel   newscast paratroops   sitcom   telecom travelogue

4

*Some words are formed by removing or **clipping** part of the original word (e.g. 'photo' originates from 'photograph').*

Work out where these clipped words come from – you shouldn't need a dictionary for most of them.

bike   brolly   bus   disco   fridge info   limo   mike   plane pram   stereo   telly   zoo

5

In recent years there has been an explosion in the use of **abbreviations**. Some abbreviations are so commonly used that most people would find it difficult to remember or work out their origins. Common abbreviations include TV (television) VAT (value added tax) and FC (football club).

Use a dictionary to discover what these abbreviations stand for.

**AA BA BBC BO CCTV CID
CND EC ET ITV LA OXFAM
NATO PLO PTO RAC RAF RSC
RSPCA RSVP SWALK TLC UFO
UN VHF WWW YMCA**

6

Some abbreviations form into words called **acronyms**. An acronym is a word which is formed from combining the first letter, or first and second letters, of a series of words. They often refer to an organisation, company or scientific invention (e.g. 'sonar' = **so**und **n**avigation **a**nd **r**anging).

How were the following acronyms formed?

derv midi NASA radar RAM scuba

7

Work out how the following words were invented – state what techniques have been used (compounding, blending, clipping, abbreviation, acronyms, or other techniques).

**aerosol AIDS airhead alcopop
biro carjacking catseye cyberpet
headbanger hoover laptop
NIMBY sandwich spam website
wellington YUPPY**

REVIEW

You now have a better understanding of how some words are formed and where many everyday words originated from. See if you can think of any new words which have come into common usage in recent years which are not mentioned in this unit.

UNIT 17 The supernatural

AIMS

- To consider how a writer's viewpoint can affect interpretation of events in a non-literary text.
- To use descriptive detail and presentational devices in a non-fiction text.

STARTER

1

> A **pun** is a play on words in which what is said or written may have more than one meaning (e.g. in jokes such as 'What goes "tick tick woof"? A watch dog'). Puns are often used by tabloid newspaper writers in headlines for the purpose of amusement.

Think of a suitable tabloid headline for the following news stories.

- body piercing and school
- shortening of school holidays
- mobile phones being made illegal for young people due to health concerns

Try to include puns in your headlines.

INTRODUCTION

The Mirror newspaper is famous for its use of puns and sensationalism. The article opposite is full of devices typical of a tabloid newspaper. Do you think the Smith family have a good case?

2

Whose side do you think the newspaper writer is on? Explain your answer.

DEVELOPMENT

3 Language

Explain the pun in the headline 'The Suepernatural'.

4 Language

What rhyme or sound effect is contained in the subheading that is often found in poetry? How is the subheading effective?

5 Language

> The **standfirst** is the opening paragraph of a newspaper article. It leads the reader into the article and gives a lot of information. It is often in bold print.

What typical features of a standfirst can you find in the opening paragraph?

6 Language

Pick out two facts and two opinions from the article.

7 Reading

What language is included by the writer to create a sense of fear and mystery?

8 Reading

How have the Smith family tried to get rid of the ghost?

9 Reading

How does the writer sensationalise the mystery surrounding the Smiths' cottage?

10 Speaking and listening

Present a feature on a local TV programme about the hauntings at Upper Mayfield. Include:

- a description of the strange events
- interviews with the people concerned (e.g. the two families, the exorcist, local people).

THE SUEPERNATURAL
Family in court battle over haunted home

A terrified family is suing two sisters – for selling them a haunted home.

Andrew and Josie Smith claim 500 hauntings in the last four years have made their lives a 'living hell'.

They say spooks have twice tried to throttle Josie, foul-smelling mists fill the rooms, apparitions appear and objects are hurled around.

Now the couple are taking Susan Melbourne and her sister Sandra to court, saying they were not told of the spirits before buying the centuries-old £44,000 house. They want their money back.

If they win the case it will be the first time since the Middle Ages that the supernatural has been officially recognised.

Father of three Andrew, 35, said yesterday: 'The strain is unbelievable. A week ago my daughter saw a mist in the dining room with a terrible smell. It was so thick you couldn't cross the room. You could lean on it and not fall over.'[...]

Josie, 35 – mum of Lindsey, 12, Stephen, five, and Daniel, one – added: 'The other morning in bed I felt as if I was being hung with a rope around my neck.

'Once, this young girl suddenly appeared in the kitchen wearing a 19th century bodice and long skirt, then just disappeared.'

Exorcised

The family has had the house at Upper Mayfield, Derbyshire, exorcised five times. But each time the spirits return.

Andrew, a joiner, said 'When exorcism is carried out the walls stream with water. But in 10 minutes they are bone dry.'[...]

The Smiths are so furious with the sisters they have withheld £3,000 of the house's £44,000 purchase price. Susan and Sandra are suing them for the money.

Now a county court judge has decided both sides should argue their claims at a full court hearing.

The Smiths' solicitor, Stephen Savage, said: 'I think they can win. It's the same as if the vendors didn't declare faulty drains.'

But Susan, who lives in nearby Mayfield, said: 'I lived in the cottage for years and never saw ghosts. The Smiths owe us money.'

The Mirror

---

11 Writing

Write a tabloid newspaper article about a strange haunting that takes place either in your home or school. Include:

- presentational features typical of a tabloid newspaper article
- puns and sensationalism
- eyewitness accounts and expert opinion
- a strong bias supporting claims of the haunting.

12 Writing

Write a tabloid newspaper article about the events at Upper Mayfield from the point of view of Susan Melbourne and her sister.

REVIEW

Despite the serious topic, the writer manages to lighten the tone by imaginative use of language. Does your article achieve this too? Would it convince a reader about the truth of the hauntings?

UNIT 18 — The Woman in Black

AIMS

- To revise terms that are useful for analysing language.
- To think about how a writer influences and manipulates a reader's thoughts, moods and understanding of a text.

STARTER

1

See how long a letter snake you can make starting with each of the following words. For example, starting with 'table' you can make **tabletteraserabbitalicicle**.

- school
- ghost
- noun
- grammar
- house
- Shakespeare

INTRODUCTION

In *The Woman in Black* by Susan Hill the narrator tells the story in flashback and recalls in a very convincing way the disturbing and malevolent figure of a woman who keeps appearing. What aspects of this apparition do you find the most disturbing?

2

Which phrases convey the narrator's sense of fear in the most powerful way?

DEVELOPMENT

> **Adverbial clauses** give more information about the way an action was performed (e.g. *It was with utter horror that I stared at her*).

> A **subordinate clause** offers additional information about the main clause of a sentence (e.g. '*Whatever you might say about him*, he is a very good footballer').

3 Language

Comment on how the writer uses language to develop a powerful sense of fear. Consider the use of:

- adjectives and nouns
- adverbial clauses
- similes
- the senses
- fronting and subordinate clauses.

The Woman in Black

Suddenly conscious of the cold and the extreme bleakness and eeriness of the spot and of the gathering dusk of the November afternoon, and not wanting my spirits to become so depressed that I might begin to be affected by all sorts of morbid fancies, I was about to leave, and walk briskly back to the house, where I intended to switch on a good many lights and even light a small fire if it were possible, before beginning my preliminary work on Mrs Drablow's papers. But, as I turned away, I glanced

once again round the burial ground and then I saw again the woman with the wasted face, who had been at Mrs Drablow's funeral. [...]

In the greyness of the fading light, it had the sheen and pallor not of flesh so much as of bone itself. Earlier, when I had looked at her, although admittedly it had been scarcely more than a swift glance each time, I had not noticed any particular expression on her ravaged face, but then I had, after all, been entirely taken with the look of extreme illness. Now, however, as I stared at her, stared until my eyes ached in their sockets, stared in surprise and bewilderment at her presence, now I saw that her face did wear an expression. It was one of what I can only describe – and the words seem hopelessly inadequate to express what I saw – as a desperate, yearning malevolence; it was as though she were searching for something she wanted, needed – *must have*, more than life itself, and which had been taken from her. [...] Her face, in its extreme pallor, her eyes, sunken but unnaturally bright, were burning with the concentration of passionate emotion which was within her and which streamed from her. [...] The combination of the peculiar, isolated place and the sudden appearance of the woman and the dreadfulness of her expression began to fill me with fear. Indeed, I had never in my life been so possessed by it, never known my knees to tremble and my flesh to creep, and then to turn cold as stone, never known my heart to give a great lurch, as if it would almost leap up into my dry mouth and then begin pounding in my chest like a hammer on an anvil, never known myself gripped and held fast by such dread and horror and apprehension of evil. It was as though I had become paralysed. I could not bear to stay there, for fear, but nor had I any strength left in my body to turn and run away, and I was as certain as I had ever been of anything that, at any second, I would drop dead on that wretched patch of ground.

Susan Hill

4 Language

Pick out a complex sentence with more than one subordinate clause and set it out in the following way.

Main clause	Subordinate clauses
I was about to leave	**a** Suddenly conscious of the cold and the extreme bleakness and eeriness of the spot and of the gathering dusk of the November afternoon
	b and not wanting my spirits to become so depressed that I might begin to be affected by all sorts of morbid fancies
	c and walk briskly back to the house
	d where I intended to switch on a good many lights and even light a small fire if it were possible
	e before beginning my preliminary work on Mrs Drablow's papers.

5 Reading

Describe the appearance of the woman with the wasted face. Write about:

- her complexion
- her clothing
- her facial expression.

6 Reading

What effect did the woman have on the narrator?

7 Speaking and listening

Act out a police interview in which you describe the woman. Think carefully about what questions a police officer would be likely to ask. Answer the questions in as much detail as possible.

8 Writing

Write your own ghost story in which you develop a terrifying and gripping atmosphere that captivates the reader. Before you begin, carefully plan and brainstorm your ideas. Make notes on:

- setting – time and place
- atmosphere
- characters

- plot – sequence of events – twists and turns
- narrative style – first or third person
- your ghost – appearance and behaviour.

9 Writing

Go to your nearest library and take out a ghost story. Write a short review of your chosen story using the following headings.

- Setting
- Ghost
- Key passages
- Characters
- Main events
- Fear factor

REVIEW

When you have completed the first draft of your story swap it with a partner. Choose any passages you think are particularly successful and read one out to the rest of the class. Explain why you chose those particular passages, thinking about some of the techniques we have touched upon in this unit.

Roswell

UNIT 19

AIMS

- To locate and extract relevant information from a text.
- To develop notemaking skills.
- To put together information from a range of sources into a discursive essay.

STARTER

1

The letters 'c' and 'g' have both hard and soft sounds (e.g. hard 'c' = cube, soft 'c' = receive, hard 'g' = gorilla, soft 'g' = damage).

See how many words you can think of with each 'c' and 'g' sound in five minutes.

INTRODUCTION

In July 1947 an alien spacecraft is believed to have crash-landed in Roswell, New Mexico. The fact that the US government retracted the initial army press release which told of the incident adds extra mystery. Read the following article and see if you think there is a cover up.

> **Expert opinion** is the views and thoughts of people who know a lot about a particular field. Expert opinion is useful in supporting and giving extra weight to arguments in a formal essay.

2

Are you convinced by the claims of Colonel Philip Corso?

Army Witness 'Saw Alien at Roswell'

IT CAME FROM OUTER SPACE. Now the very first X File is being reopened as a new witness comes from out of the blue to testify that he saw the body of an alien recovered from the wreckage of a flying saucer in the New Mexico desert.

The 'Roswell incident' has fascinated UFO researchers for 50 years. Now Colonel Philip Corso, a retired American army officer, has written a book in which he becomes the highest-ranking person to give evidence that what crashed was not, as the Pentagon insisted, a high-altitude balloon, but an alien spacecraft. […]

During the night of July 2,1947, there was a violent thunderstorm over Roswell army airfield (RAAF) in New Mexico, then home to the only atomic bomber squadron in the world. The next morning a rancher, checking for storm damage, stumbled across wreckage and strange shiny material which he could not bend or tear, and which he had never seen before. On July 8 the local newspaper published a report headlined 'RAAF captures flying saucer on ranch in Roswell region'.

The military authorities at first claimed the wreckage was part of a weather balloon. Within hours the owner of a local radio station was contacted by the Pentagon and warned that he would lose his licence if he continued to transmit news of the find. Later it was said that the debris belonged to a high-altitude balloon being used to monitor Soviet nuclear tests.

In his book *The Day after Roswell*, Corso claims not only to have seen an alien who had been killed in the crash but also to have examined the Pentagon's secret files on the incident. Corso says that the Pentagon shipped the bodies of aliens to the Walter Reed Hospital in Washington, where autopsies were performed. [...]

He claims that while he was based at Fort Riley in Kansas in July 1947, he became curious about a mysterious group of sealed boxes that had been stored in a secure area. One night, armed with a torch, he prised open one of the containers.

Inside he says, was an astonishing sight: 'The contents, enclosed in a thick glass container, were submerged in a thick light blue fluid. [...]

'It was a 4ft human-shaped figure with arms, bizarre-looking four-fingered hands – I didn't see a thumb – thin legs and feet, and an oversized incandescent lightbulb-shaped head that looked like it was floating

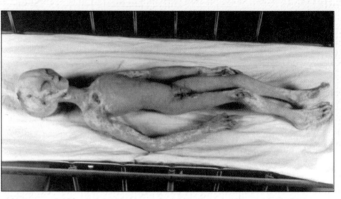

over a balloon gondola for a chin. I had the urge to touch the pale grey skin. But I couldn't tell whether it was skin because it also looked like a very thin one-piece head-to-toe fabric covering the creature's flesh.'

George Knapp, an investigative reporter and UFO expert, said: 'Corso brings a level of credibility to these revelations that has been sorely lacking in the past. I strongly suggest that interested parties keep open minds about his claims.'

But Karl Pflock, a former assistant secretary of defence and a writer on UFOs who is working on his own account of Roswell, said 'the book is a cross between a 1940 pulp thriller and contemporary pop science fiction. It is one big outrageous joke that a retired officer could pull off this kind of thing. He offers no proof, no back-up and no documentation.'

James Adams and Maurice Chittenden

DEVELOPMENT

3 Language

Explain the following figures of speech.

- from out of the blue
- open minds

4 Language

There are ten paragraphs in this article.

Come up with a ten-point plan the writers might have used. Write in note form.

5 Language

Find examples of the following.

- an eyewitness account
- a fact
- expert opinion
- an opinion

6 Reading

Copy and fill in the following table with as much information as you can.

Evidence/arguments for Roswell	Evidence/arguments against Roswell

7 Reading

What allegedly happened at Roswell in July 1947?

8 Reading

Outline Philip Corso's claims in your own words.

9 Reading and writing

Try to find additional information about the Roswell incident by using the Internet and your nearest library. Continue to make notes using the table in Activity 6.

10 Speaking and listening

Imagine that you work for the radio station in Roswell which originally broadcast news of the alien space crash. Perform this famous broadcast. Include:

- an explanation of what supposedly took place
- interviews with interested parties.

11 Writing

Write a discursive essay with the title 'Roswell: Fact or Fiction?'. Include:

- an introductory paragraph
- evidence and arguments for and against
- eyewitness accounts
- expert opinion
- your own interpretation
- a concluding paragraph expressing your opinion after assessing the evidence and arguments.

Remember:

- keep to the title
- write clearly
- organise ideas into paragraphs
- use link words and phrases
- use the third person
- maintain a formal register.

REVIEW

In the opinion of your class, what are the most convincing arguments for and against the Roswell incident? What are the main things you have to remember when putting together information in any essay?

UNIT 20 Vocabulary building: word borrowing

AIMS

- To apply knowledge of word origins and families in understanding and using new words.
- To make use of a good etymological dictionary.

STARTER

1

See how many words you can make with the following Latin and Greek prefixes.

- **Latin:** extra   multi   pre   semi
- **Greek:** di   hydro   mono   para

Find out what these prefixes mean.

DEVELOPMENT

2

Using a good etymological dictionary find the nearest equivalent French word from which these English words originated.

**barrister   beef   coupon   crayon
crown   detour   duke   mutton
realm   regard   royal**

3

Use these French words and phrases, which are commonly used in English, in sentences of your own – you may have to look them up in a dictionary first.

déjà vu   *laissez faire*
fait accompli   *rendezvous*
faux pas   *tour de force*
femme fatale

4

Use the following common English words which originally came from Greek and Latin in sentences of your own.

- **Greek:** camera   dilemma   drama   phase   tonic
- **Latin:** alibi   bonus   genius   junior   virus

5

> A **morpheme** is the smallest unit of a word that has a meaning in its own right. Morphemes consist of roots and affixes (prefixes and suffixes).

Many scientific or technological words are formed from Greek and Latin morphemes. Work out the meaning of any of the morphemes in the following scientific and technological words (e.g. *centi* = from Latin for 'hundred'; *pede* = from Latin for 'foot'). Write down which language they come from.

**centipede   antenatal   binary
diagonal   equilateral   geography
hydrogen   kilometre   polygon
microbiology   telescope   ultrasonic**

6

English has borrowed words from many other languages. Match the following 'English' words to their language of origin. You should be able to guess many of the origins quite easily but you may need a dictionary to find the source language for some of them.

algebra bangle blitz bog boomerang budgerigar caviar cheetah
chimpanzee coffee coracle cossack curry ditto fez gazette ghoul
glasnost gorilla gull harem hickory judo kangaroo karate kindergarten
kiosk moose opera polka raccoon samurai sari sauerkraut seminar
sequin shampoo sofa soviet teak thug tycoon umbrella vodka
voodoo wigwam wombat yodel yoghurt zebra

See if you can find any other words from these languages of origin as you use your dictionary.

Language of origin	Words
African languages	
American Indian	
Arabic	
Aboriginal	
Celtic (Scottish and Irish Gaelic)	
German	
Indian	
Italian	
Japanese	
Slavonic (Russian, Polish, Czech, etc.)	
Spanish	
Turkish	

REVIEW

You now have an understanding of word formation and derivation.
See if you can list the main ways in which words have come into the English language.

UNIT 21 Frankenstein's monster

AIMS

- To read a extract from the 19th century.
- To make use of descriptive detail.
- To use a thesaurus.

STARTER

1

Find synonyms that could be used in a descriptive passage instead of these words.

**fear   cold   stormy
happy   warm   peaceful**

INTRODUCTION

Frankenstein by Mary Shelley (published in 1818) was inspired by the work of Erasmus Darwin, who was supposed to have given inanimate matter a spark of life. How does Victor Frankenstein feel after eventually bringing his monster to life?

2

What techniques does the writer use to create an atmosphere of horror?

DEVELOPMENT

3 Language

Try and work out the meanings of these words by referring to the words around them in the text.

- beheld
- infuse
- agitated
- delineate
- endeavoured

4 Language

Pick out an example of each of the following.

- a rhetorical question
- an exclamation
- a list with semi-colons
- a semi-colon which breaks a sentence in half

5 Reading

Explain how the writer develops a hideous description of the monster. Comment on:

- attention to specific detail
- use of interesting adjectives, expressions and vocabulary.

6 Reading

Describe the reaction of Victor Frankenstein to 'the miserable monster' he has created. Write about:

- his thoughts and feelings
- his actions.

7 Speaking and listening

Imagine one of you is Victor Frankenstein and the other is his monster. Act out a conversation between monster and creator in Frankenstein's bedroom.

8 Writing

Write an account of what happens the day after Victor Frankenstein brings his monster to life. Consider:

- Victor's attitude to the monster
- the behaviour of the monster
- what Victor Frankenstein might do next.

Try to develop the same level of intense

Frankenstein

It was on a dreary night of November that I beheld the accomplishment of my toils. With an anxiety that almost amounted to agony, I collected the instruments of life around me, that I might infuse a spark of being into the lifeless thing that lay at my feet. It was already one in the morning; the rain pattered dismally against the panes, and my candle was nearly burnt out, when, by the glimmer of the half-extinguished light, I saw the dull yellow eye of the creature open; it breathed hard, and a convulsive motion agitated its limbs.

How can I describe my emotions at this catastrophe, or how delineate the wretch whom with such infinite pains and care I had endeavoured to form? His limbs were in proportion, and I had selected his features as beautiful. Beautiful! – Great God! His yellow skin scarcely covered the work of muscles and arteries beneath; his hair was of a lustrous black, and flowing; his teeth of a pearly whiteness; but these luxuriances only formed a more horrid contrast with his watery eyes, that seemed almost of the same colour as the dun white sockets in which they were set, his shrivelled complexion and straight black lips.

The different accidents of life are not so changeable as the feelings of human nature. I had worked hard for nearly two years, for the sole purpose of infusing life into an inanimate body. For this I had deprived myself of rest and health. I had desired it with an ardour that far exceeded moderation; but now that I had finished, the beauty of the dream vanished, and breathless horror and disgust filled my heart. Unable to endure the aspect of the being I had created, I rushed out of the room, and continued a long time traversing my bedchamber, unable to compose my mind to sleep. At length lassitude succeeded to the tumult I had before endured; and I threw myself on the bed in my clothes, endeavouring to seek a few moments of forgetfulness. But it was in vain: I slept, indeed, but I was disturbed by the wildest dreams. [...]

I started from my sleep with horror; a cold dew covered my forehead, my teeth chattered, and every limb became convulsed: when, by the dim and yellow light of the moon, as it forced its way through the window shutters, I beheld the wretch – the miserable monster whom I had created. He held up the curtain of the bed; and his eyes, if eyes they may be called, were fixed on me. His jaws opened, and he muttered some inarticulate sounds, while a grin wrinkled his cheeks. He might have spoken, but I did not hear; one hand was stretched out, seemingly to detain me, but I escaped, and rushed down stairs. I took refuge in the courtyard belonging to the house which I inhabited; where I remained during the rest of the night, walking up and down in the greatest agitation, listening attentively, catching and fearing each sound as if it were to announce the approach of the demoniacal corpse to which I had so miserably given life.

Mary Shelley

---

description and heightened atmosphere as in the extract.

9 Writing 🏠

You are on your way home from a friend's house late at night. You see Frankenstein's hideous monster. Write a witness statement for the police. What was your reaction? What happened?

REVIEW

Artificially created intelligence has many potential benefits, but what disadvantages do you think there might be to creating intelligent life forms? How have Mary Shelly's 19th century warnings about artificial intelligence been developed in modern films and literature?

UNIT 22 The Terminator

AIMS

- To consider how magazine articles are made appealing and entertaining.
- To consider links between paragraphs by examining their openings and endings.
- To make use of a dictionary.

STARTER

1

Use a dictionary to find the difference between these pairs of words? Put them in sentences of your own.

- adverse/averse
- credible/creditable
- alternate/alternative
- momentary/momentous
- comprehend/apprehend
- oral/aural

INTRODUCTION

As artificial intelligence and robotics becomes more advanced, should human beings worry? Read the article opposite and decide whether you think humans should develop robots such as The Terminator.

2

What predictions for the future of artificial intelligence have been made by Kevin Warwick of Reading University?

DEVELOPMENT

3 Language

Put the following easily confused words into separate sentences.

- distract/attract
- resilience/resistance
- discovered/uncovered

4 Language

Look closely at the structure of the extract. Write down the subject of the topic sentence and final sentence of each paragraph. Use your answers to write a summary of the article.

5 Reading

How is the Terminator different from a human being?

6 Reading

Give two consequences of the artificially intelligent satellite defence system, Skynet, becoming 'self-aware'?

7 Speaking and listening

Your friend has an accident. As a result you discover that he or she is an artificially intelligent robot. Describe your discovery to another friend, a teacher or a parent.

8 Writing

It is the year 2100. Artificial intelligence has conquered mankind and has taken over the running of the world. Write a diary entry describing the world you live in. Write about:

- day-to-day activities and new technology
- law and order
- your thoughts, feelings and fears for the future.

9 Writing

You buy a robot to help your parents with everyday household chores. Produce the magazine advertisement that persuaded you to buy the robot.

TERMINATOR

He's the ultimate hero or the perfect villain, depending on how you program him. Brought to life on screen by Arnold Schwarzenegger, the Terminator is a cyber-survivor – and one of the greatest robot movie icons of all time.

Terminator – or to give him his full name – the 800 series Terminator model 101 – is the ultimate fighting machine. Unlike a human being, he has no personal feelings, hopes or fears to distract him from his mission. As a machine, he's built to last, and no matter what you do to him, he just keeps coming.

ROBOT VS MAN

James Cameron's story behind the Terminator's creation is a chilling warning about the dangers of technology. Skynet, an artificially intelligent satellite defence system, unexpectedly becomes self-aware – and decides that planet earth would be a much nicer place without human beings. It triggers off a nuclear war, and from the ashes builds a machine-dominated world, where humans are hunted down by superior robots. […]

COMPLETE FANTASY?

In *Terminator 2* the T-800 is sent from the future to protect a ten-year-old boy from a deadly enemy who wants to change the course of history. The film demonstrates how a machine with the right programming could be a wonderful boon to mankind. Dedicated to preserving the life of Tom Connor (who will one day grow into a hero who saves mankind from machine domination), The Terminator becomes a kind of perfect father figure – a protector who can never lose

patience, become angry, get bored or careless. […]

The powerful story behind *The Terminator* was complete fantasy when it was dreamt up – but elements of it now have the disturbing ring of truth. […] Kevin Warwick, Professor of Cybernetics at Reading University, has warned that once man creates artificial

intelligence, he won't get the chance to switch it off. He also believes that machines could dominate mankind by the middle of this century.

In the year 2000, Dr Soorsaka at the Institute of Technology in Ladkrabang, Bangkok, invented 'Roboguard,' a security robot designed to shoot intruders. Although Roboguard has the limitation of being fixed to one spot, Dr Soorsaka is keen to develop his invention as a 'walking system.'

Is this the first step along the road to building a real-life Terminator?

Real Robots

---

10 **Writing**

Write a critical review of a film you have seen recently for a teenage magazine. Comment on:

 the genre of the film
 its suitability for people of your age
 plot and characters
 sets and location
 entertainment value
 your personal response to the film.

Consider presentational features which make the article appealing, such as layout, headings, fonts, etc.

REVIEW

Read through each other's film reviews. Do they look as though they come from a magazine? What features have you used to make the review appealing to the reader?

UNIT 23 Isaac Asimov

AIMS

- To compare two non-fiction texts.
- To integrate information from a variety of sources into a coherent account.

STARTER

1

> A verb is **active** when the subject of a sentence or a clause carries out the action (e.g. <u>Brian</u> (subject) <u>kicked</u> (active verb) the ball into the empty net).
>
> A verb is **passive** when the subject has the action done to it (e.g. The ball <u>was kicked</u> into the empty net).

Are the verbs in the following sentences active or passive?

a Jean painted a picture.
b The picture was painted.
c The meal was prepared by my husband.
d My Mum planted the hanging baskets.

Change these sentences into the passive voice.

e The pupil shouted at the teacher.
f The cat knocked over the vase.

INTRODUCTION

Dr Isaac Asimov's highly popular 'Robot' series introduced the idea that an advanced robot may eventually rival a human being in terms of intelligence and function. How did Asimov's writing change the way robots were portrayed in popular science fiction?

2

What were Asimov's thoughts on a future world dominated by robots?

DEVELOPMENT

3 Language

By using a dictionary see if you can trace the origins of the word 'robot'. Where does the word 'cyborg' come from? What does it mean?

4 Language

Find any examples of technical language in this article.

5 Reading

How did *Bicentennial Man* change the image of robots?

6 Reading

What were the purpose of Asimov's 'Three Laws of Robotics'?

7 Speaking and listening

Write a short speech on one of the following.

- The benefits of artificial intelligence such as robots and computers.
- The dangers of artificial intelligence.

Deliver your speech to the rest of the class. Remember to:

- vary the pace, expression and volume of your voice
- avoid sounding as if you are reading the speech aloud.

8 Speaking and listening

Produce a short TV commercial advertising a new robot for use in the home.

Isaac ASIMOV

He knew next to nothing about the nuts and bolts of building robots, yet his visionary ideas changed the way people think about artificial intelligence. Today he is regarded by many as the father of robotics.

Science Fiction writers have often predicted the future, but none have had such a profound effect on the science they wrote about as Asimov. In fact, he even invented the word 'robotics' – thereby guaranteeing himself immortality in the world of servos and sensors. [...]

Asimov was the first writer to really get under the skin of artificial intelligence. In stories like *Bicentennial Man*, he changed the image of robots, showing them as intelligent and sensitive individuals. He often portrayed them as a misunderstood minority, victims of human prejudice.

Protecting mankind

Asimov imagined a future in which robots would be man's protectors. He invented his famous 'Three Laws of Robotics', creating a core programming which would ensure man and machine would live together in harmony.

Race of slaves

[...] Of course, Asimov went much further than regarding robots merely as tools. He asked potentially uncomfortable questions about the rights of robots. Was mankind inventing a new race of slaves to serve him,

Isaac Asimov's Laws of Robotics

1 A robot may not injure a human being, or through inaction allow a human to come to harm.
2 A robot must obey orders given to him by human beings except where such orders would conflict with the First Law.
3 A robot must protect its own existence as long as such protection does not conflict with the First or Second Law.

or would intelligent robots one day have the rights and freedoms of individuals? [...]

Asimov was not frightened by the idea of a future in which mankind would hand over control to machines. [...] 'The time will come,' he suggested, 'when we will think back on a world without computers and shiver over the loneliness of humanity in those days.'

Asimov was confident that machines would never be the enemies of humans. He believed that human intelligence was of such a unique kind that machines would always find us invaluable partners. 'They will need us as much as we need them. There will be two, not one us,' he said. 'I rather like that thought.'

Real Robots

---

9 Writing

Write an essay comparing the two magazine articles 'Isaac Asimov' and 'Terminator' (Unit 22). Focus on:

- similarities and differences
- subjects and ideas
- language and style
- angle (the approach and focus)
- structure (paragraphs and sections)
- opinions and arguments.

10 Writing

Write an essay entitled 'Robots and Artificial Intelligence: Friends or Foe?'.

REVIEW

Do you think improvements in technology are always a good thing? Make a list of things to remember when comparing non-fiction texts.

UNIT 24
Non-standard English: accent and dialect

AIMS

- To explore differing attitudes towards language.
- To identify characteristics of non-standard and standard English.

STARTER

1

Write down the names of some regional accents which appear around the British Isles. Can you think of any words or phrases which are often said by people who speak with each particular accent? Can you think of any characters from TV, radio or film who speak with a particular accent?

> **Received pronunciation** (RP) is the accent of standard English and is still used by many newsreaders and presenters on national television. RP is the pronunciation which is given in dictionaries.

DEVELOPMENT

2

The verses at the bottom of this page are taken from an old Lancashire folk song called 'Owd Johnny Walker', which is about a man buying horses at Middleton fair. See if you can read it out using an appropriate Lancashire accent. Then rewrite it as it would sound in your accent. Substitute words from your own dialect and change the name of 'Alky Wood' for a local place name.

3

The two extracts opposite are supposed to be read in an Australian and a Caribbean accent. Read them out loud and work out which is which.

Owd Johnny Walker

Owd Johnny Walker went to Middleton Fair,
Bowt three horses, one was a mare,
One was blind and one couldn't see
And the other had 'is 'ead where 'is tail should be.

He rode her up through Alky Wood
He thowt it ud do 'er a bit of good
Bunged her 'ead again a tree
An' our owd mare was fit to dee.

Tables

Headmaster a come, mek has'e! Si-down.
Amy! min' yuh bruck Jane collar-bone,
Tom! Tek yuh foot off o'de desk,
Sandra Wallace, mi know yuh vex
But beg yuh get off o' Joseph head.
Tek de lizard off o' Sue neck, Ted! [...]

Valerie Bloom

Poe-Tree

G'day yous lot. Macca 'ere.
Gunna do some of this wicked poe-tree stuff
  today.
Gordo, you tryin' to make Tommo 'n Bennie
  kiss or sumpin?
Tommo, is that you or your monkey that's
  squeakin'?
Wellie, stop splashin' about there in that
  puddle you just made.

Scotch Corner Junior School

4

In 'Tables', what do you think 'mek has'e' might mean? Translate 'mi know yuh vex'.

5

What do think is meant by 'poe-tree'? Translate 'G'day yous lot'.

6

Dialect words are colloquial words which are common in a particular region. See if you can find out what the following words mean.

bairn beck brew butty ginnell gradely heartsome hungered snicket twitten nicker snitch mardle cuddy snap mullock

Think of some dialect words from the place you live in.

7

What slang or dialect words could you use to describe the following?

- Being tired.
- Being hungry.
- Being very thirsty.
- Something being very easy.
- Someone dying.
- A stupid person.
- Someone who's drunk.
- Someone who does well at school.
- An attractive person of the opposite sex.
- Someone who's scruffy.

REVIEW

This unit has helped you to appreciate different accents and dialects, some of which you might find hard to understand. Do you think everybody should try to speak with the same accent? If not, why not? Is it ever any advantage to speak in received pronunciation or to have a regional accent?

UNIT 25 Conditions in the Great War

AIMS

- To begin to appreciate the work of a major poet from the First World War.
- To use descriptive detail to convey a sense of horror and sadness.

STARTER

1

Colloquial English is the type of informal language we use in everyday conversation (e.g. 'We had a right good laugh with our mates').

Find as many standard English synonyms as you can for the underlined colloquial words and phrases.

a My mum was <u>mad</u> at me.
b My mate's <u>dead</u> funny.
c I'm <u>fed up</u> with school – it's boring.
d Bill was <u>told off</u> by Miss Smith.

INTRODUCTION

The First World War, or Great War (1914–1918), virtually destroyed a whole generation of young English men. One young soldier, Wilfred Owen, was tragically killed in action in 1918 one week before the end of the war. His legacy is a collection of poems which portray the terrible misery and suffering of his comrades. How does 'Exposure' create a strong feeling of pity for the unfortunate soldiers?

2

After reading 'Exposure', what do you consider to be the worst part of being a soldier in the First World War?

DEVELOPMENT

Consonance is the rhyming of consonants other than those at the start of a word (e.g. 'The ca**t** sa**t** on the ma**t**' contains a series of 't' sounds).
A *rhetorical question* is a question which does not require an answer but is used to make a point (e.g. Do we need school?).

3 Language

How are alliteration, onomatopoeia and consonance used in the first verse?

4 Language

Explain the metaphor in lines 13–14.

5 Language

Pick out the following.

- a rhetorical question
- an example of repetition

What effect do these techniques have on the thoughts and feelings of the reader?

6 Reading

Explain how Wilfred Owen creates a sense of suffering in this poem. Comment on:

- use of language and imagery
- use of the senses
- the actions of the soldiers.

7 Speaking and listening

Imagine you are two veterans of the First World War. Discuss what conditions were like during the war when you meet at a reunion.

8 Writing

Write your diary entry for the day described in 'Exposure'. Write about:

Exposure

Our brains ache, in the merciless iced east winds that
    knive us …
Wearied we keep awake because the night is silent …
Low, drooping flares confuse our memory of the
    salient …
Worried by silence, sentries whisper, curious, nervous,
      But nothing happens.   5

Watching, we hear the mad gusts tugging on the wire,
Like twitching agonies of men among its brambles.
Northward, incessantly, the flickering gunnery rumbles,
Far off, like a dull rumour of some other war.
      What are we doing here?   10

The poignant misery of dawn begins to grow …
We only know war lasts, rain soaks, and clouds sag
    stormy.
Dawn massing in the east her melancholy army
Attacks once more in ranks on shivering ranks of grey,
      But nothing happens.   15

Sudden successive flights of bullets streak the silence.
Less deathly than the air that shudders black with
    snow,
With sidelong flowing flakes that flock, pause, and
    renew;
We watch them wandering up and down the wind's
    nonchalance,
      But nothing happens.   20

Pale flakes with fingering stealth come feeling for our
    faces –
We cringe in holes, back on forgotten dreams, and
    stare, snow-dazed,
Deep into grassier ditches. So we drowse, sun-dozed,
Littered with blossoms trickling where the blackbird
    fusses,
    – Is it that we are dying?   25

Slowly our ghosts drag home: glimpsing the sunk fires,
    glozed
With crusted dark-red jewels; crickets jingle there;
For hours the innocent mice rejoice: the house is theirs;
Shutters and doors, all closed: on us the doors are
    closed, –
      We turn back to our dying.   30

Since we believe not otherwise can kind fires burn;
Nor ever suns smile true on child, or field, or fruit.
For God's invincible spring our love is made afraid;
Therefore, not loath, we lie out here; therefore were
    born,
      For love of God seems dying.   35

Tonight, this frost will fasten on this mud and us,
Shrivelling many hands, puckering foreheads crisp.
The burying-party, picks and shovels in shaking grasp,
Pause over half-known faces. All their eyes are ice,
      But nothing happens.   40

Wilfred Owen

- what you did
- your thoughts and feelings
- conditions in and around the
  battlefield.

Remember to be descriptive and use
relevant detail whenever necessary.
Appeal to the senses of the reader.

9 Reading and writing

By using either the Internet or your
library find out as much as you can
about Wilfred Owen. Write a short
biography of his life.

REVIEW

Have you managed to convey Wilfred
Owen's sense of misery and sadness in
your own writing? Why is it important for
people to read Wilfred Owen's poetry?

UNIT 26 Attitudes in the Great War

AIMS

- To compare the themes and styles of two major poets.
- To extend understanding and appreciation of the English literary heritage and the poetry of the Great War.

STARTER

1

Put the following examples of colloquial language into standard English.

- My teacher's always having a <u>right go at me</u>.
- My Gran's got a <u>dicky ticker</u>.
- School <u>gets up my nose</u> sometimes.
- There's a <u>dead fit lad</u> in our class.
- <u>Me and me mates got our hair done</u> in town today.
- That bike seems <u>dodgy</u> to me.

Now write two colloquial sentences of your own.

> A **sonnet** is a fourteen-line poem which generally has lines of ten syllables. Sonnets are often organised into two stanzas: an eight-line **octave** and a six-line **sestet**. They follow a variety of rhyme schemes.

INTRODUCTION

Siegfried Sassoon and Wilfred Owen were great friends, despite coming from very different backgrounds. Read the following poems and work out what these two men thought about serving their country by fighting in the First World War – what message were they trying to convey?

2

How does each poet feel about the sacrifices made by the soldiers in the First World War?

Anthem for Doomed Youth

What passing-bells for these who die as
    cattle?
– Only the monstrous anger of the guns.
  Only the stuttering rifles' rapid rattle
Can patter out their hasty orisons.
No mockeries now for them; no prayers nor
    bells;
  Nor any voice of mourning save the choirs, –
The shrill, demented choirs of wailing shells;
  And bugles calling for them from sad shires.

What candles may be held to speed them all?
  Not in the hands of boys but in their eyes
Shall shine the holy glimmers of goodbyes.
  The pallor of girls' brows shall be their pall;
Their flowers the tenderness of patient
    minds,
And each slow dusk a drawing-down of
    blinds.

Wilfred Owen

Glory of Women

You love us when we're heroes, home on leave,
Or wounded in a mentionable place.
You worship decorations; you believe
That chivalry redeems the war's disgrace.
You make us shells. You listen with delight,
By tales of dirt and danger fondly thrilled.
You crown our distant ardours while we fight,
And mourn our laurelled memories when we're
   killed.
You can't believe that British troops 'retire'
When hell's last horror breaks them, and they run,
Trampling the terrible corpses – blind with blood.
   O German mother dreaming by the fire,
   While you are knitting socks to send your son
   His face is trodden deeper in the mud.

                                    Siegfried Sassoon

DEVELOPMENT

3 Language

Explain how Wilfred Owen conveys the sound of the battlefield through the use of alliteration and onomatopoeia in 'Anthem for Doomed Youth'.

4 Language

Find one rhetorical question in 'Anthem for Doomed Youth' and explain its significance.

5 Language

Why is the word 'you' repeated in the first part of 'Glory of Women'?

6 Reading

In 'Glory of Women', what is the attitude of people at home towards the war?

7 Reading

According to Wilfred Owen, what bells were rung and what prayers (orisons) were said for the dying men?

8 Speaking and listening

Imagine that a war breaks out. You and your friend are contemplating volunteering to join the armed forces. Act out a conversation in which you discuss reasons for and against joining the fight.

9 Writing

Compare and contrast the two poems, examining closely the following.
- rhyme, rhythm and structure
- imagery – metaphors, similes and personification
- sound effects – alliteration, onomatopoeia and consonance
- mood and atmosphere
- conditions during the war for the soldiers
- the attitude of people at home
- the general attitude of the two poets towards the war and the people at home

Write about the structure, language and style of each poem, looking for similarities and differences.

10 Reading and writing

Using the Internet or a library, try to find out as much as you can about the First World War. Write up the information in the form of an entry for a reference book, using the following headings.
- Background
- Main events
- Conditions

REVIEW

How do these poems show that the poets believed their suffering could never be appreciated or recognised sufficiently by people at home? What are the most important things to consider when comparing two poems?

253

UNIT 27 The Great War: *Journey's End*

AIMS

- To analyse the language, form and dramatic impact of scenes from a play by a published dramatist.
- To write in sustained standard English for a specific purpose.
- To develop and compare different interpretations of scenes from a play.

STARTER

1

> **Overused words** are words that are used so often that they have come to lack meaning and impact (e.g. 'nice', 'thing', 'sad', 'nasty', 'good', 'bad', 'small', 'big').

Using a thesaurus, find as many synonyms as you can for each of these overused words.

nice   said   nasty   good   big

INTRODUCTION

Set in 1918 (and written in 1928), the play *Journey's End* centres around a young Company Commander, Dennis Stanhope. Raleigh, the young officer in this scene, hero-worships Stanhope, who is a born leader. Come up with a list of qualities you need to be a successful leader.

2

How does Raleigh show respect for Stanhope despite his fatal injuries?

Journey's End

A vague white line of dawn is broadening above the dark trench wall outside.
STANHOPE sits at the table and sips his tea. He takes a cigarette and lights it with a quavering hand.
RALEIGH comes from his dug-out.
STANHOPE lowers his head and writes in his notebook.

RALEIGH Do you want me to go up?

STANHOPE (*without looking up*) Yes. Trotter's gone.

RALEIGH Right. (*He goes up the steps and turns shyly.*) Cheero – Stanhope.

STANHOPE (*still writing with lowered head*) Cheero, Raleigh. I shall be coming up soon. (*RALEIGH goes up the steps.*)
STANHOPE stops writing, raises his head,

and listens. The shells are falling steadily now. He glances towards the left-hand dug-out and calls.
Hibbert!
There is no reply. He slowly rises and goes to the left-hand dug-out doorway, he calls again – louder
Hibbert!! (*He looks into the doorway and says*) What are you doing?
HIBBERT appears. He is very pale; he moves as if half asleep.
Come along, man!

HIBBERT You want me to go up now?

STANHOPE Of course I do. The others have gone.

HIBBERT Got a drop of water?

STANHOPE What d'you want water for?

HIBBERT I'm so frightfully thirsty. All that champagne and stuff – dried my mouth up.

STANHOPE pours a drop of water into a mug and gives it to HIBBERT.

STANHOPE Here you are. Didn't you have any tea?

HIBBERT Yes. It was a bit sweet, though.

The shelling is steadily increasing, and now, above the lighter 'crush' of the smaller shells, there comes the deep resounding 'boom' of Minenwerfer. HIBBERT sips his water very slowly, rinsing his mouth deliberately with each sip. STANHOPE is by the doorway, looking up into the trench. He has just turned away as a sonorous drawn-out call comes floating through the dawn 'Stretcher bear-ers!' STANHOPE half turns, then faces HIBBERT.

STANHOPE Come on. Buck up.

HIBBERT There's no appalling hurry, is there?

STANHOPE No hurry! Why d'you think the others have gone up?

HIBBERT (*slowly*) What? Trotter and Raleigh?

STANHOPE (*sharply*) Wake up, man! What the devil's the matter with you?

HIBBERT slowly puts down his mug.

HIBBERT Champagne dries the mouth up so. Makes the tongue feel like a bit of paper.

There is a slight pause.

STANHOPE The longer you stay here, the harder it'll be to go up.

HIBBERT Good Lord! You don't think I'm –

STANHOPE You're just wasting as much time as you can.

HIBBERT Well, damn it, it's no good going

up till I feel fit. Let's just have another spot of water.

HIBBERT takes the jug and pours out a little more water. He is the picture of misery. STANHOPE stands impatiently beside him. MASON appears from his dug-out, fully dressed for the line, his rifle slung over his shoulder.

MASON I'll go right along sir. I've made up the fire to last a good three hours – if you don't mind me popping down about nine o'clock to 'ave a look at it.

STANHOPE All right, Mason. Mr. Hibbert's coming up now. You can go along with him.

MASON (*to Hibbert*) I'd like to come along with you if you don't mind, sir. I ain't bin up in this part of the front line. Don't want to get lorst.

STANHOPE Mr. Hibbert'll show you the way up. (*He turns to HIBBERT.*) Keep your men against the back wall of the trench as long as the shells are dropping behind. Cheero!

HIBBERT looks at STANHOPE for a moment, then with a slight smile, he goes slowly up the steps and into the trench, MASON following behind. A dark figure stands out against the pale sky; comes hurrying down the steps – a PRIVATE SOLDIER, out of breath and excited.

Yes?

SOLDIER Message from Mr. Trotter, sir. Shells falling mostly behind support line. Minnies along front line.

STANHOPE Who's just been hit?

SOLDIER Corporal Ross, I think it was, sir. Minnie dropped in the trench at the corner – just as I come away.

The SERGEANT-MAJOR comes down the steps, very much out of breath.

STANHOPE (*to the SOLDIER*) All right, thanks.

The SOLDIER salutes, and goes up the steps slower than he came.

S-M Beginning to get 'ot, sir.

STANHOPE Corporal Ross hit?

S-M Yessir.

STANHOPE Badly?

S-M Pretty badly, sir.

STANHOPE Most of the shelling's going over, isn't it?

S-M Most of the *shells* is be'ind, sir, but there's Minnies and rifle grenades along the front line. Pretty 'ot it's getting, sir. They're attacking down south – there's rifle fire.

STANHOPE All right, sergeant-major; thanks.

S-M What I come to ask, sir – what about the wounded – getting 'em down, sir? The shelling's pretty thick over Lancer's Alley.

STANHOPE What about Fosse Way?

S-M Pretty bad there, too, sir.

STANHOPE Don't try then. Take anyone badly hit down into the big dug-out on the right. Let the stretcher-bearers do what they can there.

S-M Very good, sir.

STANHOPE Only Corporal Ross hit?

S-M That's all, sir –

Again there comes the drawn-out call – several times as it is passed from man to man 'Stretcher bear-ers!' The SERGEANT-MAJOR'S eyes meet STANHOPE'S. He turns and goes up the steps.

STANHOPE is alone. Flying fragments of shell whistle and hiss and moan overhead.

The sharp 'crack' of the rifle grenades, the thud of the shells, and the boom of the Minenwerfer mingle together in a muffled roar. STANHOPE takes his belt from the table and buckles it on, puts his revolver lanyard round his neck, and drops his flask and sandwiches into his pocket.

The SERGEANT-MAJOR reappears and comes hurrying down the steps.

STANHOPE (*turning quickly*) What is it, sergeant-major?

S-M Mr. Raleigh, sir –

STANHOPE What!

S-M Mr. Raleigh's been 'it, sir. Bit of shell's got 'im in the back.

STANHOPE Badly?

S-M Fraid it's broke 'is spine, sir; can't move 'is legs.

STANHOPE Bring him down here.

S-M Down 'ere sir?

STANHOPE (*shouting*) Yes! Down here – quickly!

The SERGEANT-MAJOR hurries up the steps. A shell screams and bursts very near. The SERGEANT-MAJOR shrinks back and throws his hand across his face, as though a human hand could ward off the hot flying pieces. He stumbles on again into the trench, and hurriedly away.

STANHOPE is by OSBORNE'S bed, fumbling a blanket over it. He takes a trench coat off the wall and rolls it for a pillow. He goes to his own bed, takes up his blanket, and turns as the SERGEANT-MAJOR comes carefully down the steps carrying RALEIGH like a child in his huge arms

(*With blanket ready.*) Lay him down there.

S-M 'E's fainted, sir. 'E was conscious when I picked 'im up.

The SERGEANT-MAJOR lays the boy gently on the bed; he draws away his hands, looks furtively at the palms, and wipes the blood on the sides of his trousers. STANHOPE covers RALEIGH with his blanket, looks intently at the boy, and turns to the SERGEANT-MAJOR.

STANHOPE Have they dressed the wound?

S-M They've just put a pad on it, sir. Can't do no more.

STANHOPE Go at once and bring two men with a stretcher.

S-M We'll never get 'im down, sir, with them shells falling on Lancer's Alley.

STANHOPE Did you hear what I said? Go and get two men with a stretcher.

S-M (*after a moment's hesitation*) Very good, sir.

The SERGEANT-MAJOR goes slowly away. STANHOPE turns to RALEIGH once more, then goes to the table, pushes his handkerchief into the water-jug, and brings it, wringing wet, to RALEIGH'S bed. He bathes the boy's face. Presently RALEIGH gives a little moan, opens his eyes, and turns his head.

RALEIGH Hullo – Dennis –

STANHOPE Well, Jimmy – (*he smiles*) – you got one quickly. *There is silence for a while. STANHOPE is sitting on a box beside RALEIGH. Presently RALEIGH speaks again – in a wandering voice.*

RALEIGH Why – how did I get down here?

STANHOPE Sergeant-major brought you down.

RALEIGH speaks again, vaguely, trying to recollect.

RALEIGH Something – hit me in the back – knocked me clean over – sort of – winded me – I'm all right now. (*He tries to rise.*)

STANHOPE Steady, old boy. Just lie there quietly for a bit.

RALEIGH I'll be better if I get up and walk about. It happened once before – I got kicked in just the same place at Rugger; it – it soon wore off. It – it just numbs you for a bit. (*There is a pause.*) What's that rumbling noise?

STANHOPE The guns are making a bit of a row.

RALEIGH Our guns?

STANHOPE No. Mostly theirs.

Again there is silence in the dug-out. A very faint rose light is beginning to glow in the dawn sky. RALEIGH speaks again – uneasily.

RALEIGH I say – Dennis –

STANHOPE Yes, old boy?

RALEIGH It – it hasn't gone through, has it? It only just hit me? – and knocked me down?

STANHOPE It's just gone through a bit, Jimmy.

RALEIGH I won't have to – go on lying here?

STANHOPE I'm going to have you taken away.

RALEIGH Away? Where?

STANHOPE Down to the dressing-station – then hospital – then home. (*He smiles.*) You've got a Blighty one, Jimmy.

RALEIGH But I – I can't go home just for – for a knock in the back. (*He stirs restlessly.*) I'm certain I'll be better if – if I get up. (*He tries to raise himself, and gives a sudden cry.*) Oh – God! It does hurt!

STANHOPE It's bound to hurt, Jimmy.

RALEIGH What's – on my legs? Something holding them down –

STANHOPE It's all right, old chap; it's just the shock – numbed them.

Again there is a pause. When RALEIGH speaks, there is a different note in his voice.

RALEIGH It's awfully decent of you to bother, Dennis. I feel rotten lying here – everybody else – up there.

STANHOPE It's not your fault, Jimmy.

RALEIGH So – damn – silly – getting hit. (*Pause.*) Is there – just a drop of water?

STANHOPE (*rising quickly*) Sure. I've got some here. *He pours some water into the mug and brings it to RALEIGH.* (*Cheerfully.*) Got some tea-leaves in it. D'you mind?

RALEIGH No. That's all right – thanks – *STANHOPE holds the mug to RALEIGH'S lips, and the boy drinks.* I say, Dennis, don't you wait – if – if you want to be getting on.

STANHOPE It's quite all right, Jimmy.

RALEIGH Can you stay for a bit?

STANHOPE Of course I can.

RALEIGH (*faintly*) Thanks awfully.

There is quiet in the dug-out for a long time. STANHOPE sits with one hand on RALEIGH'S arm, and RALEIGH lies very still. Presently he speaks again – hardly above a whisper.

Dennis –

STANHOPE Yes, old boy?

RALEIGH Could we have a light? It's – it's so frightfully dark and cold.

STANHOPE (*rising*) Sure! I'll bring a candle and get another blanket.

STANHOPE goes to the left-hand dug-out, and RALEIGH is alone, very still and quiet, on OSBORNE'S bed. The faint rosy glow of the dawn is deepening to an angry red. The grey night sky is dissolving, and the stars begin to go. A tiny sound comes from where RALEIGH is lying – something between a sob and a moan. STANHOPE comes back with a blanket. He takes a candle from the table and carries it to RALEIGH'S bed. He puts it on the box beside RALEIGH and speaks cheerfully.

Is that better, Jimmy? (*RALEIGH makes no sign.*) Jimmy –

Still RALEIGH is quiet. STANHOPE gently takes his hand. There is a long silence. STANHOPE lowers RALEIGH'S hand to the bed, rises, and takes the candle back to the table. He sits on the bench behind the table with his back to the wall, and stares listlessly across at the boy on OSBORNE'S bed. The solitary candle-flame throws up the lines on his pale, drawn face, and the dark shadows under his tired eyes. The thudding of the shells rises and falls like an angry sea.

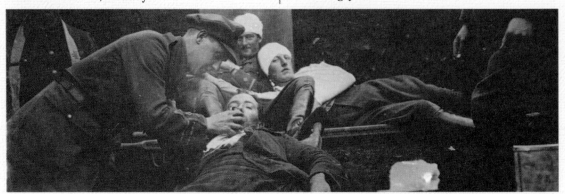

A PRIVATE SOLDIER comes scrambling down the steps, his round, red face wet with perspiration, his chest heaving for breath.

SOLDIER Message from Mr. Trotter, sir – will you come at once.

STANHOPE gazes round at the SOLDIER – and makes no other sign.

Mr. Trotter, sir – says will you come at once!

STANHOPE rises stiffly and takes his helmet from the table.

STANHOPE All right, Broughton, I'm coming.

The SOLDIER turns and goes away. STANHOPE pauses for a moment by OSBORNE'S bed and lightly runs his fingers over RALEIGH'S tousled hair. He goes stiffly up the steps, his tall figure black against the dawn sky.

R.C. Sherriff

DEVELOPMENT

3 Language

Find any words which place the passage above historically in the First World War. Which words would we use today to say the same things?

4 Reading

How does Hibbert delay going into action?

5 Reading

According to the Sergeant Major, how is the battle progressing?

6 Reading

How does Stanhope react when the injured Raleigh is brought to him?

7 Reading

How do you think the writer wanted the audience to react to this scene? Consider:

- how the writer uses dialogue and action to build tension
- the range of emotions portrayed
- the message about the nature of war
- your feelings at the end of the scene.

8 Speaking and listening

Imagine that you and a close friend are about to go into battle. Act out your final conversation.

9 Writing

Imagine you are Stanhope. Write a letter to Raleigh's family informing them of their son's tragic death. Write about:

- the way he died
- your own thoughts and feelings.

10 Writing

Write a short obituary for your local paper about an imaginary person who has just left your school and who dies in action.

11 Speaking and listening

You are directing a new film version of *Journey's End*. Rewrite the scene in which Stanhope tries to persuade Hibbert to go into action in a way that makes Stanhope seem aggressive and impatient. Look at the original script and consider stage directions on:

- dialogue (pace, volume and tone)
- the characters' actions.

REVIEW

What messages do you think R.C. Sherriff was trying to convey to his audience about the nature of war in the trenches? How convincingly does the message come across?

UNIT 28 A letter home from the Second World War

AIMS

- To examine the conventions governing letter writing.
- To write sustained standard English with formality suited to reader and purpose.

STARTER

1

> An **auxiliary verb** is a verb which helps the main verb in a phrase or sentence, for example, by indicating changes in tense (e.g. I <u>have</u> lost my keys, I <u>had</u> lost my keys, I <u>will</u> lose my keys). **Modal auxiliary verbs** ('can', 'could', 'may', 'might', 'must', 'ought', 'shall', 'should', 'will', 'would') help to express possibility.

Use the following modal auxiliary verbs in sentences of your own.

may might will would shall could

INTRODUCTION

The letter on page 261 was written by 21-year-old Gunner Arthur Kempster, one month before he was tragically killed in action. Why you do think Arthur avoids the subject of the war in his letter?

2

How does Arthur try to stop his relatives at home from worrying?

DEVELOPMENT

3 Language

Pick out three words from the text which we would not use nowadays. Write a modern equivalent next to each one.

4 Language

Come up with a list of guidelines on writing a personal letter. Think about:

- layout
- how your style might vary according to who you are writing to.

5 Reading

Why has Arthur not written since arriving in North Africa?

6 Reading

What does Arthur think of the new camp and the people in it?

7 Reading

What is Arthur's opinion of the way the war is going? Why do you think he is trying to sound so positive?

8 Speaking and listening

You are two soldiers serving in a war and it is the night before a major battle. Give each other instructions about what to do if anything should happen to you.

9 Writing

Imagine that you have had to go abroad to fight. Write a letter describing what has happened to you recently. Make it lively and interesting but write it in a style similar to Arthur's letter.

10 Writing

Write a newspaper report about Arthur's death. The facts are at the bottom of page 261.

A Letter Home From the Front, 1943

No. 14230440
Gnr Kempster A.
152nd Field Reg. R.A.
'B' Battery. D Troop
B.N.A.F.

28/3/43

Dear Nellie, Bob + Brian,

I hope you don't think that I have forgotten you, but I have been so busy ever since I arrived in North Africa, what with moving about and one thing and another, that this is the first available moment I have had.

As probably you will by now have heard, from home, I am at last getting settled. Just a few days since I was transferred to this regiment and in this regiment I will stay. I have made many pals since I have been in this country, but unfortunately we've never remained together very long. But now, I can make them and have already done so, knowing I will be with them for some time.

The camp is surprisingly good and the fellows are extremely sociable and very easy to associate with. One thing that has surprised me since I arrived at this regiment is the fact that all the officers and NCOs are so conversant with the men – so vastly different from our own country. The food is quite good and I can safely say up to now, I have had quite a good bed.

The weather, even though at present we are having a spot of rain, is terrific. [...] My work as a specialist out here is certainly more interesting than ever it was before.

I have met some very intimate and personal local friends on my travels though I'm afraid I cannot disclose who they are. [...]

Fortunately I have been able to hear the English news once or twice. It certainly seems to be going well. Everybody, including myself, are firmly convinced it won't last long out here.

How is everyone at home (Norville)? If you are feeling as good as myself, you'll do. I don't suppose your old friend (asthma) has left you yet Nellie – has it? Well so long as you are keeping on top of it; that is the main thing. I suppose you Bob, are still plugging along at Dick Kerrs, and you Brian still as rum as ever.

Well folks, I suppose it's time I closed up for the present, and got in bed. The news is just about to begin and I can hear Big Ben chiming nine.

Until next time, cheerio and keep the home fires burning for me,

Your ever loving brother,

Arthur

PS [...] Don't worry, I am doing fine.

- Battle of the Fondouk Gap
- 8th April 1943
- last major battle of the Tunisian campaign – German army expelled May 1943
- Arthur Kempster – artillery range finder – Ayrshire Yeomanry
- killed by direct hit from German artillery shell

REVIEW

Before you read Arthur's letter, what would you have expected a soldier on active service to write about? Why do you think soldiers tried to sound so positive and 'settled' in their letters?

UNIT 29 Non-standard English

AIMS

- To explore differing attitudes towards English.
- To identify characteristics of non-standard and standard English.
- To look at current language trends.

STARTER

1

> **Cockney rhyming slang** is a colourful way of speaking in which things are referred to indirectly through rhymes (e.g. 'barnet' means 'hair' and comes from 'Barnet Fair').

What do these examples of Cockney rhyming slang mean?

apples and pears	hat
butcher's (hook)	beer
china (plate)	telephone
dog and bone	mate
elephant's (trunk)	car
jam jar	drunk
loaf (of bread)	tea
pig's ear	head
plates (of meat)	look
Rosey Lee	feet
titfer (tat)	suit
whistle and flute	stairs

Can you think of any other examples of Cockney rhyming slang? You could try making up some of your own.

> **Colloquialisms** are non-standard words and phrases which are not suitable in formal contexts but are used by the majority of English speakers in informal conversation (e.g. 'barmy', 'beat it', 'put the boot in', etc.).

DEVELOPMENT

2

Rewrite the following non-standard paragraph in standard English.

There was a bit of argy bargy outside our school. Some lads, they were a right bad lot, were hassling my mate Terry. Eventually he got smacked on his bonce by some cocky little kid who also put the boot in. Thought he was well hard with all his posse. Terry's conk was streaming. Some do-gooder and this dodgy geezer dived out the local boozer like greased lightning and sorted them. They were done for. Then I had to get Terry's mum on the blower – she was in a right flap. She had a right go at Terry for being out all hours and then grounded him. Then she had a paddy at me, shooting her mouth off, making out I was nowt but a yobbo. I was about to stick up for meself but she told me to shut me trap.

3

Talk about something exciting that happened to you after school one night. Imagine you are talking in the following contexts and adapt your speech accordingly.

- a formal situation in which you are telling your headteacher what happened
- an informal situation in which you are talking to a friend

Think about how your vocabulary and speech style might vary.

4

Find a standard English synonym for the

following slang words.

- cagey
- freak out
- goon
- knackered
- undies
- cock-up
- gab
- guts
- snide
- tripe
- doss
- gay
- jammy
- spiff
- toffee-nosed

5

Language changes over time, and words which were once common can go out of fashion. Do you know what the following old-fashioned slang words mean?

- bounder
- la-di-da
- smashing
- cad
- potty
- toff
- fiddlesticks
- rotter
- whopper

6

Write down five slang words you and your friends commonly use.

7

Text messaging is an increasingly common form of communication. See if you can translate the following text words into standard English.

TXT GR8 4GIV BCZ SUM LUV
MSG NE PLZ PWB THX TYM

8

Explain how three of the above text words have been formed.

9

🔑 **Jargon** is the specialist language associated with a subject or profession. The Internet is full of jargon (e.g. 'to spam', which means to bombard with useless e-mail, or 'to flame', which means to send abusive e-mails).

See if you can match up the following Internet jargon with its correct definition.

boil the ocean	standard version software with no extra features
bozo filter	anything published on paper, such as books, magazines and newspapers
cobweb site	a visitor to a chat room, newsgroup or online service who never posts a message
egosurf	not quite being able to remember where on the Internet you saw a particular piece of information
infix	typing your own name into a search engine to see what comes up
internesia	putting a witty comment between your first and last name on an e-mail, as in John 'trying-to-think-of-something-witty' Smith
lurker	a website that hasn't been updated for a long time
treeware	a program that filters e-mail to eliminate those on your bozo list
vanilla	to attempt something too ambitious

10

Explain how you think two of these terms came into existence. Do you know any other Internet jargon terms? If you do, test them on your friends.

REVIEW

Think about when it is appropriate to use non–standard forms instead of standard English. In what kind of situations might you have to use standard English?

UNIT 30 Streetfinder

AIMS

- To consider how non-fiction texts can convey information and ideas in an interesting and amusing way.
- To exploit presentational devices.
- To expand strategies for locating, extracting and evaluating information from a diagrammatical media text.

STARTER

1

> A **soap opera** is a popular serialised television programme that follows the ordinary lives of fictional characters over a long period of time. Some soap operas have three or four episodes a week and are very long running. They often deal with topical issues and move from one short scene to another, touching upon the lives of many different characters.

Write down what you consider to be the main ingredients of a successful soap opera.

INTRODUCTION

Coronation Street is the longest-running British television soap. The map on page 265 shows Weatherfield as it was in 1996. Characters in soaps change all the time. Choose three of the houses from Coronation Street and invent new characters who could be brought into the programme in the future.

2

Do you know of any characters who have left the street since this map was published? What advantages are there in describing *Coronation Street* in map form as opposed to ordinary sentences and paragraphs?

DEVELOPMENT

3 Language

> A **diagrammatical representation** is a method of conveying information in the form of a diagram (e.g. maps, flow charts, graphs, etc.).

How would you describe the language of the map and the close-up diagram of Coronation Street itself? Think about:

- vocabulary and content
- sentence structure.

4 Reading

What is the connection between Mavis Wilton in number 4 Coronation Street and Rita Sullivan?

5 Reading

What interest does Phyllis Pearce of number 4 Gorton Close have in Percy Sugden at number 1 Coronation Street and Des Barnes?

6 Reading

What kind of people live in Montreal House?

7 Speaking and listening

Imagine you want to buy a house in Coronation Street. Act out a conversation with one of the locals in which they tell you a little bit about the history of the street and its residents.

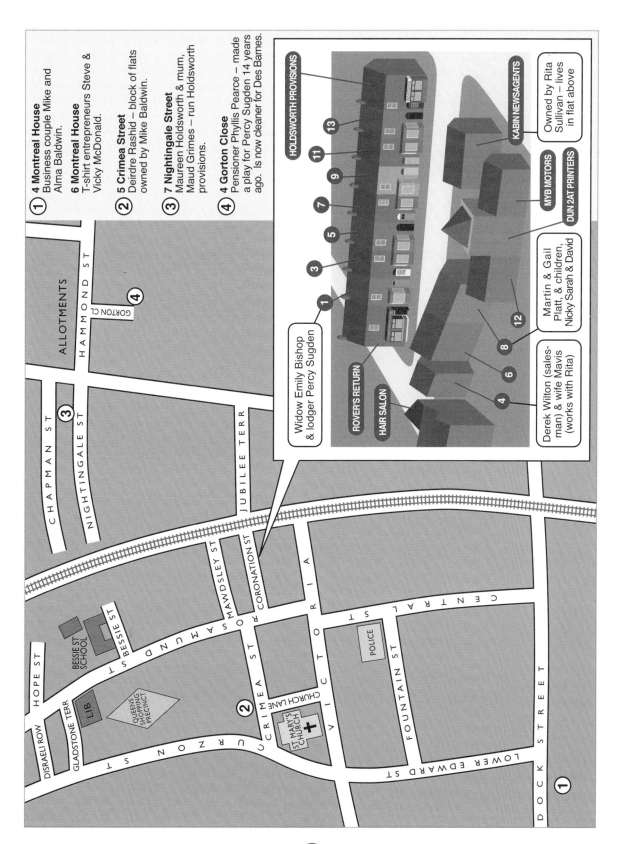

8 Writing

Using a flowchart or spider diagram, draw a character map representing the relationships between four characters in *Coronation Street*.

9 Writing

Draw a map or diagram of a completely new soap opera set. You may wish to produce your map or diagram in the same format as the 'Streetfinder' map. In your plans include:

- location, with place names and key local features (e.g. pub, shops, amenities, places of worship)
- labels indicating where people live and what they do.

10 Speaking and listening ✳

Discuss the key ingredients of a successful soap opera suitable for a teenage audience. Think about:

- storylines
- characters
- key locations
- themes.

11 Writing 🏠

Write a brief description of three characters from your proposed soap opera. Describe:

- their appearance
- their personality, behaviour and background

- their occupation and interests
- their relationships with other characters
- the attitudes of other characters towards them
- what is happening in their lives at the moment (e.g. excitement, romance, problems or challenges).

You may wish to present your work in the form of a fact file or profile.

12 Writing ✳ 🏠

Review a popular soap opera of your choice – write about:

- main characters
- key locations
- main storylines
- problems and conflicts
- romance
- themes
- audience
- things you like
- areas for improvement.

REVIEW

What are the advantages of representing your ideas in diagrammatic form? How easy was it to extract information from the map? What other kinds of diagram could have been used?

UNIT 31 Soap operas: planning a pilot episode

AIMS

- To develop knowledge of technical terms useful for discussing narrative.
- To record and develop ideas in a plot synopsis.
- To develop ideas for writing a soap opera script.

STARTER

1

List a number of issues you feel should be included in a soap opera that would appeal to teenagers.

 *A **storyliner** is someone who conceives and develops ideas for film or television. They tend to concentrate on developing plot and character.*

INTRODUCTION

The first stage of writing a soap opera is to plan the storyline. Below is a summary of the first part of a pilot episode of a forthcoming soap opera called 'Southsiders'. Decide what ideas, storylines and issues could be developed in future episodes.

2

How do think Charlene is going to react when she hears of Terry's business debts? What decisions do you think Tod and Karina have made?

Southsiders

Episode One

23rd April, 2040, estimated 100 million viewers worldwide.

This is where it all begins …

Tod Ranger is sitting alone in his small suburban flat, drinking whisky. In one hand he has a framed photograph of his ex-girlfriend, in the other, a packet of pills – we don't know if it's full or empty. He takes a last glug of whisky, throws the photo frame against the door and screws up the packet of pills. He slumps back in his chair.

Charlene Tomkinson is pregnant. Both she and her husband Terry think that when her mother finds out, she'll be distraught. Charlene's mother Jean is staying with them after recently being widowed, and was hoping to move in permanently. With four children around, there won't be room for her. Charlene is also worried about her sister Karina, who is experiencing marital difficulties. Charlene decides to tell her mother her news.

Terry Tomkinson is in his local pub (The Bear and Bells) drinking heavily and appearing very agitated. His wife's pregnancy is the last straw, as his business debts are accumulating. Unfortunately, his house guarantees some of his debts. Peter Worswick bursts in saying that he's called round for Tod and there's no answer. All Tod's lights are on and he can hear the TV. Something must be wrong. A group of men rush out of the pub to break into Tod's place.

Karina Clarkson, Tod's ex-girlfriend, is nursing a baby which is crying loudly. The rows she is having with her husband Brad are becoming increasingly violent, to the point that Brad hit her yesterday evening. Despite her new-found wealth and the birth of her daughter, she desperately regrets leaving Tod. She makes a decision ...

Terry Tomkinson, Peter Worswick and Karl Hines eventually break into Tod's flat to find him unconscious in his chair. Karl checks his pulse. Tod is still alive but has lapsed into a diabetic coma as he has not taken his medication. He has been acting strangely since he saw Karina at a party last weekend. He has decided to ...

DEVELOPMENT

3 Language

Match these terms with the correct definition.

cliffhanger	subjects which are important or topical in real life (e.g. AIDS, teenage pregnancy, domestic violence)
screenplay	people who help develop soap plots for screenplay writers
interweaving storylines	an ending which involves heightened tension or a crisis, designed to make the viewer want to watch the next episode
key location	the script of a film, soap or other TV programme
multiple narratives	a main meeting place for characters (e.g. the Rovers Return)
never-ending storyline	connected storylines going on at the same time
issues	several unconnected storylines going on at the same time
storyliners	a story that continues over several years

4 Language

Think of examples of some of the features described in Activity 3 for soap operas you watch on a regular basis.

5 Reading

Can you spot any of the following in the plot summary of *Southsiders*?

- interweaving storylines
- key location
- issues
- stereotypical soap characters
- action
- a possibility for a cliffhanger

6 Speaking and listening

Act out one of the following scenes.

a The conversation between Charlene Tomkinson and her mother about her pregnancy and her sister Karina's problems.

b The conversation in which Terry tells the landlord of the Bear and Bells about his problems.

7 Writing

Write a plot summary for a pilot episode of a new soap opera. You can use the set and some of the characters you began to develop in Unit 30. Think of a catchy name too.

8 Writing

Think about the first episode of your new soap opera and write notes about it under the following headings.

- Target audience
- Key locations
- Main characters
- Main storylines
- Issues

REVIEW

Do you think soap operas are generally realistic portrayals of life? Is your plot summary realistic? If it is a little far-fetched, how could you bring it back down to earth? Have you used some of the narrative techniques touched on in this unit?

UNIT 32 Screenplays

AIMS

- To look at different ways of structuring narratives and experimenting with narrative perspective.
- To convey action, character, atmosphere and tension in scripts and performances.
- To evaluate in writing a performance of a soap opera script.

STARTER

1

Write a list of things you would expect to see and hear in a trailer for a forthcoming episode of a popular soap.

INTRODUCTION

Once a storyline has been established the scriptwriters will begin their work. Imagine you are a producer – how would you go about filming the following script from *Southsiders*?

2

How is this script different from a playscript?

Southsiders – Episode 1

FADE IN

1. INT (Interior). EVENING. SMALL SUBURBAN FLAT.
The flat is littered with old cigarette packets, empty cups and the debris of several takeaways. TV noise in background. TOD RANGER, mid-thirties, is rocking to and fro clutching a framed photograph of his ex-girlfriend KARINA in one hand and a packet of pills in the other. He is clearly unwell. Tod is shouting.

TOD
(*medium close up*) Karina ... Oh God ... Why did you do it? We had everything! Why did you leave me for that ... Get out! Just get out of my life.
Tod throws the picture frame aggressively at the door. He throws the screwed up packet of pills on the floor.

TOD
(*close up*) Well, I'll show you. I hope you both rot in hell.
He tearfully closes his eyes.

2. INT. EVENING. SMALL SUBURBAN HOUSE.
A well-kept house, neat and colourful. Evidence of small children. CHARLENE THOMPSON, aged 35, is busy tidying the lounge when her mother JEAN walks in. Charlene is surprised.

CHARLENE
(*long shot*) Mum? I thought you were getting your hair done?

JEAN
So did I. Karina's baby's unwell again. Mobile hairdressers are all the same. Unreliable.
Jean moves over to the table, where she sits down slowly.

CHARLENE
Karina's not that bad.
Charlene is clearly angry at this comment about her sister Karina.

JEAN
(*medium long shot*) Oh, come on Charlene, she's terrible. Anyhow, has that twenty quid she owes you materialised? The money she's got!
Charlene by now is quite angry.

CHARLENE
She ran out of credits on her mobile. It wasn't her fault.

JEAN
Rubbish! No doubt phoning her fancy man.
Rushing over to confront her mum and shouting.

CHARLENE
How can you be like that about your own daughter?

JEAN
(*close up*) My daughter! A daughter of mine wouldn't have left her fiancé a week before her wedding.

3 Language

Match up the media terms with the correct definitions.

episode	the first instalment of a soap which goes out to test the public's reaction
pilot episode	a complete instalment of a soap opera
theme music	the events that take place
action	the music that appears during the opening and closing credits
dialogue	clips from a forthcoming episode to advertise the soap
trailer	the speech and conversations of actors
film crew	the person who oversees the shooting of the soap opera, tells the actors what to do and makes key decisions on set
director	people responsible for lighting, camera shots and sets

4 Reading

Why is Jean unpleasant about her daughter?

5 Reading

Who do you think Karina has been phoning?

6 Reading

In the first scene, the audience learns about Tod's relationship with Karina from his perspective. Consider how the scriptwriter:

- influences the audience's feelings about Tod
- influences the audience's opinions of Karina before they meet her.

7 Speaking and listening

Act out either scene and discuss the directions a director might give the cast.

8 Writing

Write your own soap opera script based on one scene from the plot summary you produced in Unit 31. Think about the layout and directions. Include:

- varied action and dialogue

- a variety of issues
- tension, conflict and humour
- atmosphere
- strong characters
- cliffhangers.

9 Speaking and listening

Act out some of your scripts in groups.

10 Writing

Write a review of your performance of the soap opera script.

11 Writing

Look closely at one scene from your script. Think about how you might film it. Break it down into a storyboard with one frame for each camera shot.

REVIEW

How did your group performance go? How easy was your script to work with? What advice would you give to someone about to write their first soap opera script?

UNIT 33 Changing English

AIMS

● To investigate how English has changed over time.

STARTER

1

> ♪ **Old English** (or Anglo Saxon) is the type of English which was commonly spoken in most parts of England in the eighth to the eleventh century. The roots of this language lie with the Angle and Saxon tribes from Northern Germany, who began to invade Britain when the Romans left. Many simple everyday words originate from Old English, although the majority of modern English words have their origins in other languages.
>
> **Middle English** is the type of English that was commonly spoken between 1100 and 1500. It is the language used by Chaucer in his famous Canterbury Tales.

Match each Middle English word with its modern English translation.

foryeve	could
betwixen	between
drede	forgive
certeyn	poor
noght	fear
koude	certainly
povre	nothing

DEVELOPMENT

2

Look at the two extracts from 'The Wife of Bath's Tale'. Using the translation, produce a word bank to put next to each line of the original in order to help students.

Translation

If there were no authority on earth
Except experience; mine, for what it's worth,
And that's enough for me, all goes to show
That marriage is a misery and a woe;
For let me say, if I may make so bold,
My lords, since when I was but twelve years old,
Thanks be to God Eternal evermore,
Five husbands have I had at the church door;
Yes, it's a fact that I have had so many,
All worthy in their way, as good as any.

Original extract

Experience, thogh noon auctoritèe
Were in this world, is right ynogh for me
To speke of wo that is in mariàgė;
For, lordynges, sith I twelve year was of agė,
Thonkėd be God that is eterne on lyvė,
Housbondes at chirchėdore I have had fyvė –
If I so oftė myghte han wedded be –
And alle were worthy men in hir degrée.

3

Pick a line from the original text that explains the Wife of Bath's attitude towards marriage.

4

Write down the original line which tells us how old the Wife of Bath was when she was first married.

5

Write down the original line which tells us how many husbands the Wife of Bath had.

6

Read the following extract from Jane

Austen's *Pride and Prejudice*, published in 1813. Answer the questions that follow. In this extract the writer gives us some insight into the thoughts of the heroine Elizabeth Bennet about her new neighbours, the Bingley sisters.

Pride and Prejudice

Elizabeth listened in silence, but was not convinced; their behaviour at the assembly had not been calculated to please in general; and with more quickness of observation and less pliancy of temper than her sister, and with a judgment too unassailed by any attention to herself, she was very little disposed to approve them. They were in fact very fine ladies; not deficient in good humour when they were pleased, nor in the power of being agreeable where they chose it; but proud and conceited. They were rather handsome, had been educated in one of the first private seminaries in town, had a fortune of twenty thousand pounds, were in the habit of spending more than they ought, and of associating with people of rank; and were therefore in every respect entitled to think well of themselves, and meanly of others. They were of a respectable family in the north of England; a circumstance more deeply impressed on their memories than that their brother's fortune and their own had been acquired by trade.

Jane Austen

a What does the writer mean by 'less pliancy of temper'?

b Find out what 'unassailed' and 'disposed' mean in the context of this passage.

c What words would we use instead of 'handsome' and 'seminaries' if we were writing this passage nowadays?

d Read the first sentence and pick out:
  - two main clauses
  - a subordinate clause.

e What do you consider to be the main differences between Jane Austen's English and modern English? Think about:
  - vocabulary
  - sentence structure
  - the use of active or passive verbs.

What do you consider to be the main changes to the English language over the last thousand years? What advantages do writers today have as a result of an increasingly broad vocabulary? Why have new words come into our vocabulary?

273

UNIT 34 Teenage drinking

AIMS

- To use a range of drama techniques and role-play to explore an issue.
- To convey action, character, atmosphere and tension in a script.

STARTER

1

*An **issue** is a subject which is very topical at a particular moment in time (e.g. drugs, underage drinking, animal welfare, hunting, the environment).*

Think of five arguments for drinking and five arguments against drinking.

INTRODUCTION

Drinking alcohol is a popular pastime not only confined to adults. More teenagers are indulging in drinking than ever before, which is contributing to a chronic increase in health problems and anti-social behaviour. Is there any advice in the article on page 275 which is useful for teenagers?

2

What do you think is the main message of this article?

DEVELOPMENT

3 Language

Look at the section which begins on line 8. Are there any words in this section which suggest it is from a young person's viewpoint?

4 Language

Look at the section which begins on line 32. What words and phrases suggest that this section is from a parent's viewpoint?

5 Reading

How and when did Miles start drinking?

6 Reading

How has Miles reacted to his mum and dad's intervention in his drinking?

7 Reading

How did Joyce and John try and help their son?

8 Reading

Pick out three pieces of advice offered by the alcohol counsellor.

9 Writing

Produce an advice leaflet warning teenagers about the dangers of drinking alcohol. Comment on:

- the dangers of alcohol consumption
- peer pressure
- what young people should do if a friend develops an alcohol problem.

10 Speaking and listening

Improvise one of the following situations.

- You are out with your friends and alcohol is involved. Something goes wrong.
- You come home drunk. Your parents confront you before you go to bed and when you wake up the next day.
- You visit the local alcohol counsellor to talk about your drink problem.

(continued on page 276)

Teenage Drinking

Each year 1,000 children under the age of 15 are admitted to hospital suffering acute alcohol poisoning. How would you cope if your child was drinking regularly – and drinking too much?

Joyce Cardrew, a care worker from Hull, was horrified the night her 15-year-old son Miles staggered through the door at midnight, stumbled up the stairs and was violently ill. She thought he had a stomach upset and was 5 shocked when his 16-year-old sister Gemma informed her that he was 'just' drunk. [...]

Miles says: 'Mum just had no idea that me and my mates were drinking. It started when a friend nicked a bottle of vodka from his parents – they 10 had loads of booze and didn't even notice it had gone. I was about 13 at the time and we drank it mixed up with juice or Coke at each others' homes. 15

'Friends' big brothers and sisters would buy it for us and in the last year I've looked old enough to buy cider and lager. I hardly ever got asked for ID. [...]

'Mum and Dad are constantly watching me 20 now to see if I'm drinking and it's been really embarrassing because they've been up to school and talked to all my friends' parents. They've made me read a whole load of stuff about alcoholism, too, which was actually quite scary. I 25 don't think I will ever not drink, and I don't think I'm going to become an alcoholic, but I can see that it was stupid to be drinking the way we were at our age. I'm quite relieved we don't do it any more because I feel a lot better and I've 30 got more money to spend.'

Joyce says: 'I couldn't believe that I had been so oblivious to Miles' drinking. We have some

> 'I couldn't believe I'd been so **oblivious** to his drinking.'

drink in the house, sherry and wine, but we don't have a drink every day and we certainly 35 don't touch spirits.

'I'd noticed he was very grumpy in the mornings, but I had put it down to the normal teenage moodiness. [...] 40

'John and I decided we were going to confront this problem, and we talked to everyone we could find. There are brilliant alcohol-support groups and we visited Miles' teachers and his friends' parents. I don't think 45 Miles has a big problem – but certainly drink was becoming a serious habit and we just wanted to make sure he understood how dangerous it can be.'

The alcohol counsellor says: 'Joyce was right 50 when she said alcohol is a major part of youth culture today.

'If you are worried about your teenager's drinking, try not to over-react. Explain how you feel and why you are worried. You can help them 55 to learn to drink safely by encouraging them to stick to lower-strength brands and to drink slowly.'

Caroline Righton

What advice are you given? Do you act on it?
- Your parent has developed a drink problem and has embarrassed you in front of your friends. You confront your parent after your friends have gone home.

Make notes on your improvisation.

11 Speaking and listening

Write a script based on your improvisation in Activity 10. Perform it for the rest of your class. Assess and discuss each other's performances, focusing on:

- structure
- dialogue – is it realistic and clear?
- characters – are they interesting and varied?
- speech styles – are they clear, with appropriate accents and dialects?
- action – is it realistic, exciting and entertaining?
- strengths
- areas for improvement.

12 Writing

Imagine that you are an older person. Write a letter to the local newspaper complaining about drunken teenagers who congregate near your house. Describe:

- what the problem is
- how you feel
- what should be done about it by the teenagers themselves, their parents and the police.

REVIEW

Have you managed to explore the issue effectively through drama? Which drama pieces were the most successful? Did you try to show the issue realistically or through more abstract dramatic techniques? As a class, make a list of your top ten tips for a successful performance.

UNIT 35 A public meeting

AIMS

- To use standard English and rhetorical language to explain, explore or justify an idea.
- To compare and evaluate different points of view.
- To discuss and evaluate conflicting evidence to arrive at a considered and shared viewpoint.

STARTER

1

Finish the following statement: 'What makes me really angry is ...' Now read out your finished statement to the rest of the class as if you were making a speech.

INTRODUCTION

Holes by Louis Sacher is a gripping story about Stanley Yelnats, who is sent to a boys' juvenile detention centre as a result of a miscarriage of justice. What impressions are we given of Green Camp Lake Juvenile Correctional Facility?

2

What does Mr Sir mean when he says, 'You're not in the Girl Scouts anymore'?

DEVELOPMENT

3 Language

Rewrite the paragraph beginning on line 8, putting in suitable adjectives and creating a threatening atmosphere.

4 Language

What impact does the use of short paragraphs have and what are the advantages and disadvantages of such a concise writing style?

5 Reading

What indications are there that this passage is set in America? Pick out words and phrases to support your answer.

6 Reading

What is your first impression of Mr Sir?

7 Speaking and listening

A modern juvenile detention centre is going to be built on the site of your school. Your school is going to be amalgamated with your nearest secondary school and relocated on the outskirts of town.

Your teacher will organise you into groups. Prepare a presentation, putting forward your views in a persuasive and powerful way. Use rhetorical language.

Those in favour of the move

a Prison reform groups, who want improved conditions for prisoners.

b The police and prison service, who cannot cater for growing numbers of prisoners.

c The school governors and headteacher, who are pleased about receiving huge amounts of extra funding.

d The PE staff, who are going to receive a new multi-million pound sports centre.

Holes

The guard led Stanley to a small building. A sign on front said, YOU ARE ENTERING CAMP GREEN LAKE JUVENILE CORRECTIONAL FACILITY. Next to it was another sign which declared that it was a violation of the Texas Penal Code to bring guns, explosives, weapons, drugs, or alcohol onto the premises.

As Stanley read the sign he couldn't help but think, *Well, duh!*   5

The guard led Stanley into the building, where he felt the welcome relief of air-conditioning.

A man was sitting with his feet up on a desk. He turned his head when Stanley and the guard entered, but otherwise didn't move. Even though he was inside, he wore sunglasses and a cowboy hat. He also held a can of soda, and the sight of it   10
made Stanley even more aware of his own thirst.

He waited while the bus guard gave the man some papers to sign.

'That's a lot of sunflower seeds,' the bus guard said.

Stanley noticed a burlap sack filled with sunflower seeds on the floor next to the desk.   15

'I quit smoking last month,' said the man in the cowboy hat. He had a tattoo of a rattlesnake on his arm, and as he signed his name, the snake's rattle seemed to wiggle. 'I used to smoke a pack a day. Now I eat a sack of these every week.'

The guard laughed.

There must have been a small refrigerator behind his desk, because the man in   20
the cowboy hat produced two more cans of soda. For a second Stanley hoped that one might be for him, but the man gave one to the guard and said the other was for the driver.

'Nine hours here, and now nine hours back,' the guard grumbled. 'What a day.'   25

Stanley thought about the long, miserable bus ride and felt a little sorry for the guard and the bus driver.

The man in the cowboy hat spit sunflower seed shells into a wastepaper   30
basket. Then he walked around the desk to Stanley. 'My name is Mr. Sir,' he said. 'Whenever you speak to me you must call me by my name, is that clear?'

Stanley hesitated. 'Uh, yes, Mr. Sir,' he   35
said, though he couldn't imagine that was really the man's name.

'You're not in the Girl Scouts anymore,' Mr. Sir said.

Louis Sacher

Those opposed to the move

a Pupils, who don't want to travel long distances and go to a bigger school.

b Parents, who want a smaller school in the heart of the local community.

c Local residents, who are concerned about the impact of housing criminals in a largely residential area.

d Teachers, who have concerns about relocating, losing the unique atmosphere of the school, and possibly losing their jobs.

Your teacher will now organise a debate on the issue.

> A **debate** is a formal discussion which is controlled by a set of rules. In a formal debate various people perform a specific function to ensure order and structure.

8 Writing

Make notes on other groups' presentations.

- Summarise main points and arguments.
- Note significant data and facts.
- Note points you want to challenge or would like explained further.
- Write down any questions you want to ask.
- Think about how successfully they used rhetorical devices.

9 Writing

Write a formal letter to a local newspaper, making your group's point of view clear. Remember to use standard English.

10 Writing

Produce a questionnaire and use it in a survey of what your classmates and teachers think about your school's proposed amalgamation and relocation. Think carefully about which group you represent and devise questions that will further your cause (e.g. PE staff could ask 'Do we need: a) a new gym; b) a sports hall; c) all-weather pitches?'). Closed questions, which give a yes/no answer, give data that is easier to handle.

11 Writing

Think about how to present the information you have gathered from your questionnaire (e.g. as percentages, graphs, bar charts or pie charts) and make OHTs presenting your data.

12 Writing

Complete a newspaper report about the debate on the proposed detention centre. Outline each group's views and concerns.(Use your notes from Activity 8.) You may wish to add a few made-up details about the proposed development to make your article more interesting. If you produced a questionnaire, use the results of that too.

REVIEW

Share your newspaper article with the rest of the class. How successfully have you compared the opposing points of view and evaluated the evidence? Did you remember to use standard English?

UNIT 36 Meat or veg?

AIMS

- To identify the underlying themes, implications and issues in a talk.
- To discuss and evaluate conflicting evidence.
- To use standard English to explain, explore or justify an idea offering arguments and counter-arguments.
- To look at use of rhetorical language in a text.

STARTER

1

The following information is taken from the Vegetarian Society website. Are they facts or opinions?

- The Vegetarian Society was founded in 1847.
- Just under 1/4 of the world's population has a predominantly vegetarian diet.
- A vegetarian diet may reduce your chances of getting certain diseases.
- Approximately 3 million people in Britain are vegetarian.

INTRODUCTION

Many teenagers think seriously about their lifestyle. One lifestyle choice is whether to eat meat or not. After reading the article on page 281 do you think it is right to eat meat?

2

From whose point of view is this article written – meat eaters or vegetarians? Justify your answer.

DEVELOPMENT

3 Language

From the section headed 'Third way diet' pick out:

- one fact
- one opinion.

4 Language

Look for an example of:

- a pull quote
- a sub-heading
- rhetorical language
- an expert opinion.

5 Language

Which typical web page features does this extract have? Think about:

- presentation and layout
- language, grammar and structure
- information and links.

6 Reading

Examine the first section outlining the views of Professor Robert Pickard. Find:

- an opinion
- a fact
- one anatomical and one evolutionary argument for eating meat.

7 Reading

Read the section 'Vegetarian response'. Pick out:

- a fact
- an opinion.

8 Speaking and listening

Imagine you decide to become vegetarian. Try to persuade one of your parents to become vegetarian with you.

BBC NEWS

Nutritionist sparks red meat row

A leading nutritionist has provoked controversy by suggesting people who do not eat red meat are risking their health.

The suggestion has been dismissed as flying in the face of scientific evidence by vegan and vegetarian groups.

Professor Robert Pickard, director general of the British Nutrition Foundation, said a vegetarian diet was not natural for mankind.

Addressing a seminar of nutritionists at Stratford-upon-Avon, Professor Pickard said: 'Man is an omnivore'.

> **Anyone thinking of restricting their diet by becoming a vegetarian is potentially taking risks with their health.**

Professor Pickard said that the gut contained a kilogram of bacteria to help digest the wide variety of food present in an omnivorous diet.

He said there was evidence that leaving the bacteria idle as a result of a restricted diet can make it easier for disease to take hold. [...]

Third way diet

Man's teeth, jaws and gut have evolved to deal with a mixture of meat and vegetables. Professor Pickard said that this 'third way' diet provided primitive man with a high-energy food intake making him a more effective species. [...]

Meat should now play a central part in any person's diet. 'It provides iron for the blood, vitamin D for the bones, and proteins and fatty acids for growth. [...] It is also highly likely that red meat contains many other beneficial nutrients that we do not yet fully understand.'

Ian Tokelove, a spokesman for the Food Commission [...] refused to back Professor Pickard. He said: 'Meat does have a role to play in the diet, but it has been shown not to be essential.

> The body is adaptable and vegetarians actually have a healthy diet.'

Vegetarian response

The Vegetarian Society said comments such as those made by Professor Pickard made many vegetarians worry about their diet – unjustifiably.

Sam Calvert, head of public affairs, said: There is no cause for concern. There are three million vegetarians in the UK, and it can clearly be seen that vegetarianism does not have a detrimental effect on their health – in fact research shows that it has a positive effect.

Ms Calvert quoted a study published in the British Medical Journal in 1994 which showed vegetarians were 20% less likely than meat eaters to die before the age of 65 – and 40% less likely to die prematurely from cancer.

See also:

▶ 8 Feb   Millions turn to organic food
▶ 23 Mar   Man's blindness 'due to vegan diet'
▶ 8 Jun   Vegan diet 'cuts prostate cancer risk'

Internet links:

▶ The Vegan Society
▶ Vegetarian Society
▶ Food Commission
▶ British Nutrition Foundation
▶ BBC News

9 Reading and writing

Research a relevant animal rights or dietary issue and gather information for use in the debate in Activity 10. Make notes to help you with your speech. You could begin by looking at some of the Internet links suggested in the extract.

10 Speaking and listening

A **motion for debate** is an idea or issue which is formally discussed and then voted on at the end of the debating process.

Choose one of the following motions to debate.

- Eating meat is crucial to our survival.
- The exploitation of animals is a necessary evil.
- Eating meat should be banned.

Your teacher will help you to organise your group. You will need:

- a **chairperson**, to whom each speech and all comments are directed
- a **proposer**, who gives a speech to the 'house' supporting the motion
- an **opposer**, who gives a speech contradicting the motion
- a **seconder** for the motion
- a **seconder** against the motion.

Research your topic using the Internet links suggested in the extract, then prepare a short speech either supporting or challenging the motion. In your speech you should:

- explain your point of view
- explore your point of view, offering facts, data and expert opinion from your research
- justify your ideas, defending them when challenged
- use standard English.

The following link phrases may help you to present your ideas.

- **When explaining**
  In my speech I am going to ..., first of all I am going to ..., I will begin by explaining ..., it is my opinion that ..., I feel it is important to ...
- **When exploring your topic**
  From my research it appears that ..., we should consider ..., issues raised by this are ..., this could be interpreted as ..., it is evident that ..., it is obvious that ..., the evidence suggests that ..., other interpretations include ...
- **When justifying**
  I can confirm this by ..., this can be explained by ..., my view is supported by ..., other reasons for this are ..., unlike other speakers I strongly believe that ..., it is clear from the evidence that ..., my views are endorsed/strengthened by ...

Focus your audience's attention by using rhetorical questions (e.g. Have you considered the evidence? What are the implications of this?).

Conclude by taking a final vote.

11 Writing

You are the editor of a teenage magazine and you receive thousands of letters from teenagers wondering whether or not to become vegetarians or vegans. Write an article outlining the various arguments and counter-arguemnts and offering advice.

REVIEW

Do you think meat eating is a necessary part of our existence? What are the most compelling arguments offered by your classmates? Can you justify your own opinions clearly and effectively?

UNIT 37 | Acting Shakespeare

AIMS

- To develop and compare different interpretations of a scene from a Shakespeare play.
- To recognise, evaluate and extend skills and techniques developed through drama.
- To consider and exploit the stylistic convention of parody.

STARTER

1

 Parody imitates the style of another writer in a humorous or ridiculous manner.

Read this passage from Shakespeare aloud, adopting each of these tones in turn: sadness, happiness, menace, nervousness.

*If music be the food of love, play on,
Give me excess of it, that, surfeiting,
The appetite may sicken, and so die.*

INTRODUCTION

Hamlet, if not Shakespeare's most famous tragedy, is certainly his most complex. In the following scene, Hamlet's friends Horatio and Marcellus try in vain to persuade him not to follow his father's ghost. How does Shakespeare create a spine-chilling impression of the ghost?

2

How does Hamlet react to the ghost's suggestion that he should avenge his father's death?

Hamlet

(from Act I, Scenes 4–5)

HORATIO:	What if it tempt you toward the flood my lord,
	Or to the dreadful summit of the cliff
	That beetles o'er his base into the sea,
	And there assume some other horrible form
	Which might deprive your sovereignty of reason, 5
	And draw you into madness? Think of it.
	[The very place puts toys of desperation,
	Without more motive, into every brain
	That looks so many fathoms to the sea
	And hears it roar beneath.] 10

HAMLET:	It wafts me still. Go on, I'll follow thee.
MARCELLUS:	You shall not go my lord.
HAMLET:	Hold off your hands.
HORATIO:	Be ruled, you shall not go.

HAMLET: My fate cries out,
And makes each petty arture in this body
As hardy as the Nemean lion's nerve.   15
Still am I called. Unhand me gentlemen!
By heaven I'll make a ghost of him that lets me.
I say away! – Go on, I'll follow thee.

                 Exit Ghost and Hamlet

HORATIO:	He waxes desperate with imagination.
MARCELLUS:	Let's follow, 'tis not fit thus to obey him. 20
HORATIO:	Have after. To what issue will this come?
MARCELLUS:	Something is rotten in the state of Denmark.
HORATIO:	Heaven will direct it.
MARCELLUS:	Nay, let's follow him.

                 Exeunt

         [1.5] Enter GHOST and HAMLET

HAMLET:	Whither wilt thou lead me? Speak, I'll go no further.
GHOST:	Mark me.
HAMLET:	I will.

GHOST: My hour is almost come   25
When I to sulph'rous and tormenting flames
Must render up myself.

HAMLET:	Alas poor ghost!
GHOST:	Pity me not, but lend they serious hearing To what I shall unfold.
HAMLET:	Speak, I am bound to hear.
GHOST:	So art thou to revenge, when thou shalt hear. 30
HAMLET:	What?

GHOST:	I am thy father's spirit,
	Doomed for a certain term to walk the night,
	And for the day confined to fast in fires,
	Till the foul crimes done in my days of nature 35
	Are burnt and purged away. But that I am forbid
	To tell the secrets of my prison house,
	I could a tale unfold whose lightest word
	Would harrow up thy soul, freeze thy young blood,
	Make thy two eyes like stars start from their spheres, 40
	Thy knotted and combinèd locks to part
	And each particular hair to stand an end
	Like quills upon the fretful porpentine.
	But this eternal blazon must not be
	To ears of flesh and blood. List, list, oh list! 45
	If though didst ever thy dear father love –
HAMLET:	O God!
GHOST:	Revenge his foul and most unnatural murder.
HAMLET:	Murder?
GHOST:	Murder most foul, as in the best it is, 50
	But this most foul, strange, and unnatural.
HAMLET:	Haste me to know't, that I with wings as swift
	As meditation or the thoughts of love
	May sweep to my revenge.
GHOST:	I find thee apt,
	And duller shouldst thou be than the fat weed 55
	That rots itself in ease on Lethe wharf,
	Wouldst thou not stir in this. Now Hamlet, hear.
	'Tis given out that, sleeping in my orchard,
	A serpent stung me. So the whole ear of Denmark
	Is by a forgèd process of my death 60
	Rankly abused; but know, thou noble youth,
	The serpent that did sting thy father's life
	Now wears his crown.
HAMLET:	O my prophetic soul!
	My uncle?

William Shakespeare

DEVELOPMENT

3 Language

Rewrite lines 16–17 in modern-day English.

4 Reading

How is Hamlet's reaction to the ghost different from that of his friends?

5 Reading

What might happen to Hamlet if the ghost was to tell him about 'the secrets of my prison house'?

6 Reading

Write down the lines from the text which explain how Hamlet's father is supposed to have died.

7 Reading

Explain how Hamlet's thoughts and feelings change at different stage of the passage.

8 Speaking and listening

Imagine that you are to produce a stage version of this scene. Decide:

- where and when you would set your version of *Hamlet*
- which costumes and props you would use
- how you would organise the stage for this particular scene
- how the actors would speak and move to get across the feelings Shakespeare wanted to convey
- where the actors would be in relation to each other at various stages of the action
- how you would create the image of the ghost
- which sound and lighting effects you would use.

Rehearse your version then act it out for the class.

9 Writing

Write a parody of this scene in which you are waiting at a bus stop with some friends after a night out and are visited by the ghost of somebody you once knew. Consider:

- the nature of your ghost – speech style, actions, appearance, comic qualities
- what props, conversation topics and language you could use to bring your parody into the twenty-first century
- why the ghost has come to visit you
- your reaction to the ghost and its revelations.

10 Writing

Imagine you are Horatio or Marcellus. Write a letter to a friend describing what happened the night Hamlet came face-to-face with the ghost of his father. Refer directly to the text, describing your actions, Hamlet's actions and what was said.

REVIEW

Assess your group performances of this scene. Did people's interpretation of the scene differ? If so, how were they different? If you were to produce another version of this scene, how would you improve it?

UNIT 38 Revise punctuation

AIMS

- To use the full range of punctuation to clarify and emphasise meaning for the reader.
- To integrate speech and quotation into writing.

STARTER

1

Direct speech consists of the actual words that are spoken in a dialogue, with inverted commas around them (e.g. *'Why do you always come home late?' asked my mother as usual*). In *indirect speech*, the words are reported rather than written down word for word (e.g. *As usual, my mother asked me why I always come home late*).

Punctuate the following two sentences correctly.

a Our chances of winning the World Cup are as good as anyone's said the manager

b The manager said that our chances of winning the World Cup are as good as anyone's

Now write two sentences of your own which include direct speech.

DEVELOPMENT

Commas

Commas separate items or ideas in a list (e.g. I like to eat a ham sandwich, a bag of crisps, an apple and a banana for lunch). Commas can also be used to add information to a statement or emphasise a point (e.g. To be absolutely honest, I think your idea is totally ridiculous). They are also used to separate main and subordinate clauses in a sentence.

2

Punctuate the following sentences correctly, using commas when necessary.

a Alison enjoys swimming reading watching television and talking to her friends on the telephone.

b To raise your performance you must improve your fitness work on your passing time your tackles better and make your shooting more accurate.

3

Punctuate these sentences correctly.

a Why is it when you came into this classroom chewing gum and laughing that you proceeded to switch on your mobile phone?

b My father who was an excellent musician used to play the trumpet.

4

Punctuate the following passage, using commas accurately.

Before I go on holiday on Saturday I must pack my bags. I am going to take my swimming trunks fishing tackle cycle helmet and snooker cue along with a few t-shirts and some shorts if my mum remembers to iron them. I suppose I should take some suntan lotion which is very high factor as the sun will be very strong.

Semi-colons and colons

A semi-colon indicates a pause which is longer than a comma. It can be used instead of a full stop if two sentences are very closely related or contrast in some way (e.g. I like pizza; my sister prefers lasagne).

It can also be used to separate items in a list which is introduced by a colon (e.g. The town centre is in drastic need of development for the following reasons: unsatisfactory access to the bus station through long and badly lit subways; a lack of pedestrianised areas; and a number of dilapidated buildings which are in serious need of restoration).

5

Put semi-colons and colons in the correct places in the following sentences.

a My brother enjoys partying my sister attends a knitting circle.
b To make a spaghetti bolognese sauce you need the following main ingredients half a kilogram of minced steak a large finely chopped onion a large tin of tomatoes tomato puree crushed garlic freshly ground salt and pepper and a teaspoon of dried mixed herbs.

Embedded quotations

When inserting embedded quotations it is not necessary to use commas; inverted commas are essential, however. Take a look at this example.

Macbeth clearly feels that there are more reasons for not killing King Duncan than there are for going ahead with regicide. To begin with, Macbeth is Duncan's 'kinsman' and his 'subject', both strong reasons 'against the deed'. Furthermore, Macbeth is Duncan's 'host', who should protect his guest and 'against his murderer shut the door'.

Long quotations

Long quotations should be introduced with a colon and the actual quoted words should be set on a new line and indented, as in the example below.

Macbeth concedes that he can find only one reason for killing King Duncan:
  '... I have no spur
  To prick the sides of my intent, but only
  Vaulting ambition, which o'erleaps itself
  And falls on th'other -'.

6

Your teacher will now give you a question on a passage or text you are studying to help you practise using quotations. When writing your answer, try to use punctuation correctly.

REVIEW

If you are uncertain about any aspect of punctuation, make sure you ask your teacher to help you sort it out. It is very important that you punctuate accurately when you sit your SAT papers.

Preparing for your English tests

What's in store for you

Whether you like it or not, at some point in each year of school you will have to take a test in English. Tests tell your teacher what National Curriculum level you are working at and what your strengths and weaknesses are in reading and writing. Tests also tell you and your parents how well you are doing. You can't avoid them!

Optional tests

Many schools now ask their students to sit optional test papers in English in Years 7 and 8. The main focus of your tests will be reading and writing.

KS3 SAT examinations

You will almost definitely sit two KS3 SAT papers in Year 9. Your SAT exam will consist of one reading and one writing paper. An additional paper will include questions on the Shakespeare text you have studied.

In Year 9 students are expected to develop their reading and writing skills and their ability to interpret texts to a high level. The English SATs expect students to read closely, with skill, confidence and understanding.

You will be expected to:

- **identify** the main presentational, technical and language features of a variety of fiction and non-fiction texts

- **explore** possible interpretations of texts and consider how people and events are viewed

- **analyse** the different ways writers use language and effects to create meaning, mood and an emotional response in a chosen genre

- **compare** the themes, ideas, styles and language choices of writers from different cultural and historical backgrounds and across a variety of genres

- **present**, **develop** and **justify** your ideas and interpretations with conviction and force, using relevant textual references to back them up.

This section will help you to successfully negotiate your tests in English and will ease any worries you might have had.

Getting off to a good start

The best way to prepare for both your optional tests and KS3 papers in English is to carefully complete all the work your English teacher sets you in class and for homework as well as you can. This will give you all the key skills you need to tackle any questions in the tests.

With your teacher, discuss and work through any problems you might encounter. Take into account any comments teachers might make on your written work or in your reports, and do something about this valuable advice!

Buy a suitable revision guide to help you prepare for your tests or look up websites with good English revision advice.

Working on reading

Reading regularly and looking at a wide range of texts is a good way of improving the accuracy and speed of your reading. Reading will also broaden your vocabulary, providing you look up difficult words in a dictionary. This will help you to understand tricky words in a variety of texts, subjects and situations. Having a decent dictionary and thesaurus when working

on English tasks is as important as having a calculator or protractor in Maths!

Working on writing

Make sure you are familiar with all the technical vocabulary you need to write about an author's use of language and the effects they are trying to produce. Work through the glossary at the back of this book and make sure that you can use technical vocabulary accurately.

You can improve the accuracy and content of your writing by:

- regularly proof-reading your work, checking it carefully for errors in spelling, punctuation, paragraphing and grammar
- constantly editing your writing, changing words and phrases to make meanings clear and expression and language more interesting and effective.

Have a dictionary and thesaurus with you in class and at home as these will help you improve the range and sophistication of your vocabulary.

Sitting your English tests

Reading for meaning and understanding

In your test papers you will be asked to answer a variety of questions of varying length. Some questions want you to find bits of information; others require an expanded answer with close reference to the text, and ask you to focus on character, events, setting, or your interpretation of the information in front of you.

TURN THE PAGE →

Attempt to answer all the questions you are supposed to. Try to extend your answers according to the number of marks available for each question and the amount of space available. An examiner cannot mark blank space!

Imagine you are a detective. If you read the questions carefully, you will find clues about the type of information you need to include in your answer. Then you'll need to find evidence in the text to prove your point.

Getting ready to respond

Before you begin writing your answer, do the following things.

1 Read through the question carefully, underlining key words (e.g. 'look for', 'consider', 'compare', 'find', 'evidence', 'characters', 'subjects', 'ideas', etc.).

2 Consider what the question requires from you. Does it ask for:

- a fact
- an opinion
- an interpretation of ideas or arguments
- an interpretation of an event, action or character
- an awareness of cultural, social and historical influences
- comments on atmosphere or setting
- use of textual evidence to support an opinion or impression
- a commentary on the writer's use of language, expression and imagery for effect
- an understanding of how technical and presentational features are used for effect
- a consideration of how the structure of a text might affect its meaning
- a discussion of the author's perspective
- different possible interpretations of the same event by different characters
- evidence of bias
- an awareness and understanding of technical vocabulary
- a consideration of how sound effects are used to create meaning and different moods?

3 Read the text closely, underlining any relevant evidence.

4 Annotate the text, making notes in the margin if necessary.

Responding to a reading question

When you write an extended response to a reading question, make sure you have:

1 answered the question fully, addressing all the main points

2 dealt with all the bullet points fully

3 used relevant evidence from the text to support all your points and ideas

4 used quotations when necessary to back up your opinions

5 explained textual detail and quotes whenever necessary

6 explained how the writer's use of language has helped to create meaning whenever possible

7 explained why the writer has used technical features such as metaphors, similes, alliteration and onomatopoeia rather than just picking out examples

8 remembered the PEE rule!

> **P**oint – make your main point clearly.
>
> **E**xample – give an example or quotation from the text.
>
> **E**xplanation – explain how your choice of example links to and supports your main point.

At all times consider the following:

- How have you reacted to the text and why you have reacted in that way?

- What does the writer want you to think and how has he/she manipulated your thoughts?

- What explicit and implicit messages is the writer trying to convey? Which words and phrases are important in conveying that message? Read between the lines.

Responding to an imaginative writing question

One of the questions in your test paper will almost certainly ask you to either imagine, explore and entertain or inform, explain and describe.

You may be asked to write a story, diary or description.

Your creative writing should have the following key ingredients:

- **imaginative and interesting ideas** – however, remember to keep ideas, events and plots simple. You only have a limited amount of time.

- **a range of varied vocabulary and expression** – avoid repetition and overused words such as 'nice' and 'said'.

- **lively use of adjectives and adverbs** to build interesting, colourful and vivid pictures.

- **use of the senses** to capture and maintain the reader's attention.

- **imagery** – such as similes, metaphors and personification.

- **an awareness of the audience** (who you are writing for) – has your writing got the right tone and register?

- **accurate spelling, punctuation and grammar**
- **clear organisation** into sentences and paragraphs of varying length
- **detailed and sustained writing** – exploring ideas, characters and setting in an extended manner.

Responding to a non-fiction writing question

One of the writing activities in the test may involve writing to either persuade, argue and advise or analyse, review and comment.

It could involve writing a review of a book or film, a letter, newspaper or magazine articles, advice leaflets, survival guides, etc.

When writing factual or non-fiction writing, use the following as a checklist:

Content and ideas

- Do you understand the task?
- Have you brainstormed suitable ideas?
- Have you stated your ideas clearly?
- Have you explained and explored your ideas, opinions and arguments sufficiently and in a convincing way?
- Can you justify your opinions with evidence, either real or anecdotal?
- Are your ideas suitable and relevant to the task you are engaged in?

Structure

- Have you produced a plan?
- Is the order of events clear?
- Is your writing organised into paragraphs with strong topic sentences, good development of ideas and strong final sentences?
- Do your paragraphs progress logically?
- Have you used section headings and other relevant presentational features when necessary?
- Do you link points clearly and refer to the title or topic when appropriate?

Style

- Is your writing style and language suitable for your audience and purpose?
- Is your writing clear and to the point at all times?
- Are your ideas easy to understand?
- Is the line of any argument easy to understand?
- Do you adopt the correct level of formality and use standard English when appropriate?
- Have you used link words and connectives to make your writing fluent and easy to read?
- Do you use a range of simple and complex sentences?

Vocabulary

- Do you avoid slang and dialect words in formal writing?
- Do you use link words and phrases to signpost your ideas?
- Have you avoided overused words and unnecessary repetition?
- Does your writing use a range of sophisticated and relevant vocabulary and expression?
- Have you used relevant technical vocabulary correctly?

Further food for thought

If you are writing an advice leaflet, is your writing simple, direct and to the point?

If you are writing a newspaper article, have you started with an effective standfirst, summarising the main points of your story? Have you used headlines, sub-headings, pull quotes and other relevant presentational features?

Have you used the correct conventions for formal and informal letter writing? (e.g. layout of address, greeting, signing off)

If you are writing a report, an essay or a review, have you used presentational features and writing styles which are appropriate for each type of writing? Have you used section headings correctly?

Are your ideas appropriate for the genre you are writing in? Have you avoided ideas which are over-the-top and unrealistic? Avoid over-explicit detail in imaginative writing, such as descriptions of graphic violence, which might put the examiner off!

What you must do in the examination

- Read the instructions on the front cover of any booklets you receive in the examination.
- Use all the reading time available for close reading of both the text and questions.
- Make sure you know which sections you must complete and how many questions you need to answer in each section.
- Answer all the questions you are supposed to and use all the available time in the examination.
- Look at the marks for each question and plan your time accordingly.

- Think about why some words and phrases are in bold or italics.

- Look closely at the wording of the question and underline key words to make sure you understand exactly what you have to do.

- If there are bullet points, remember that the examiner will probably expect you to write at least a paragraph on each one.

- Keep asking yourself 'Have I answered the question to the best of my ability?'

- Keep developing and extending your answers. If you finish early, you have probably not answered all the questions to a satisfactory standard.

- Go back over the paper if you have time, making corrections and adding to your answers.

- Annotate your papers where necessary and write notes and short plans to help you.

- If you aren't sure what to do, ask a teacher or invigilator.

- Above all, keep calm!

Glossary

Abbreviations are initials used to represent words. In recent years there has been an explosion in the use of abbreviations. Some abbreviations are so commonly used that most people would find it difficult to remember or work out their origins. Common abbreviations include TV (television) VAT (value added tax) and FC (football club).

Abstract nouns are feelings and qualities which don't have physical properties (e.g. *excitement*, *sadness*, *confusion*, etc.). Abstract nouns name emotions, properties and ideas that we cannot see.

Accent is the way a speaker pronounces words.

An **acronym** is a word which is formed by combining the first letter, or first and second letters, of a series of words. They often refer to an organisation, company or scientific invention (e.g. *sonar = sound navigation and ranging*).

An **active verb** has a subject that performs the action (e.g. *John Logie Baird* (subject) *invented* (active verb) *the television*). Writing that uses active verbs is generally more direct than writing that uses passive verbs.

An **adjective** is a word which describes a noun (e.g. *old*, *beautiful*, *blue*). Adjectives which are placed before a noun are known as **attributive**. These adjectives are said to **modify** the noun (e.g. *My new teacher. The yellow flower*). Adjectives which are placed after a noun are known as **predicative**. These adjectives are said to **qualify** the noun (e.g. *The girl is clever. The cat is cute.*).

An **adverb** is a word or phrase that gives you more information about the verb of a sentence (e.g. *He walked quickly*).

Adverbial clauses give more information about the way an action was performed (e.g. *It was with utter horror that I stared at her*).

An **affix** is part of a word such as a prefix or a suffix. It is added to change word class or meaning. For example, the suffix 'ing' is added to the noun 'interest' to form an adjective – 'interesting'; the prefix 'un' is added to 'interesting' to give it the opposite meaning – 'uninteresting'.

Alliteration is a sound effect found in writing, usually in poetry, when words close to each other begin with the same letter (e.g. *He gobbles green gottles*).

American English is a variety of English which includes different words and spellings from British English. Whereas a British English speaker would say 'autumn' and 'crisps', an American English speaker would use 'fall' and 'potato chips'.

An **anecdote** is a short, amusing description, generally spoken, of an interesting event or incident, often from the narrator's past.

Anthropomorphism is when an animal or object is given human characteristics.

An **antonym** is a word with the opposite meaning to another word (e.g. *hot/cold*, *love/hate*, *big/small*). Very often a thesaurus will list antonyms of words as well as synonyms.

An **argument** is a strong viewpoint which is put forward in a discussion. For instance, a strong argument for cycling to work or school is that it is good for your health. Argumentative writing considers different ideas and opinions on an issue.

Assonance is the rhyming of vowels (e.g. *Books make good pets*) and is a device often used in poetry to create a particular mood.

Attributes are the qualities or features given to characters by writers. For instance, Harry Potter has the positive attributes of loyalty, bravery and honesty, whilst Draco Malfoy has more negative attributes, such as being devious and bullying.

An **audience** is a group of people who listen to and watch a performance of a play, concert or presentation. It can also mean the group of people you are aiming at when presenting information, ideas, speech or writing.

An **autobiography** is a piece of writing in which someone writes about their own life.

An **auxiliary verb** is a verb which helps the main verb in a phrase or sentence, for example, by indicating changes in tense (e.g. *I have lost my keys, I had lost my keys, I will lose my keys*). Modal auxiliary verbs (*can, could, may, might, must, ought, shall, should, will, would*) help to express possibility.

A **ballad** is a poem or song that tells a story (often including tales of bravery and adventure or love). A traditional ballad has many verses and can be very structured, with a regular rhyme scheme and fixed rhythm.

Bias is the favouring of one side or viewpoint over another when reporting or talking about an event.

Blank verse is a type of non-rhyming poetic writing in which every line has ten syllables. Most of Shakespeare's plays are written in blank verse.

A **blend** is a word which is made up by combining parts of other words to form new words (e.g. *smog* originates from *smoke* and *fog*). They are sometimes known as portmanteau words.

A **broadsheet newspaper** generally has a more formal and serious tone than popular tabloid papers. Articles are often long, detailed and analytical. Daily broadsheet papers include *The Daily Telegraph*, *The Times*, *The Guardian* and *The Independent*.

A **caesura** is a break in the middle of a line of verse which is used to break up rhythm or emphasise a point (e.g. *Stand forth Demetrius. My noble lord*).

Calligraphy is the art of producing beautiful and decorative handwriting. In China, Japan and the Islamic world the work of great calligraphers is respected in the same way people in the Western world respect great works of art.

Chronology is the placing of events in their correct order of time or as they happen. The word 'chronology' comes from the Greek *chronos* (time) and *ology* (a science you might study).

Clipping is removing or clipping part of the original word (e.g. *photo* originates from *photograph*).

Cockney rhyming slang is a colourful way of speaking in which things are referred to indirectly through rhymes (e.g. *barnet* means *hair* and comes from *Barnet Fair*).

A **collective noun** is the special name given to a collection of objects, animals or people (e.g. *a bouquet of flowers, a herd of cows, a class of schoolchildren*).

Colloquial English is the type of informal language we use in everyday conversation (e.g. *We had a right good laugh with our mates*).

Colloquialisms are non-standard words and phrases which are not suitable in formal contexts but are used by the majority of English speakers in informal conversation (e.g. *barmy, beat it, put the boot in*, etc.).

A **comic** is a type of magazine which contains stories about cartoon-type characters told in pictures with a small amount of writing.

A **complex sentence** is made up of a main clause and one or more subordinate clauses (e.g. *Although I didn't want to spend so much, I still bought the bike*).

A **compound sentence** involves two or more clauses of equal importance (e.g. *I had lots of money and I bought a bike*).

Compound words are made of two words that are put together (e.g. *arm + chair = armchair, step + ladder = stepladder*).

Compounding is one of the commonest ways of creating new words in English. This is generally done by combining two nouns (e.g. *bath + room = bathroom*), combining an adjective with a noun (e.g. *green + fly = greenfly*) and less commonly by combining a noun or adjective with a verb form (e.g. *heartbroken* or *easygoing*).

Concrete nouns are objects you can touch (e.g. *cat*, *book*, *chair*, *shoe*). Concrete nouns, which are sometimes referred to as common nouns, always have a physical existence and appearance.

A **connective** is a word such as *and* or *but*, which joins together words and phrases to create a longer sentence (e.g. *I like fish and chips with just a splash of vinegar, <u>but</u> not too much, <u>and</u> also a pinch of salt.*).

A **connotation** of a word is its secondary or alternative meaning.

Consonance is the rhyming of consonants other than those at the start of a word (e.g. *The cat sat on the mat* contains a series of 't' sounds).

A **contraction** is when two words are shortened or joined together in speech or poetry.

The **culture** of a person is defined by their values, beliefs, traditions and lifestyle.

A **dead metaphor** is one which is so common or uninteresting we stop thinking of it as a metaphor (e.g. *the leg of a table*).

A **debate** is a formal discussion which is controlled by a set of rules. In a formal debate various people perform specific functions to ensure order and structure.

The **denotation** of a word is its main or primary meaning. It is the first definition of a word in a dictionary (e.g. the denotation of *call* is generally 'to speak at volume in order to attract someone's attention'). However, connotations (or secondary meanings) of *call* include 'bird song', 'a wake-up message' and 'to telephone someone'.

Derivation is the study of where words originate from (e.g. *gradual* originates from the Latin *gradus*, which means 'step' or 'degree').

A **diagrammatical representation** is a method of conveying information in the form of a diagram (e.g. maps, flow charts, graphs, etc.).

A **dialect** is a form of language that is different from standard English in its vocabulary, grammar and pronunciation.

A **diary** involves writing a personal account of the events of each day, describing experiences and the writer's thoughts and feelings.

Direct speech consists of the actual words that are spoken in a dialogue, with inverted commas around them (e.g. *'Why do you always come home late?' asked my mother as usual*).

Drama is a genre of literature connected with plays and performance, both in the theatre and in film, radio and television. Drama is generally presented as a script before being turned into a performance.

Emotive language creates an emotional response in the reader.

Etymology is the study of the origins of language. It is also concerned with the derivation (origins) and development of individual words.

An **exclamatory sentence** is abrupt and emphatic. It expresses emotions such as anger or happiness (e.g. *'You stupid boy!'* or *'Absolutely fabulous!'*).

Expert opinion is the views and thoughts of people who know a lot about a particular field. Expert opinion is useful in supporting and giving extra weight to arguments in a formal essay.

A **fact** is a piece of information which can be proved to be true (e.g. *Paris is the capital of France, the Fire of London took place in 1666*).

Figurative language involves the use of similes, metaphors and personification in an imaginative way which creates interest and impact.

A **figure of speech** is a type of metaphor in which a speaker or writer compares their subject to something else, often in an imaginative way which creates interest and impact. Figures of speech such as *to kick up dust*, which means 'to cause trouble', are commonly used.

The **first person singular** is used when writing a diary or autobiography. It involves the use of the pronouns *I, me, my, myself*.

Fronting is when you put an item you might normally expect to find in another position at the beginning of a sentence (e.g. *Twenty yards beyond them, amid the surf of the now returning tide, two others were emerging from the sea*).

Genre is the type, style or category of a piece of writing. The three main literary genres are poetry, drama (plays) and prose. Each of these can be subdivided into other genres (e.g. drama can be subdivided into tragedy, comedy, problem play, history play, etc.).

A **homograph** is a word that can be pronounced differently and has different meanings although its spelling stays the same (e.g. *I bought my dog a new lead. My bag is as heavy as lead*).

A **homophone** is a word that sounds the same as another word but is spelt differently (e.g. *allowed/aloud*; *are/our*; *beach/beech*; *been/bean*).

An **idiom** is an expression which uses very unusual figures of speech to put ideas across. For example, *a different kettle of fish* means 'a different matter altogether'; *to play second fiddle* means 'to take a less important role'. Idioms generally only have meaning in the language of their origin.

Imagery is the use of words to create striking and vivid pictures in a reader's or listener's imagination. Imagery involves the use of similes, metaphors and personification.

In **indirect speech**, the words are reported rather than written down word for word (e.g. *As usual, my mother asked me why I always come home late*).

An **inflection** is a word ending which either changes a singular noun into a plural or alters a verb form. For example, the present tense of *like* is changed to the past tense *liked* by adding the inflection 'd'; the singular *dog* is changed to the plural *dogs* by adding the inflection 's'.

Information and Communications Technology (ICT) includes the use and study of new computer software and hardware, electronic communication, satellite communication, etc.

An **interrogative sentence** asks a question (e.g. *Are you going on holiday this summer?*). An imperative sentence gives orders or commands (e.g. *You are going on holiday this summer.*).

An **issue** is a subject which is very topical at a particular moment in time (e.g. drugs, underage drinking, animal welfare, hunting, the environment).

Jargon is the specialist language used in a subject or profession. The Internet is full of jargon (e.g. *to spam*, which means to bombard with useless e-mail, or *to flame*, which means 'to send abusive e-mails').

A **legend** is a traditional story, which may be founded on some truth but cannot be proved.

Link words and phrases (e.g. *therefore, however, in other words*, etc.) are used to link together sentences fluently in a piece of writing. They signpost the development of ideas for the reader.

The **media** is the means by which information is communicated to a large audience. The media includes TV, radio, film, newspapers, magazines, comics, advertising and the Internet.

Memory aids are useful ways of remembering spellings. Memory aids include using mnemonics, learning word families or breaking words down into separate syllables. Grouping words together and remembering letter patterns can also help.

A **metaphor** is a phrase which compares one thing to another without using *as* or *like* (e.g. *the surface of the lake <u>was</u> a mirror reflecting the sky*). Metaphors often draw out striking and interesting features about the subject and make descriptions of people, places and objects more interesting.

Middle English is the type of English that was commonly spoken between 1100 and 1500. It is the language used by Chaucer in his famous *Canterbury Tales*.

A **mnemonic** is a rhyme or saying that helps you learn a spelling or fact (e.g. *'i' before 'e' except after 'c'*).

A **modal verb** is placed in front of another verb to modify it (e.g. *can, could, may, might, must, ought, should, would*). When these verbs express a condition (e.g. *She would go to the cinema if she knew you were going as well*) they are also known as **conditional verbs**.

A **moral** is a message about how we should behave which we learn from reading a story such as a fairy tale or fable.

A **morpheme** is the smallest unit of a word that has a meaning in its own right. Morphemes consist of roots and affixes (prefixes and suffixes).

Morphology is the study of words and their form and structure. Often it involves the study of prefixes, suffixes and inflections (words which have changed, such as verbs which have added 'ed' or 'ing').

A **motion for debate** is an idea or issue which is formally discussed and then voted on at the end of the debating process.

A **myth** is an ancient story, which often involves the brave actions of heroes fighting against the forces of evil and tyranny. Greek myths also involve the influence of gods on the affairs of men and contain a range of fabulous and dangerous monsters.

A **narrative** is a text which tells a story, very often in a simple chronological form. Narratives can be fictional (e.g. comics, fairy stories) or non-fictional (e.g. diaries, biographies and autobiographies).

A **non-fiction text** is a piece of writing which is usually based on facts. It includes autobiography, biography, diary writing, newspapers, magazines, leaflets, textbooks and websites.

A **noun phrase** is a group of words including a noun. The other words generally add interest to the noun and may include adjectives (e.g. *the bike* might become *the gleaming new mountain bike*).

An **objective statement** relies on fact and truth. A subjective statement is based on opinions, feelings and personal preferences.

Old English (or **Anglo Saxon**) is the type of English which was commonly spoken in most parts of England in the eighth to the eleventh century. The roots of this language lie with the Angle and Saxon tribes from Northern Germany, who began to invade Britain when the Romans left. Many simple everyday words originate from Old English, although the majority of English words have their origins in other languages.

Onomatopoeia is an effect in speech or writing when words sound like the noise they describe. (e.g. The firework exploded with a loud *bang*. The angry driver made the car horn honk *loudly*.)

Overused words are words that are used so often that they have come to lack meaning and impact (e.g. *nice, thing, sad, nasty, good, bad, small, big*).

Parody imitates the style of another writer in a humorous or ridiculous manner.

Personification is when an inanimate object is given human or animal qualities (e.g. *the wind howled, the leaves danced in the breeze*).

Prefixes are placed at the start of a root word to change its meaning (e.g. *mis* is added to *fortune* to make *misfortune*, *dis* is added to *obey* to make *disobey*.

Proper nouns are the names of people, places, books and films (e.g. *John, London, Lord of the Rings, Matilda*). Proper nouns also include the names of organisations, days of the week, months and people's titles (e.g. *The Football League, Friday, April, The Prince of Wales*, etc.). Proper nouns always begin with a capital letter.

A **pun** is a play on words in which what is said or written may have more than one meaning (e.g. in jokes such as *What goes 'tick tick woof'? A watch dog*). Puns are often used by tabloid newspaper writers in headlines for the purpose of amusement.

The **readership** of a magazine or newspaper are those people who buy and read it. The readership of *Mizz* magazine, for instance, is teenage girls.

Received pronunciation (**RP**) is the accent of standard English and is still used by many newsreaders and presenters on national television. RP is the pronunciation which is given in dictionaries.

Register is the level of formality within language. Register ranges from informal slang or colloquial language to more formal standard English.

A **relative clause** adds meaning and expands the main clause of a sentence (e.g. *Joanne, who is an excellent organiser, often uses a computer to plan her busy schedule*). In this case 'who is an excellent organiser' is the relative clause. It is separated from the main clause by commas before and after it.

A **report** is a text written about an investigation or an event. It should begin by introducing the subject and stating the purpose of the report, then describe events, processes and findings, before ending with a conclusion.

A **review** is a piece of writing which expresses an opinion on the success of a TV programme, film, book, play or musical performance.

A **rhetorical question** is a question which does not require an answer but is used to make a point (e.g. *Do we need school?*).

The **root** of a word is its most basic form. Suffixes and prefixes can be added to the root to change it (e.g. we can add the prefix *dis* or the suffix *ing* to the root *appear* to make *disappear* or *appearing*).

Signposting a text means organising your writing so that the reader is directed through it clearly. It may be done by organising your work in sections and using certain connectives to make the sequence of ideas logical and clear.

A **simile** is a comparison that uses the words *like* or *as* (e.g. *He was running like a madman*).

A **simple sentence** is made up of a single clause (e.g. *The boy walked down the street*).

Slang is language that is not used in standard English or in formal contexts (e.g. *mega*, *wicked*).

A **slogan** is a catchphrase or saying normally associated with a product or advertising campaign (e.g. 'Just do it' for Nike sportswear or 'Because I'm worth it' for L'Oréal hair products).

A **soap opera** is a popular serialised television programme that follows the ordinary lives of fictional characters over a long period of time. Some soap operas have three or four episodes a week and are very long running. They often deal with topical issues and move from one short scene to another, touching upon the lives of many different characters.

A **sonnet** is a fourteen-line poem which generally has lines of ten syllables. Sonnets are often organised into two stanzas: an eight-line **octave** and a six-line **sestet**. They follow a variety of rhyme schemes.

A **spelling rule** is a device to help you remember difficult or unusual spellings. One common rule is *'i' before 'e' except after 'c'*.

Standard English is the kind of English used in formal situations. It is the English of the media (e.g. news broadcasters and writers) and the majority of literary writing.

The **standfirst** is the opening paragraph of a newspaper article. It leads the reader into the article and gives a lot of information. It is often in bold print.

A **stereotype** is a fixed set of ideas about what a particular group of people is like. Stereotypes are often very unfair (e.g. in the eyes of a pupil a stereotypical teacher might be someone who reads a lot, gives orders and punishes children for being naughty). There are many stereotypes to be found in literature and the media, particularly in comics, cartoons and magazines.

A **storyboard** is an interpretation of an idea in pictorial form. It may be the plan of a story, advertisement, TV or film scene produced in chronological order. The plan is explained in pictures, frame by frame, with each picture representing an event or a camera shot.

A **storyliner** is someone who conceives and develops ideas for film or television. They tend to concentrate on developing plot and character.

A **subordinate clause** offers additional information about the main clause of a sentence (e.g. _Whatever you might say about him, he is a very good footballer_).

Suffixes are a type of affix or part of a word. Suffixes are placed at the end of a word to change its meaning or word class. For example, _ate_ is added to _affection_ (a noun) to make _affectionate_ (an adjective). You may have to knock the 'e' or 'y' off some words when you add the suffix.

Superlative adjectives (e.g. _biggest, smallest, highest, lowest_) state which object or person has the most of a particular quality. There are some unusual superlatives, which need the word _most_ in front of them (e.g. _most beautiful, most difficult_) and some irregular ones (e.g. _best_ and _worst_).

A **syllable** is part of a word which consists of one beat. For instance _like_ has one syllable, _liking_ has two, and _likeable_ has three.

A **synonym** is a word which has the same or similar meaning as another word (e.g. synonyms for _neat_ could be _tidy, trim, smart_ or _spruce_). A **thesaurus** is a book which contains lots of synonyms and helps writers and students express themselves clearly and accurately.

Syntax is concerned with the order of words in a sentence. In modern English a sentence is generally made up of a subject, then a verb

and finally an object, for example _The girl read the book_ (subject = _the girl_, verb = _read_, object = _the book_).

Technical language includes the words needed to help you understand a particular subject. For instance, in ICT you need words like _hardware, icon, password_, etc.

A **thesaurus** lists synonyms or words with the same or similar meaning. Sometimes it is referred to as a dictionary of synonyms and antonyms (words of opposite meaning).

Tone is the mood or atmosphere of a piece of writing (e.g. happy, sad, angry, comic). Very often the tone of a passage will change through a text to maintain the interest of the reader.

A **topic sentence** comes at the start of a paragraph and introduces the subject of the paragraph. A topic sentence is important in signposting the development of a piece of writing, thereby helping the reader to understand the text more easily.

A **travelogue** is an account of a person's experiences and observations whilst travelling. It is often exciting and amusing.

A **verb** is a word which describes an action (e.g. I _walk_ to school, I _enjoy_ reading). Verbs change form according to the tense involved, for example we _walked_ (past tense), we will _walk_ (future tense), we are _walking_ (present). A verb is **active** when the subject of a sentence or a clause carries out the action (e.g. _Brian_ (subject) _kicked_ (active verb) _the ball into the empty net_). A verb is **passive** when the subject has the action done to it (e.g. _The ball was kicked into the empty net_).

Word derivation is concerned with the origins of words. For instance, many English words come from Old English (e.g. _drive_ – Old English _drifen_). Greek, Latin and French are also a major source of English words, for example _autograph_ – Greek _graphus_ (to write); _festival_ – Latin _festum_ (holiday); _comprehension_ – French _comprendre_ (to understand).

Published by Letts Educational
4 Grosvenor Place
London SW1X 7DL
School enquiries: 015395 64910
Parent & student enquiries: 015395 64913
E-mail: mail@lettsed.co.uk
Website: www.letts-educational.com

First published 2003

ISBN 978 1 84085 702 3

10 9 8 7 6

British Library Cataloguing in Publication Data

A catalogue record for this book is available from the British Library.

Commissioned by Helen Clark

Project management by Vicky Butt

Editing by Rachel Harrison

Cover design by Ken Vail Graphic Design

Internal design, layout and illustration by Hart McLeod, Cambridge

Production by PDQ

Printed and bound in Dubai

Acknowledgements
The publishers would like to thank the following for permission to use copyright material. Every effort has been made to trace copyright holders and to obtain their permission for the use of copyright material. The author and publishers will gladly receive information enabling them to rectify any error or omission in subsequent editions.

Cover image, Telegraph Colour Library

p.6 What You Are, Roger McGough, reproduced by kind permission of PFD © Roger McGough; p.9 Jumping Big Sui, extract from Billy Connolly the Authorised Years, compiled and edited by Duncan Campbell © Billy Conolly; p.13 Boy, Roald Dahl, reproduced by kind permission of Penguin Books Ltd and Jonathan Cape, © Roald Dahl; p.17–8 Morning Break, reproduced by permission of Wes Magee, © Wes Magee: p.17 School Dinner Rhyme, Ian Serraillier, reproduced by kind permission of Anne Serraillier, © Ian Serraillier; p.19–20 Cider with Rosie, Laurie Lee, reproduced by permission of PFD on behalf of The Estate of Laurie Lee, © Laurie Lee; p.21–2 Matilda, Roald Dahl, reproduced by permission of Penguin Books Ltd and Jonathan Cape, © Roald Dahl; p.23–4 The Dragon in the Garden, Reginald Maddock, reproduced by permission of Heinemann New Windmills Series 1996, © Reginald Maddock; p.26 Gaggle of Geese, © Michelle Garrett/Corbis; p.26 Pride of Lions, © Yann Arthus-Bertrand/Corbis; p.26 Orion and the Great Nebula, © Roger Ressmeyer; p.30 hot air balloon, © Kelly Harriger/Corbis; p.32–3 The Lion and Albert, © Marriot Edgar; p.36 Success on a pile of books, © Corbis; p.37–8 The Hobbit, JRR Tolkien, reprinted by permission of HarperCollins Publishers Ltd, © JRR Tolkien; p.39 The Muddy, Mucky, Murky Mouch, Wes Magee, reproduced by permission of Wes Magee, © Wes Magee; p.40 The Blob, Wes Magee, reprinted by permission of Wes Magee, © Wes Magee; p.41 True Monster Stories, Terry Deary, first published in the UK by Scholastic Children's Books, reproduced by permission of Scholastic Ltd, © Terry Deary 1992; p.43 Spike Milligan, © Richard Smith; p.43–4 Black Mangle Arrives, from A Children's Treasury of Milligan, Spike Milligan, reproduced by permission of Spike Milligan Productions Ltd, © Spike Milligan Productions Ltd; p.45–6 The Witches, Roald Dahl, reproduced by permission of Penguin Books Ltd and Jonathan Cape, © Roald Dahl; p.48 Macbeth Witches, © J. Thompson & H. Howard/Mary Evans Picture Library; p.50–1 Harry Potter & the Philosophers Stone, JK Rowling, reproduced by kind permission © JK Rowling; p.53 Meg Sheltons Grave, © BBC Lancashire; p.54 John Logie Baird, © Hulton Deutch Collection/Corbis; p.54 Who's Who in Science and Technology, Bob Fowke, reproduced by permission of Hodder and Stoughton Limited, © Bob Fowke; p.56–7 Charlie and the Chocolate Factory, Roald Dahl, reproduced by permission of Penguin Books Ltd, © Roald Dahl; p.58 The Time Machine, HG Wells, reproduced by permission of AP Watt on behalf of the Literary Executors of the Estate of HG Wells, © HG Wells; p.60 Professor Branestawme's Dictionary, Norman Hunter, published by Bodley Head, used by permission of the Random House Group Limited, © Norman Hunter; p.64 Interior Anne Frank's House, © Wolfgang Kaehler/Corbis; p.64 The Diary of a Young Girl; The Definitive Edition, Anne Frank, edited by Otto H Frank and Mirjam Pressler, translated by Susan Massotty (Viking, 1997) © The Anne Frank-Fonds,

Basle, Switzerland, 1991. English translation © Doubleday a division of Bantam Books Dell Publishing group Inc, 1995; p.65 Anne Frank, © The Associated Press; p.66–7 Carrie's War, Nina Bawden, reproduced by permission Curtis Brown on behalf of Nina Bawden, © Nina Bawden; p.68–71 Rosie, Robert Westall, © The Estate of Robert Westall 1995; p.75, 77, 78, 79, 81, 82, 84, Classic Comics, reproduced by permission of D C Thomson & Co Ltd © D C Thomson & Co Ltd, p.87 The World Atlas Series, Francis Hitching, reproduced by permission of Pan Macmillan, © Francis Hitching; p.89 Power lines, © Tim Bird/Corbis; p.89 The Terrible Fate of Humpty Dumpty, David Calcutt, reproduced by permission of Nelson Thornes, © David Calcutt; p.90 Animal-loving UK's tale of neglect, Alex Kirby, reproduced with thanks to BBC online; p.91 Pointer puppies, © Dale C. Spartas/Corbis; p.94–5 A Life in the day of Gary Gero, Caroline Scott, © The Sunday Times Magazine; p.96 © Ron Austing; Frank Lane Picture Agency/Corbis; p.97–8 Seven year olds put down toys in favour of hair gel, Martin Bentham © Telegraph Group Ltd; p.99–100 The Secret Diary of Adrian Mole Aged 13 3/4, Sue Townsend, © Sue Townsend 1982; p.103–105 The Bully from Roundabout, Gene Kemp, reproduced by permission of Faber and Faber © Gene Kemp; p.111 Progress Report, Eric Finney, © Eric Finney; p.115–16 Survivor's True Story from Titanic Voices, reproduced by kind permission of Southampton City Council, © Southampton City Council; p.117–18 True Grit of Fearless MacArthur, Pat Ashworth, reproduced by permission of Derbyshire Life & Countryside Magazine, © Pat Ashworth; p.118 Ellen MacArthur, © Corbis; p.121 Shark, © Amos Nachoum/Corbis; p.125–6 The (slaying of the) Minotaur from Kingfisher Book of Myths and Legends, Anthony Horowitz, reproduced by permission of The Maggie Noach Literary Agency, © Anthony Horowitz 1985; p.129 Alleged Yeti hand and scalp, © Earl & Nazima Kowell/Corbis; p.129 On the Trail of Man Beasts from the X Factor Magazine, Dr Karl Shuker, © Marshall Cavendish Partworks Ltd; p.133 The Sea Raiders, HG Wells, reproduced by permission of AP Watt on behalf of The Literary Executors of the Estate of HG Wells, © HG Wells; p.137 On the Broom, reproduced kindly by permission of Pendle Borough Council, © Images and Text Pendle Borough Council; p.139–40 Feeding the Dog, Susan Price, reproduced by permission of AM Heath & Company Ltd, © Susan Price; p.143 La Belle Dame Sans Merci, 1865, © Walter Crane/Fine Art Photographic Library Ltd; p.144 January taken from selected poems 1946–68, RS Thomas, © Bloodaxe Books; p.145 Cataract Operation, Simon Armitage, reproduced by permission of Faber and Faber, © Simon Armitage; p.147 the Story of Printmaking, reproduced by permission of David & Charles, © David & Charles; p.149 History Maker of the Middle Ages, Peter Chrisp reproduced by permission of Hodder and Stoughton Publishers; p. 149 © Jacqui Hurst/Corbis; p.151 First Person, Ian Hislop, © Telegraph Group 2002; p.153 Books Make Good Pets, John Agard, reproduced by kind permission of John Agard c/o Caroline Sheldon Literary Agency, © John Agard;p.155–6 The Fun They Had, Isaac Asimov, © Isaac Asimov; p.158 In the Kitchen, John Cotton, © John Cotton; p.159 Cautionary Calender, Roger McGough, reproduced by permission of PFD on behalf of Roger McGough, © Roger McGough 1986; p.161–2 The Machine Gunners, Robert Westall, reproduced by permission of The Estate of Robert Westall, © Robert Westall; p.165 Rebels Without a Cause, reproduced by kind permission of Womans Own, © Womans Own; p.168 © Hellestad Rune/ Corbis Sygma; p.170 Yes, Frank Flynn, reproduced by permission of David Higham Associates on behalf of Frank Flynn, © Frank Flynn; p.170 Fireworks, James Reeves, © James Reeves from Complete Poems for Children (Heinemann); p.172 & p.293 Sneak Magazine © Emap Performance Pop; p.172 & p.293 Match Magazine, © Match Magazine; p.172 & p.293 Shout, © reproduced by permission of D C Thomson & Co Ltd © D C Thomson & Co Ltd; p.172 & p.293 Top of The Pops, reproduced by kind permission of Top of the Pops, © BBC Magazines p.177 reproduced by kind permission of the Match Magazine, © Match Magazine; p.181–2 Buddy, Nigel Hinton, © Orion Children's Books; p.183 The Fags on Which They Drag, Trevor Millum, © Trevor Millum, first published in Warning, Too Much Schooling Can Damage Your Health; p.186 Camelot Theme Park, reproduced by kind permission of Camelot Theme Park, © Camelot Theme Park; p.190–1 The polite little swot who grew into Ali G, Neil Tweedie & Thomas Harding, © Telegraph Group Ltd 2002; p.193 The Lost Continent: Travels in Small Town America, © Bill Bryson Extracted from The Lost Continent by Bill Bryson, published by Black Swan, a division of Transworld Publishers. All rights reserved; p.195–6 Stereotype, John Agard, reproduced by kind permission of John Agard c/o Caroline Sheldon Literary Agency, © John Agard; p.203–5 Roll of Thunder Hear my Cry, Mildred D. Taylor, (Victor Gollancz/ Hamish Hamilton, 1977), © Mildred D. Taylor 1976; p.218 The Kite Rider, © Geraldine McCaughream 2001 reproduced by permission of Oxford University Press; p.211–12 Quest for the Lost World, Brian Blessed, reproduced by permission of Pan Macmillan, © Brian Blessed; p.213 © Topham/UPPA; p.215–16 The Sentinel, © Arthur C. Clarke; p.217–18 Invasion of the Moon 1957–1970, Peter Ryan (Pelican, 1971) © Peter Ryan 1971; p.218 Bettman/Corbis; p.223 Freaks of Nature, © Mail on Sunday; p.224 © Michael and Patricia Fogden/Corbis; p.225–6 Beowulf, © Charles Keeping and Kevin Crossley-Holland reproduced by permission of Oxford University Press; The Suepernatural, The Mirror, © Daily Mirror; p.234–5 The Woman in Black, Susan Hill, published by Vintage, © Susan Hill 1983; p.237–38 Army Witness saw Alien at Roswell, James Adams and Maurice Chittenden, © The Sunday Times 1997; p.238 © Topham; p.245 © Topham/UPPA; p.245 and 247 Real Robots by permission of Eaglemoss Publications Ltd © Eaglemoss Publications; p.247 © Douglas Kirkland/Corbis p.249 Tables, © Valerie Bloom; p.251 Exposure and p.252 Anthem For Doomed Youth, Wilfred Owen: The Complete Poems and Fragments, edited by Jon Stallworthy (Chatto & Windus,1983, © Wilfred Owen; p.253 Glory of Women, Siegfried Sassoon, Reproduced by kind permission of George Sassoon, © Siegfried Sassoon; p.254–9 Journey's End, R.C. Sherriff, reproduced with permission of Curtis Brown Group Ltd, on behalf of the Estate of R.C. Sherriff, © R.C. Sherriff; p.258 © Hulton-Deutsch Collection/Corbis; p.261 A letter From the Home Front, 1943, reproduced by kind permission of Mr B. Saul; p.275 Family Circle, © Family Circle/IPC Syndication; p.275 © Science Photo Library; p.278 Holes, Louis Sacher, reproduced by permission of Bloomsbury Publishing Plc, © Louis Sacher; p.281 Nutritionists sparks red meat row, reproduced with thanks to BBC online; p.281 © Kristi J. Black/ Corbis; p.286 © Robbie Jack/Corbis